For the
Love
of Rome

For the *Love* of Rome

Memories, Musings, and Anecdotes

John Ferris

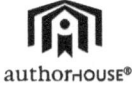

authorHOUSE®

AuthorHouse™
1663 Liberty Drive
Bloomington, IN 47403
www.authorhouse.com
Phone: 1-800-839-8640

Published by AuthorHouse   05/28/2013

ISBN: 978-1-4817-5246-6 (sc)
ISBN: 978-1-4817-5245-9 (hc)
ISBN: 978-1-4817-5244-2 (e)

Library of Congress Control Number: 2013908667

Contents

Part III. Echoes and Re-Echoes

Part IV. At the Heart of Rome

Author's Note

ome was founded in 753 BC by shepherds, farmers, artisans, and their leaders who came down from the Alban hills twenty miles to the east and settled on the Palatine, one of the city's seven traditional hills. The colony, ruled by kings, thrived and in 510 BC became a republic. Through the centuries its dominion extended rapidly. In 27 BC Rome became an empire. It reached the height of its power in 117 AD and ruled the western world from the English border of Scotland to the Black Sea.

Roman law and language became standard. Wherever Romans went they built: roads, temples, monuments, aqueducts, bridges, arenas, theaters. The empire fell in the fifth century, largely because of barbarian pressure and the Romans' own moral corruption. For five centuries the Christian church had been growing in strength and importance, and when the empire disintegrated the papacy took over power, at first spiritual, then temporal. The vast lands once governed by Rome and the papacy went their own way and became large independent countries much as we know them today—France, Germany, North Africa, and the Middle East. The Italian peninsula itself broke up into separate units; but through all these changes the pope's spiritual power was dominant, though it gradually diminished throughout the Reformation. Italy as a European state came to be regarded as second-rate, but in 1870, having fought numerous internecine wars, it finally was united.

In this brief summary I have used certain dates and landmarks but said nothing about the wars, the persecutions, the internal struggle for power both within the Roman rule and that of the church, nothing of Rome's cultural development. The book, after all, is about the experiences of my wife and myself in Rome, and about what drew us there. We learned by seeing and reading, and from what we read I selected various odd pieces for illustrative purposes. If I refer frequently to Rodolfo Lanciani, it is because he was the leading archeologist of the latter part of the nineteenth century, an authority on Roman excavations, a man full of learning, and a writer of important books, who lectured at Harvard and was universally respected.

Prologue

La Signore and Ettore, the houseboy, were sitting in the garden at the side of the palazzo when my wife and I drove into Via Ajaccio. Nothing could have been more satisfying than the sight of those two behind the high iron fence as they rose to welcome us to the Pensione Desiree, and to Rome. What a *bella giornata*! Yes, a lovely April day.

Giving us a hand with our luggage, they showed us to a large room facing the street. It was just right for our special need of space for books and papers. They served us coffee there, and later we enjoyed a satisfactory dinner in a dining room overlooking a garden full of bushes bearing dark purple flowers. We were in Rome to stay, and soon we would be seeking more adequate quarters; but for the moment we were well pleased.

We were not strangers to Rome. We had been here a year earlier for a month, had enjoyed several operas, and in a rented car had driven far afield to Ravenna on the Adriatic, to Venice and Florence, Pisa, Verona, Orvieto, Siena, and elsewhere—about thirty towns and villages. Now we had our own Karmen-Ghia for further explorations.

Many of our friends had questioned our decision to settle in Rome, urging us instead to go to Florence. But we knew that only Rome would do, for although we would find nothing in our ancestry to link us to the city, we felt as others before us had felt—a homing instinct of the heart that drove us there.

We had met many people who disliked Rome. Venice and Pisa and other Italian cities appealed to them; Rome aroused in them a strange hostility. Did anyone really like Rome? Nobody criticized Florence or argued about Perugia or Bologna or Verona. Who liked Rome? Priests and scholars did, and government bureaucrats in fat jobs; the rich—and laymen like ourselves, who were fascinated by the mazes of history and the eternal mystery of Rome: what it was, why it was there at all when so many times it had been near death. Whatever the answers, we could not retreat. If we had doubts, we could fortify our feelings by recalling what others had felt.

Here was the French writer Stendhal, for instance, standing in the morning sun of October 16, 1832, at San Pietro in Montorio on the Janiculum, joyously looking at Rome and beyond. A few small white clouds floated above Monte Albano. A delicious warmth filled the air. There was sweetness in Stendhal and a sting in the skeptics. Still, some sort of defense seemed desirable, not because Rome demanded it, but for one's own satisfaction. Rome was indifferent. It asked nothing, and it gave everything.

PART I

Antiquity into Metropolis

CHAPTER I

Rome: An Enchantment of the Spirit

Rome was beyond love and hatred, as love and hatred are understood in Florence and Venice. It even resisted a proper definition. Paris and London could be defined and lived in for a lifetime without nagging the mind. Rome was elusive, and there was too much of it. The tourist might move through the city in five days of his allotted time, or pass three weeks there, and still not comprehend it except as an old persistent rumor given substance by a few images familiar from books or travel folders.

It was said that Pius IX, who reigned from 1846 to 1878, liked to inquire of foreigners how long they had been in Rome. If someone told him that he had been in Rome less than six months, the pope said, "So you've seen it all." He was less cynical with those who had been in the city a few months longer, remarking casually, "Then you've not seen it all." But when he spoke to someone who had been in Rome a year or longer, he smiled and said, "So now you know you can never see it all."

What one saw was often a matter of chance and mood and of knowing. It still is. From a bus, or the double tram of *Il Circolare*

Esterna Destra, which used to run an irregular course around the city, one could see San Giovanni in Laterano rising in postcard grandeur beyond a dry and dusty and sometimes littered piazza; but with luck or foreknowledge, one could come up on foot from outside the Aurelian Wall to the russet bricks of Porto Asinaria's round towers in the waning glow of an October afternoon and catch sight through a thicket of golden leaves of the figures of Christ and the saints on the basilica's roof—fifteen white restless figures, twenty-one feet high, looking as if they had just fluttered down from heaven.

Knowing was recognition of what the eye was forever finding unexpectedly, so that the distant white daubs seen from the window of a bus rolling down Via Dandolo on the Janiculum were not vague, meaningless blobs against the Alban Hills, but those same wildly distraught saints of the Laterano, as comical in their postures as the statue of Christ dangling irreverently from a helicopter in the opening scene of Fellini's *La Dolce Vita*.

Rome, as Pio Nono knew, was an endless quest of mind and imagination. It was also a snare. Byron, who may have been the ideal tourist, avoided the trap. Although he lived in Italy for seven years, he spent only three weeks in Rome, in May, 1817. The population then was 115,000—and Byron, who had little love for ruins and disliked walking because of his lameness, did most of his sightseeing on horseback.

"I have been some days in Rome the Wonderful," he said in a letter. "I am delighted with Rome. As a whole—Ancient and Modern—it beats Greece, Constantinople, everything—at least, what I have ever seen . . . As for the Colosseum, Pantheon, St. Peter's, the Vatican, Palatine, etc., they are quite inconceivable and must be seen." It was the conventional view, stated by an Englishman through the years of the Grand Tour. Later on, in the fourth and last canto of *Child Harold*,

Byron would cry in a spasm of poetic fervor, "Oh, Rome, my country! City of the soul." Quite possibly he was sincere, but he never returned. Stendhal, who was French, confessed he had wept when he stood in the Colosseum and heard birds singing in the upper tiers.

No one is likely to weep now, and few of those who see the Colosseum today can guess at the lonely majesty of the place when Stendhal's birds twittered and quarreled in the luxuriant vegetation among the ancient stones.

Two years after Byron, Shelley was enchanted by the birdsong and decay and the shattered splendor of the irrecoverable past. Time, he wrote, had transformed the Colloseum into "an amphitheater of rocky hills overgrown by the wild olive, the myrtle and the fig tree, and threaded by little paths which wind among its ruined stairs and immeasurable galleries: the copsewood overshadows you as you wander through its labyrinths and the wild weed of this climate of flowers blooms under your feet."

Before 1870 and the end of Papal Rome, botanists had collected a herbarium of 420 different species of plants growing in the Collosseum. Goethe, who came to Rome in 1786 at the age of thirty-seven regretting he had not known the city in his youth, recorded an evening of spectral beauty, when a beggar's bonfire glowed in one of the vaults, and the smoke, drifting softly on the gentle airs, shrouded all but the massive bulk looming above in the moonlight. Nowhere else in the world was the moon so highly regarded as it was in Rome when its light bathed the remnants of the ancient world: the Colosseum, the ghostly Arch of Constantine, the Arch of Titus, the eerie silent wasteland of the Forum Romanum, the dark rise of the Palatine.

There were drawbacks: the fear of Roman fever from the night air, the malaria, and the more palpable danger of thieves, pickpockets, and other criminals. Antonio Uggeri, an architect in the service of the liberal Pius VI, related that a great many skeletons of murdered men had been discovered in the excavations of the Colosseum.

"There is no doubt," he wrote, "that the Colosseum has been for centuries the safest den of Roman outlaws. This is what happened to me there in 1790. I was engaged at that time in correcting some measurements which I had taken of the building on former occasions. I arrived at the spot one afternoon an hour before sunset, climbed up, not without danger, taking advantage of the walls, and entered the main corridor on my way to the upper galleries. I had walked scarcely a hundred paces when, all of a sudden, a man sprang at me from a corner, a man very tall, entirely naked, with rags around his head and ankles, black in the face, bearded, and absolutely repulsive to look at. He caught me at the wrist, shook me violently, asking me at the same time who I was, what business I had there, and other such questions. I answered, trembling, that I was an architect, and showed him my measure and my compass as an evidence of the purpose of my expedition among those ruins. In the meanwhile, I heard a more gentle voice close by, begging him to leave me in peace; and proceding a few steps farther I discovered the rest of the company under the vault of one of the staircases. It was composed of two more men and one woman, to whose interference I most likely owed my life; all three were entirely naked, as the season was very warm. One of the men was standing; the other was cooking something at the farther end of the passage. The poor woman crouched down to conceal her nudity as well as she could."

Rodolfo Lanciani, the archeologist, wrote that in 1874, when the new Via Claudia was first opened between the Colosseum and the Navicella, he came upon a whole family nested, thirty-six feet below the level of the Temple of Claudius, in a corridor or channel six feet wide, a few yards long, with little air or light. One of the family was lying dead on some straw; the others were praying and sobbing round the corpse.

Two decades later a daring pickpocket turned up living in the attic of the Arch of Titus.

The ruins of the city had been a refuge for brigands and assassins in the Middle Ages—Rome's population had dropped to seventeen thousand in 1377 when the papacy returned from Avignon—and the perils of attack by *malviventi* (criminals) had not disappeared as the nineteenth century advanced; but travelers who had endured the tedium and sometimes the hardships and dangers of coming to Rome were not to be denied the city at any hour. Sunset and twilight and night itself deepened the strange pain and joy of the impenetrable mystery the old places imparted. The past was not merely intrusive; it had a habit of displacing the present. Reality easily slipped into the shadows.

Francis Wey, a Frenchman, brooding at the summit of the Colosseum one evening in the 1860s, heard a confusion of voices and sacred music somewhere in the depths of the arena and, like a man roused from deep sleep, was uncertain for a moment where he was. When his mind cleared, he gazed below and saw a procession of shrouded penitents carrying lighted tapers, preceded by a figure with a banner, and followed by peasants and shepherds making the Stations of the Cross in the dying day. Was the scene real? He knew it must be so, but after a while, when he had descended to the ground, the place was deserted and dark.

An enchantment of the spirit. Stendhal, burning with love of Rome, had no need of darkness. "I could clearly see Frascati and Castel Gandolfo four leagues away, and the Villa Aldobrandini where Domenichino's sublime fresco of Judith is," he wrote of a sunny October day. "A good deal farther away I could see the rock of Palestrina and the white building of Castel San Pietro which was once its fortress. Below the wall against which I am leaning are the big orange trees of the Capuchins' orchard, then the Tiber and the Maltese Priory (on the Aventine), a little beyond them on the right the Tomb of Cecelia Metella, San Paolo and the Pyramid of Cestius. Opposite me I see Santa Maria Maggiore and the long lines of the Palazzo di Monte Cavallo (the Quirinal Palace). The whole of ancient and modern Rome, from the ancient Appian Way with its ruined tombs and aqueducts to the magnificent gardens of the Pincio built by the French, lies spread before me. There is no place like this in the world, I mused, and against my will ancient Rome prevailed over modern Rome; memories of the Roman historian Livy crowded into my mind. On Monte Albano, to the left of the convent, I could see the fields of Hannibal."

Coming down to Rome from his native Venice to work and study, Giovanni Battista Piranesi, the eighteenth-century etcher and engraver, was filled with joy as he prowled through the streets examining the churches and palaces of the Renaissance and Baroque periods. The place dazzled him. For him, too, it was enchanting—most of all, the ruins.

Here were the raw materials for the creation of a city of his own, and that, in fact, is what Piranesi did—make a city of his own, real yet fantastic, ugliness mixed with beauty, with gigantic facades and the shrunken figures of men without purpose, and everywhere clutter, dirt, and neglect. From Tiepolo, Piranesi seems to have learned the uses of theatrics. He instinctively bent toward the dramatic. The plate he made of the Tomb of Cestius revealed its degradation and desolation, and its nobility as well.

The ravaged Forum Romanum and the lesser fora inspired Piranesi and imbued his work with a rich extravagance. When he walked in the Campagna, he was reminded by every overgrown hillock and arid gully of old Rome's grandeur and glory. The ruins cried out for his needle and burin. He made over one thousand plates of Rome—his city and, I must say, the Rome that existed for me through much of my boyhood, neither the Rome of Caesar, Nero, and Augustus, nor the city that grew out of Papal Rome. The *ruderi* that Piranesi came upon on the Palatine, the Caelian and the Esquiline hills were the basic elements of the Piranesian Rome—whole or fragmented marble, porphyry, granite; broken temples and shattered friezes, arches bereft of ornamentation, columns felled among twisting vines and the gnarled branches of stunted trees, headless nymphs in sunny glades, glimpses of statuary in the solitude of the hills, the Arch of Titus transformed into a hideous fortress by the Frangipani, the Arch of Septimus Severus mired to its waist in the filth of the Forum Romanum, the little Temple of Vesta, a dreary scene of impoverishment, and—what easily may be the most powerful of all his engravings—the gargantuan, menacing hulk of the Castel Sant'Angelo, which he called by its original name, the Mausoleum of Hadrian.

F. Marion Crawford, the novelist and author of *Ave Roma Immortalis*, who was born in Italy in 1854 and had known Rome before 1870, when it came under what the English writer Augustus J. C. Hare contemptuously called "the Sardinian rule," said that an appreciation of Rome was a matter of feeling, though he was as concerned as Hare, who was twenty years older, with knowing the city. Hare was a man of strong opinions, an Englishman born in Rome and educated in England.

"Those who come to it [Rome] with the least mental preparation are those best fitted to enjoy it," he wrote in his *Walks in Rome* in the 1880s. The Romans, he complained, didn't know Rome, a charge that has substance even in these times, as the weekly illustrated magazine *Epoca* indicated in an issue celebrating a century of Italian unity. A survey of the city's elementary and high schools, *Epoca* said, showed that half of the pupils had never been inside of St. Peter's nor the Colosseum.

"It must not be supposed," said Hare, "that one short residence at Rome will be sufficient to make a foreigner acquainted with all its varied treasures; or even, in most cases, that its attractions will become apparent to the passing stranger. The squalid appearance of its modern streets will in itself go far to neutralize the effect of its ancient buildings and the grandeur of historic recollections.

"It is only by returning again and again, by allowing the feeling of Rome to gain upon you, when you have constantly revisited the same view, the same temple, the same picture, under varying circumstances, that Rome engraves itself upon your heart, and changes from a disagreeable, unwholesome acquaintance, into a dear and intimate friend seldom long absent from your thoughts."

"One might remain here three or four years and still be always learning," said the French philosopher, historian, and critic Hippolyte Taine. "It is the greatest museum in the world, all centuries have contributed to it."

"But," he asked, "what can one see in a month of this grand old curiosity shop? What can one do here but study art, history, and archeology? If I did not thus occupy myself, I am satisfied that the confusion and dirt of the bric-a-brac, the cobwebs, the mustiness of so many precious objects, formerly bright and perfect but now faded, mutilated, and despoiled, would give me a fit of the blues."

"The Rome we see today," said Crawford, "owes its mystery, its sadness, and its charm to six and twenty centuries of history, mostly filled with battle, murder, and sudden death, deeds terrible in that long-past present which we try to call up, but alternately grand, fascinating, and touching now, as we shape our scant knowledge into visions and fill our broken dreams with the stuff of fancy. In most minds, perhaps, the charm lies in that very confusion of suggestions, for few indeed know Rome so well as to divide clearly the truth from the legend in her composition. Such knowledge is perhaps unattainable in any history; it is most surely so here where city is built on city, monument upon monument, road upon road, from the heart of the soil upwards—the hardened lava left by many eruptions of life; where the tablets of Clio have been shattered again and again, where fire has eaten and sword hacked and hammer bruised ages of records out of existence, where even the race and type of humanity have changed and have been forgotten twice and three times over. Therefore, unless one has half a lifetime to spend in patient study and do research, it is better, if one comes to Rome, to feel much than to try to know a little, for in such feelings there is more human truth than in that dangerous little knowledge which dulls the heart and hampers the clear instincts of natural thought. Let him who comes hither be satisfied with a little history and much legend, with rough warp of fact and rich woof of old-time fancy, and not look too closely for the perfect sum of all, when more than half the parts have vanished forever."

Crawford, the son of Thomas Crawford, one of the first American sculptors to work in Rome, had childhood memories of the Angelus ringing out in Santa Maria Maggiore down the hill from the Villa Negroni, where the Crawford family lived. The villa, adjoining the ruins of the Baths of Diocletian, was the estate put together by the poor Franciscan Felice Peretti, Cardinal Montalto, before he was elected pope in April 1585 at the age of sixty-four, taking the name Sixtus V. The Crawfords occupied a corner of the *cadina*, and in a long, low studio where the Stazione Termini, Rome's Central railroad station, now stands, Thomas Crawford modeled the statue of Freedom that crowns the Capitol in Washington, D.C. and the equestrian statue of George Washington for the city of Richmond, Virginia.

The younger Crawford recalled, in *Ave Roma Immortalis*, the villa's old gardens, the avenues of lordly cypresses, the bitter orange trees, the half-wild roses and sweet flowers. As a little boy he had stood at a window in the moonlight, listening to the night birds and watching out for the foxes that came in from the Campagna to drink at the moss-grown fountains and prowl in the deep orchard.

"On the Eve of St. Peter's Day when St. Peter's was a dream of stars in the distance and the gorgeous fireworks gleamed in the sky above the Pincio, we used to climb the tower above the house and watch the still illumination and the soaring rockets through a grated window till the last one had burst and spent itself, and we crept down the steep stone steps, half frightened at the sound of our own voices in the ghostly place."

A view of Santa Maria Maggiore as it was when the Crawfords lived in Villa Negroni survives in a drawing by Ingres, who came down from Paris in 1806, when he was twenty-six. "I certainly loathe Rome," he wrote to his fiancée. "It is very beautiful but, in a few words, everything is provincial compared to the city of Paris." Yet Rome enveloped his mind and spirit and he stayed for fourteen years. Whatever the reason, it was plain that Rome exercised a power over men's minds and spirits that made them yield to the city, and this had always been true.

Rome was rarely spared from criticism by the French, but it was criticism tinctured with good sense and love—and money. Charles de Brosses, eighteenth-century man of letters, said that one-third of the population were priests, one-third of the people did very little, and the rest did nothing at all.

It was only partly true. A census taken in 1809 listed over four hundred churches, chapels, and oratories, twenty-three seminaries, 240 monasteries, seventy-three convents, and thirty religious orders. But there were also architects, artists, and artisans, the men who created new buildings and restored the old; the sculptors, masons, woodcarvers, workers in gold, silver, ivory, brass, and alabaster; the painters, and those wonderful craftsmen whose skill could turn a wooden column, a wooden pilaster, or an altar rail into delicately veined marble, impossible to detect as false unless one rapped it with the knuckles. These men and others of their kind had left their mark in such eighteenth-century monuments as the Spanish Steps; Villa Torlonia on Via Salaria above Piazza Fiume; Palazzo Braschi, now the City of Rome Museum; Palazzo Colonna; the Church of Nome di Maria, which faces Trajan's Forum; and parts of Palazzo Odescalchi.

Taine's observations in 1864 on the squalor and inertia he beheld in Rome were so pointed that they were quoted with approval by Mussolini sixty years later, when the Fascist regime proposed demolishing some of the hideous tenements that cluttered the city and disfigured its monuments. The French made Roman life more orderly and civilized. They encouraged street paving and public lighting. They gave Rome the Church of Trinita dei Monti, begun by Louis XII and consecrated by Sixtus V. The Spanish Steps below the church were built with French money, as was the Church of San Luigi dei Francese near Piazza Navona; and it was the French, employing a Roman with a French name—Valadier, baptized Giuseppe—who transformed the old Piazza del Popolo into the most esthetically satisfying open space in the city, with the Pincian terrace rising above it.

Napoleon, who would have made Rome the second city of his empire, never saw the city, but members of his family made it their home, and his mother died in Rome. One of his most memorable tributes was the purchase of the sixteenth-century Villa Medici on the Pincio, to which the Academie Nationale de France was transferred from Paris.

On the other hand, he brazenly confiscated and sent to Paris 294 ancient statues from the Villa Albani (now the Via Salaria Villa Torlonia to distinguish it from the Via Nomentana Villa Torlonia, where

13

Mussolini lived). The statues had been assembled by J. J. Winckelmann, the German archeologist and art historian. After Waterloo most of them were sold at Munich; some were returned to Rome upon the solicitations of a diplomatic mission headed by Antonio Canova, the sculptor, who carved in white marble the half-naked figure of the Emperor's sister Pauline, wife of Prince Camillo Borghese.

Marion Crawford was sixteen when Rome fell in 1870, and within a few years, as Hare angrily wrote, the new government betrayed the aged Prince Massimo, expropriating the Villa Negroni, which he had inherited from his father, and breaking the old man's heart. The *casina* was pulled down, the beautiful trees were felled, the statues and fountains dispersed, and building crews came in as the wreckers retreated. It was one of the first acts of officially-sanctioned vandalism-for-profit by a new breed of avaricious nobles, land speculators, and real-estate promoters. The villa had passed from the Montalto-Peretti family to the Savelli and then, in 1698, to Cardinal Negroni, from whom the elder Prince Massimo bought it at the close of the eighteenth century. (One of the villa's fountains turned up years later in Trastevere, where it is called the Fountain of the Prisoner.)

Crawford's father died of cancer in 1857. A few years later his mother, who was rich in her own right, married the expatriate Connecticut painter Luther Terry and moved with him and Marion and her three daughters into rooms in the Palazzo Odescalchi on the Corso.

In Crawford's boyhood Pius IX still dwelt in the sumptuous Quirinal Palace and was familiar to the faithful and to strangers who strolled on the Pincio. The English diplomat Sir Rennell Rodd remembered His Holiness appearing in the gardens among the nursemaids and children and the stylish ladies with parasols. Ross, as a child of eight in 1866, saw the gilded coach drive slowly up the steep gradient from the Piazza del Popolo, and Pio Nono alight, a stately figure in white, Christ's vicar on earth—followed, as he walked on, by a small group of monsignori and a few Swiss halberdiers in their ballooning gold and yellow and blue pantaloons. He chatted with everyone, extending his ring to be kissed, and blessing all impartially. Another small witness of these pleasant outings on the Pincio was John Singer Sargent, the future portrait painter, who was born in Florence in 1856 to a Philadelphia surgeon and his wife.

The coaches of the rich cardinals, drawn by black horses with red trappings, rumbled along imperiously over the little square blocks of lava that people erroneously called cobblestones. Rome's population had doubled in fifty years, but the city had changed very little since Shelley found the Forum "a kind of desert full of heaps of stones and pits and though near the habitations of men . . . the most desolate place you can conceive . . . Rome is a city, as it were, of the dead, or rather of those who cannot die and who survive the puny generations which inhabit and pass over the spot which they have made sacred to eternity."

Not everyone who came to Rome cared for what he saw. Goethe was vexed by so much of the indifference he observed. "In the few weeks I have been here," he wrote, "I have already seen a number of foreigners come and go, and have been amazed by the lack of respect so many of them show for all those objects which are so worth seeing. In the future, thank God, none of these birds of passage will ever be able to impress me again. If, when I get back to the north again, one of them should start telling me about Rome, he will never again make me sick with envy. I have been here for myself and I already know more or less where I stand."

The somber aspects of the city were noted by Taine, who arrived on an evening "so dark with a few dim gaslights scattered wide apart." He thought it a funereal spectacle. "The Piazza Barberini where I lodge is like a catafalque of stone with a few forgotten tapers on it; the feeble little lights seem to be swallowed up in a lugubrious shroud of shadow, and the indistinct murmur of the fountain in the silence is like the rustling of phantoms. The nocturnal aspect of Rome cannot be described." (Two decades later Friedrich Nietzsche, the German philosopher, listening to the play of water in the same fountain, Bernini's Tritone, was so tranquilized that he composed his Canto Notturno. It was the water of Acqua Felice, named for Sixtus V, who had brought it to Rome from the Alban Hills three hundred years before.) Taine found the daytime city "corpselike," and at night "there were all the horror and grandeur of the sepulcher."

James Joyce, who lived in Rome for seven months in 1906-1907, thought the neighborhood of the Colosseum and the Forum Romana was like an old cemetery. "Rome," he wrote to his brother Stanislaus in Trieste, "reminds me of a man who lives by exhibiting to travelers his grandmother's corpse." As he had neither the time nor the wish to take up Roman studies, Joyce dismissed antiquity flippantly. "Let the ruins rot," he said.

This attitude toward the *ruderi*—and they became even more extensive after Mussolini cleared the imperial fora and by accident revealed the four Republican temples at Largo Argentina—is echoed today by many visitors who are disappointed or unimpressed or displeased, and wonder why the whole mess, as they see the ruins, is not cleaned up. Florence is so much easier to take—a few palazzi, a few noble churches, Giotto's tower, the Uffizi, the Duomo, the Boboli Gardens, Fiesole, and the Arno bridges.

How does one measure a visitor's reaction to Rome or account for it? Henry James, coming down to Rome by way of Switzerland at the age of twenty-six in 1869, deposited his luggage at the hotel Inghilterra near the Spanish Steps and, with uncontrolled energy and love, set out to tramp around the city for five hours. The Russian novelist Nikolai

Gogol, visiting Paris in 1837 when the news of Pushkin's death in a duel reached him, left at once for Rome to find some moderation of his grief. He was twenty-eight.

William Dean Howells was twenty-seven when he went down to Rome from his consular post at Venice in the winter of 1864. The Forum disappointed him. ". . . I had all along secretly hoped for some dignity of neighborhood, some affectionate solicitude on the part of Nature to redeem those works of Art from the destruction that had befallen them. But in hollows below the level of the dirty cornfield, wandered over by evil-eyed buffaloes, and obscenely defiled by wild beasts of men, there stood here an arch, there a pillar, yonder a cluster of columns crowned by a bit of frieze; and yonder again, a fragment of temple half-gorged by the façade of a hideous Renaissance church; then a height of vaulted brickwork, and, leading on to the Colosseum, another arch, and then incoherent columns overthrown and mixed with dilapidated walls—mere phonographic [*sic*] consonants dumbly representing the past out of which all vocal glory had departed . . . Modern Rome appeared, first and last, hideous. It is the least interesting town in Italy, and the architecture is hopelessly ugly—especially the architecture of the churches. The papal city contrives at the beginning to hide the imperial city from your thought, as it hides it in such a degree from your eye, and old Rome only comes to you in a sort of stupid wonder over the depth at which it is buried."

His sense of "the wildness everywhere lurking about Rome" was fortified when he walked near the Pantheon as night fell and saw a group of peasants cooking their supper over a brushwood fire almost within the portico of the building. The filth and smells of the streets disgusted him, but when he went out to the Campagna his spirit changed. He caught the Roman fever, as he wrote, not the physical malady that sometimes was fatal, but "the longing that burns one who has been in

Rome to go again—that will not be cured by all the cool contemptuous things he may think or say of the Eternal City; that will fill him with fond memories of its fascination and make it forever desired."

It was indeed a deeply buried past. Nathaniel Hawthorne wrote in 1860 that, if we connected the Rome of his time with ancient Rome, it was only because the city we saw was built over the old one's grave; and Lanciani noted that, when the new Treasury buildings were constructed in 1874 in Via Venti Settembre, the engineers had to dig through forty-one feet of debris before they struck solid ground. Lanciani himself was to see the city's true extent as a cemetery when acres of tombs were dug up, great stacks of housed skeletons were revealed by chance, and columbaria, holding the ashes of men, women, and children who had died in the Augustan age, were bared and deep masses of gelatinous flesh exhumed in ancient ditches.

The thought could be overpowering if one gave it rein. It was Eliot drawing on Dante's words: I had not thought that death had undone so many.

Above ground the signs of man's mortality were abundant everywhere. The churches had their tombs and relics—fingers, arms, legs, severed heads, and complete shriveled bodies in ghastly masquerade of facial mask, gloves, and colored garments. Yet death when it was old in time never seemed real. The tombs and catacombs along Via Salaria, beyond what is now Piazza Fiume, had been looted as early as the sixteenth and seventeenth centuries. Thieves had stolen what they could from the catacombs south of the city. Disinterred sarcophagi that once held human remains were emptied and used to catch water in courtyard and street-wall fountains. The Etruscan tombs north of Rome had been excavated legally and illegally. The tombs of the Via Appia were robbed and stripped of their marble facings. Only the Jewish catacombs were safe: The Jews did not bury valuables with their dead.

Visitors who went to the Trevi fountain sometimes rested, as they still do, on the wine-stained steps of Santi Vicenzo and Anastasio, and few were aware that in a crypt of the church, labeled jars held the hearts and viscera, removed in the embalming process, of the popes who had reigned since 1590. (This was the parish church of the Quirinal residence, and the practice, which nobody in Rome appears to have thought strange, continued for some years after the official papal residence was moved to Vatican City.)

The showiest preoccupation with death was to be found in the Church of the Cappucini, Santa Maria della Concezione, in Via Veneto, where, in five chapels standing side by side, visitors could see the bones and skulls and full skeletons of more than four thousand monks, their skeletons in the dark brown Franciscan habit standing with bowed hooded skull against the wall—or lounging in recesses constructed of bones and looking like cold fireplaces—reading with eyeless sockets a breviary or faded parchment manuscripts.

The separate bones were arranged in fanciful patterns, as pendant lamps and wall designs, chandeliers, pieces of grotesquerie, tasteless and somehow failing in their purpose, if the aim was to make death edifying. Then as today, there was a strain of unfathomable humor in the greeting of the monks assigned to welcome callers and extract from them small donations. From the depths of their rough cowls, not by accident pulled low, they smiled gently and murmured, "Accommodatevi" (Make yourself at home).

While the cardinals and popes and nobility had their monumental tombs and marble effigies, a man greater than most of his contemporaries lay behind two feet of masonry in the Pantheon. Vasari and Lorenzo Lotto had written that Raphael's body had been placed in Santa Maria Rotonda, or Santa Maria ad Martyres, as the Pantheon is known in ecclesiastical records, but the exact spot of his entombment was conjectural. Nineteenth-century curiosity and zeal settled the matter. On September 9, 1833, 313 years after Raphael's passing at the age of thirty-seven, a committee of artists, prelates, and public notaries began a search that ended five days later when an opening made in the wall exposed the skeleton of the painter, who had died in 1520. The frequent floodings of the Tiber, even this far inland, had penetrated the wall. The cheap deal coffin had decayed, and a layer of mud partly covered the bones. The skeleton was measured, an artist made a drawing, and after several days of public exposure in a glass case, the remains were returned to the wall. Even then, death seemed remote.

A feeling of triumph, usually vague, often inexpressible, and never to be forgotten, was in the hearts of almost all new arrivals in Rome, such a feeling that one sees reflected today in the shining eyes and half-parted lips of foreign nuns and even those Italians making their first visit to Rome, as they alight from buses and march across St. Peter's Square in quick breathless squads to the basilica.

"At last for the first time I live," Henry James told his brother William.

"The city is an enchantress," wrote Ernest Renán in 1849. "I am no longer French."

Longfellow, returning to the city forty years after his European study days, found Rome unchanged. Hawthorne happily guided Franklin Pierce, the ex-President of the United States, on a tour of the monuments. (Born in the same year, 1804, they had attended Bowdoin College together, and one of Pierce's first acts as President had been to appoint his friend consul general at Liverpool, England.)

Henry Adams, nearing seventy when he finished his autobiography, remembered the Rome of his youth as "seductive beyond resistance." He was twenty-two then, and the month of May 1860 was "divine."

"No doubt other young men, and occasionally young women, have passed the month of May in Rome since then and conceive that the charm continues to exist," he wrote in *The Education of Henry Adams*. "Possibly it does—in them—but in 1860 the lights and shadows were still medieval and medieval Rome was alive; the shadows breathed and glowed, full of soft forms felt by lost senses. No sand-blast of science had yet skinned off the epidermis of history, thought, and feeling. The pictures were uncleaned, the churches unrestored, the ruins unexcavated. Medieval Rome was sorcery."

In Murray's *Handbook* Adams read again how the idea of writing *The Decline and Fall of the Roman Empire* had come to Gibbons' mind in October 1764, "in the close of the evening as I sat musing in the Church of the Zoccolanti or Franciscan Friars while they were singing their Vespers in the Temple of Jupiter, on the ruins of the Capitol." Adams himself more than once, as he wrote, sat on the steps of Santa Maria in Aracoeli at sunset and thought of the riddle of Rome's existence—the riddle no one has ever answered.

He was in the studio of a friend one day when a middle-aged Englishman came in, shocked by something he had just seen. While riding near the Circus Maximus, he had come unexpectedly on a guillotine where a criminal had been put to death an hour earlier. The Englishman was Robert Browning.

A month later, in the Piazza di San Lorenzo in Florence, Browning bought from a barrow of old books the "square old yellow book," an account of the Caponsacchi tragedy, a seventeenth-century Roman scandal, from which he fashioned *The Ring and the Book*, twenty thousand lines of verse published in four monthly volumes in the winter of 1868-1869.

Augustus Saint-Gaudens, born in Dublin of a French father and an Irish mother, who immigrated to New York in his infancy, came to Rome in 1870 from Paris to escape the disaster of the impending Prussian victory. He was twenty-two, full of exuberant song and soaring hopes. Installed in a studio on the grounds of the Palazzo Barberini within earshot of the Tritone Fountain—the murmuring of which had annoyed Taine—he was in time for two momentous events: the arrival of Vittorio Emanuele and his court from Florence, a royal parade down the Corso; and the biggest flooding of the Tiber in modern times. (Saint-Gaudens and Adams met in later years and became close friends, and in 1893, six years after Adams' wife committed suicide, he commissioned Saint-Gaudens to make the bronze figure of Grief in Rock Creek Cemetery in Washington, D.C., one of the most memorable sculptures ever created in America.)

Francis Wey, the Frenchman who was startled by the procession of *penitenti* in the Colosseum, walks on his first morning in Rome through Via del Tritone, which was lined with "shops for the sale of smoked and greasy meat, *trattorie* that the Germans must frequent, for you see in them a vast quantity of sausages and schoppes of beer; the common people, squatting or leaning against the wall and about the door, proud, idle, sober." He proceeds through muddy streets without footways past "arched shops with narrow doors . . . walls whose peeling plaster has received a daubing of mud from the splashings of the gutter; now and then a church with shabby façade in modern taste, set in among the houses." (A few years later, when Italian unity had become a legal fact and skeptical journalists came down from the north, one of them wrote that Rome stank. There was no denying it: Lacking public toilets and even adequate private facilities, Romans for centuries had shamelessly relieved themselves like animals in the streets, gardens, alleys, courtyards, hallways, and terraces.) Wey, picking his path carefully, finds much animation and babbling among the people—"all the women ragged, and with hair deliberately dressed, even those who have none, terrible to behold—this is what greets you at every corner."

So, with no more forewarning than an indistinct murmur like waves rising above the street noises, he comes to Trevi, is dazzled, and reaches the conclusion that the fountain is best seen from a distance, a sound observation, since part of the original idea of attaching it to the back of the Palazzo Poli was that its cooling tumbling water would be seen from the windows of the Quirinale on the hill. He wanders through narrow streets smelling of cabbage and broccoli, comes to the Corso by accident and finds it disappointing. He looks up at the column of Marcus Aurelius in the Piazza Colonna, where a daily vegetable market was installed under the windows of the Palazzo Chigi; and beyond, in the open space before Palazzo Montecitorio, he comes upon the city's coffee roasters.

He penetrates the maze of crooked streets of the Campo Marzio, encounters a friend, an abbe, and has a look at the piazza and the Borghese Palace that is shaped like a harpsichord, and is guided through the Tiberside slums to Ponte Sant'Angelo and past the castello into the Borgo and to St. Peter's.

A few years earlier, in 1859, when he was still a small boy, Crawford had seen the Prince of Wales at the Carnival in an open carriage: "a thin young man in a black coat, with a pale face and a quiet smile." Crawford had, too, an even more charming memory of that Carnival day: Franz Liszt, "not yet in orders, but dressed in a close-fitting and very fashionable gray frock coat, with a gray high hat, young then" (actually in 1859 he was forty-eight and Crawford was five) . . . "tall, athletic, and erect . . . not at all the silver-haired priestly figure the world knew so well in later years."

The Frenchman Wey was lucky that he turned westward, for Campo Narzio and the walk to St. Peter's was relatively quiet. Via del Tritone, where he started out that morning, was probably the most crowded street in Rome. It still was a mess sixty years later, when Mussolini came to power and knocked down scores of buildings between Piazza Barberini and the Church of Santa Susanna on Via Venti Settembre and built the wide curving Via Barberini and Largo Santa Susanna.

The Via del Tritone, Crawford wrote, "was the only passage through the valley between the Pincian and the Quirinal hills from the region of Piazza Colonna toward the railway station and the new quarter. During the busy hours of the day a carriage can rarely move through its narrower portions any faster than at a foot pace, and the insufficient pavements are thronged with pedestrians . . . It is as though the contents of Rome were drawn daily through a keyhole. In the Tritone are to be seen magnificent equipages, jammed in the line between milk carts, omnibuses, and dustmen's barrows, preceded by butchers' vans and followed by miserable cabs, smart dogcarts and high-wheeled country vehicles driven by rough, booted men wearing green-lined cloaks and looking like stage bandits. Even saddle horses are led that way sometimes to save time, and on each side flow two streams of human beings of every type to be found between Porta Angelica (near St. Peter's) and Porta San Giovanni (near the Lateran).

"A prince of the Holy Roman Empire pushes past a troop of dirty school children and is almost driven into an open barrel of salt codfish, in the door of a poor shop, by a black-faced charcoal man carrying a sack on his head half as high as himself. A party of jolly young German tourists in loose clothes, with red books in their hands, and their field glasses hanging by straps across their shoulders, try to rid themselves of the flower girls dressed in sham Sabine costumes, and utter exclamations of astonishment and admiration when they themselves are almost run down by a couple of the giant Royal Grenadiers, each six feet five or thereabouts, besides nine inches or so of crested helmet aloft, gorgeous, gigantic and spotless. Clerks by the dozen and liveried messengers of the ministries struggle in the press; ladies gather their skirts closely and try to pick a dainty way . . . servant girls, smart children with nurses and hoops going up to the Pincio, black-browed washerwomen with big baskets of clothes on their heads, stumpy little infantry soldiers in gray uniforms, priests, friars, venders of bootlaces and thread, vegetable sellers pushing hand-carts of green things in and out among the horses and vehicles with amazing dexterity, and yelling their cries in superhumanly high voices—there is no end to the multitude. If the day is showery, it is a sight to see the confusion in the Tritone when umbrellas of every age, material and color are all opened at once, while the people who have none crowd into the codfish shop and the liquor seller's and the tobacconist's, with traditional *con permesso* or excuse for entering though they do not mean to buy anything; for the Romans are mostly civil people and fairly good-natured. But rain or shine, at the busy hours, the place is always crowded to over-flowing with every type of humanity."

Mrs. Winthrop Chanler, née Margaret Terry and Crawford's half-sister, was around seventy years of age in 1932 when she finished her charming autobiography. (Their mother, whose maiden name was Louise Cutler Ward, was one of the three sisters of Sam Ward, "King of the Lobby" of nineteenth-century Washington, a cosmopolite who made and lost a fortune or two and was popular in rich and fashionable society in London and New York. The Wards had a big house at Broadway and Bond Street in New York, a few blocks south of the home of old Commodore Cornelius Vanderbilt. The most famous of the Ward girls, Julia, who married Dr. Samuel Gridley Howe, was the author of "The Battle Hymn of the Republic.")

As a little girl dwelling in the Palazzo Odescalchi, Mrs. Chanler and her brother, Arthur Terry, were allowed to play in the Colonna and Quirinal gardens and were taken on outings to the Pincio Hill, where, like Rennell Rodd, they saw Pius IX driving in his great coach up the slope. He would walk and make small talk with the children and their parents and nurses.

Pio Nono loved children. "He would give us his ring to kiss, speak to this one or that one," Mrs. Chanler recalled. "One day my brother and I were his favored ones: he took Arthur up in his arms and asked the nurses who we were. When told regretfully that we were Americans and Protestants, he patted our heads and promised to pray for us."

The Romans who also strolled there, the ladies with parasols, were in many cases impoverished men and women who put all the money they could scrape together into public outfits.

It was Pius IX, by the way, who promulgated the Dogma of the Immaculate Conception in 1854, and three years later raised a column at the south end of the Piazza di Spagna to commemorate the event. William Wetmore Story, remembered today less for his sculpture than for his *Roba di Roma*, a book about Roman life and customs in the years before General Cadorna's troops breached the Aurelian Wall near Michelangelo's monumental Porta Pia, left us in a few lines a vivid picture of the raising of the monolith—hundreds of galley slaves in striped brown blouses and pants turning winches and pulling on ropes as the shaft of Carystian marble was slowly hoisted to its tall pedestal. The cost of the pedestal and the statue of the Virgin Mary, which stands on top of the column, was defrayed by public subscription.

The column was a uniquely Roman matter. Nothing, as Lancini has noted, was ever wasted in Rome. Marble, gold, bronze—everything so laboriously brought to Rome by the ancient inhabitants and not stolen by invaders, nor sold nor given away, nor transported to the East—everything was used in churches and palazzi. A great deal, buried on purpose or by accident, is still being turned up. The Column of the Immaculate Conception, exhumed in Campo Marzio in 1778, lay untouched until Pio Nono thought of using it seventy-nine years later.

Drawn to the Catholic church (she later was converted), Mrs. Chanler and her half-brother Marion Crawford, who had been raised in the faith because his father Thomas Crawford was a Catholic, attended the Office of Tenebrae in Holy Week at San Giovanni in Laterano, where the Incantations of Jeremiah were sung to ancient melodies—and perhaps Hebrew threnodies, she thought.

"They are the immemorial cry of human sorrow and desolation, answered by the beautiful responsory: 'Jerusalem, Jerusalem, convertera ad Dominum Deum Tuum.' Then the singing of the Miserere in the gathering dusk when all the candles had been extinguished save the one which was hidden behind the altar, and the crowd knelt in silent recollection till the final strepitus (the banging of books and benches) broke the spell and sent us out into the tender twilight of the Roman spring, back to the present realities of our little human lives.

"Marion and I often walked home together; our way lay by all the great Roman monuments—Constantine's Basilica, the Colosseum, the Forum, the Capitol; and the pageant of Roman history seemed to have a sharper outline than the happenings of our own existence. The great Past is not dead in Rome—rather does it at times make the present seem shadowy and ephemeral; we become a part of the stream of life that has flowed for so many centuries past these same temples, arches of triumph, porticoes and palaces . . . Rome sinks into our sense of things and becomes part of our consciousness."

How deeply Rome had sunk into the consciousness of Margaret Terry Chanler, Roman by birth, not even she could know until her marriage to a scion of the Astor family was followed by a decade or more of living in the United States—in Bar Harbor, Tuxedo Park, Washington, and New York. In 1897 her mother died, and Mrs. Chanler's husband suggested they go to Rome with their five children to be with her father, who was then eighty-four.

"Rome was Paradise . . . I felt as though my body and soul had come together again after a long separation; for during my exile in the country that should have been my own, some part of me was forever there, in the Eternal City, 'alone and palely loitering' about the well-remembered place. In the midst of the hurry and high tension of American existence my living ghost had haunted the streets of Rome; at any moment, had anyone asked me the question, I could have told him just where I was—on the Piazza del Gesù, on the Spanish Steps, in the Via della Scrofa or wherever. There was no particular spot to which my thoughts were anchored; my thoughts were fully occupied with things and people about me and had nothing to do with this uninterrupted shadowy consciousness of being in Rome. It was an idle trick of memory and imagination and wholly involuntary on my part. It was part of the great magic of Rome."

Taine thought the only true industry of Rome was the renting of lodgings to strangers, either apartments in palaces or a part of one's own small house. The cost of living was modest, a household with two children and a woman servant being less than half what it was in Paris. (At the Trattoria Lepri, opposite the Caffè Greco in Via Condotti, Herman Melville dined for nineteen cents in 1857.) Taine, incidentally, regarded the Greco as no better than a third-class Paris café.

Rome had 226,000 inhabitants in 1870 and forty thousand visitors a year. Two daily newspapers, *L'Osservatore* and *Il Giornale di Roma*, published lists of apartments to rent, specifying also—beside the *rione* (the ward or zone) and the number of rooms—whether there was sufficient water to drink and to sue for washing. No city in the world had so much water, nor such good water, though the flow was not comparable to what it had been in ancient times. (In 410 AD, the year of the Gothic sack, there were 1,212 public fountains, eleven great imperial baths, and 926 public baths.)

It was a city of palazzi, commonly defined as large buildings with inner courtyards. Taine counted 150 of them and described them with a mixture of distaste, admiration, and unsatisfied curiosity—the immense inner courts, high walls like prison walls, the monumental facades: "Nobody is in the court—it is a desert; sometimes at its entrance are a dozen loungers seated on stones appearing to be pulling up the grass: You would imagine the place abandoned. This is frequently the case, its ruined master lodging in the fourth story and trying to let a portion of all the rest, all those buildings being too grand, too disproportionate to the standards of modern living and unfit for anything but museum and ministerial purposes."

Hawthorne spoke of those "immense seven-storied, yellow-washed hovels, or call them palaces," in which, in Via dei Portoghesi, close to Via della Scrofa, he placed Hilda, the gentle heroine of *The Marble Faun*. The tower where she lived and tended a shrine to the Virgin Mary is called Hilda's Tower by Americans and the English who have read Hawthorne or the guidebook references. Romans who know anything at all about the building know it was a Frangipani fortress in medieval times.

A legend attaches to the tower. In the seventeenth century, the story goes, when the Scapucci family lived in the palazzo, a pet ape carried an infant to the top of the battlements. The baby's cries attracted a large crowd, and its father swore to the Virgin that he would make a shrine on the tower and keep a light burning there forever if she saved the child. He then whistled to the ape, and the beast descended on a water pipe, cradling the baby in one arm. The shrine was built, and the light still burns on the Torre della Scimmia.

To reach Hilda's studio, one ascended from a ground floor of cook-shops, cobblers' stalls, stables, and regiments of cavalry to a middle region of princes, cardinals, and ambassadors, and finally to the upper level of artists. Taine, visiting a palazzo on a grander scale, mounts countless steps of extraordinary width and height and finds himself in a vast range of apartments. "You walk for five minutes before reaching the dining hall in which four regiments of infantry with their sappers and musicians might all be lodged; the Austrian embassy at Venice would be as much lost in one of those palaces as a nest of rats in an old mill . . . You cast your eyes out of a window and see lofty walls, moss-covered pavements, and the cornices of a mutilated and leprous roof."

Decay could hardly go farther; yet within a few years, even the meanest Roman property would rise to an undreamed-of value as a new population from outside clamored for lodgings in the new capitol.

CHAPTER 2

Roman Tourism and Thos. Cook

Visitors to Rome usually came in the autumn if they intended to stay for the winter season. The custom of newcomers was to take temporary lodgings for a week to get the feel of the city, and then to rent an apartment for several months.

There were sixty hotels and inns in the mid-nineteenth century. Several were named for the nationality of their first guests: La Locanda di Londra (the London Inn) in Piazza di Spagna served the English, La Locanda di Alemagna in Via Condotti the Germans. The Russians went to La Locanda di Russia in Via del Babuino.

Stendhal and Renan stayed at the old papal guest house, now the Hotel Minerva, behind the Pantheon and across the street from Santa Maria sopra Minerva, Rome's only early Gothic church, owned by the Dominicans and the resting place of Fra Angelico and St. Catherine of Siena. (The adjacent monastery, run by the Dominicans, where the painter lived and where Galileo was tried by the Inquisition, is now the government's Ministry of Posts and Telecommunications.)

The Romans called the visitors *forestieri*, a more pointed term than *stranieri*; and the lower classes—tradespeople and servants—divided them into two parts: the English and the painters.

Romans associated the English with money. The English had been coming to Rome for a long time: an Englishman had even been elected pope in the twelfth century (Adrian IV, Nicolas Breakspeare). Alfred the Great was sent to Rome in 853 by his father, Aethelwulf, King of Wessex, who originated the tax known as Peter's Pence. The English tradition was adorned with the names of Canute and MacBeth; Milton and Fynes Moryson, William Lithgow and the diarist John Evelyn; Sterne, Charles Burney, Smollett, Byron, Keats, Shelley, Severn, Trelawney, Ruskin, Macauley, Crashaw, Gladstone, Harvey, the Brownings, Dickens, Hardy. Turner painted the Arch of Titus before its restoration, using the brightest golds and yellows of his palette.

It was the English who kept their big traveling coaches at the north end of Piazza di Spagna at the street which became Via delle Carrozze. The neighborhood below the Spanish Steps was known as the English Ghetto. Dr. Burney, father of Fanny Burney, in Rome in 1770 in search of music, went one day to a coffeehouse where he met twenty Englishmen, most of them artists. The nobility and the cardinals loved the English. They met at Princess Borghese's palace and were entertained at Princess Colonna's and at Cardinal Alessandro Albani's villa beyond Porta Pia. But most of the English lived modestly, forever beyond the pull of Roman society. Many were poor by standards at home but able to scrape along in Rome.

"Every winter," wrote Thackeray, "there is a gay and pleasant English colony in Rome, of course more or less remarkable for rank, fashion and agreeability with every varying year. Thrown together every day, night after night; flocking to the same picture galleries, statue galleries, Pincian drives, and church functions, the English colonists in Rome perforce become intimate, in many cases friendly. They have an English library where the various meets for the week are placarded: on such a day the Vatican galleries are open; the next is the feast of St. So-and-so; on Wednesday there will be music and Vespers in the Sistine Chapel; on Thursday the Pope will bless the animals—sheep, horses and what-not; and flocks of English will accordingly rush to watch the benediction of droves of donkeys. In a word, the ancient city of the Caesars, the august fanes of the popes with their splendor and ceremony, are all mapped out and arranged for English diversion."

Forestieri of the second division included sculptors, poets, and musicians. The lines of the two classes crossed continuously, since they existed only in the Roman mind. Some of the rich were Americans, some were French, or they came from lands to the east and north. The best-known sculptor among the Americans was William Wetmore Story, born in Boston in 1819 and educated at Harvard as a lawyer. He had inherited money, and his wife was rich. They lived in apartments at the top of the Palazzo Barberini and were active in the Roman social world. Their daughter Edith, to whom Thackeray read *The Ring and the Rose*, which he wrote during her convalescence from a serious illness—composition and recuperation ran parallel courses—grew up to marry a Medici.

In 1861 Italy had two thousand kilometers or 1,250 miles of railway lines. The mileage tripled in the next nine years, and by the end of the century it was ten thousand. Even Pio Nono, who saw little to be happy about in trains, surrendered to steam and consented to the construction of a line to Frascati in the Alban Hills, about twenty miles distant. (The Pope's personal car is preserved in the Museo di Roma in Palazzo Braschi, the rear of which overlooks Piazza Navona.)

Tourism as a modern phenomenon came to Rome in 1866 when Thomas Cook, who had started his sight-seeing business in 1841 with a ten-mile excursion in a primitive English train—the customers, riding in an open car, being showered with hot cinders and ashes from the fiery locomotive—conducted a party of fifty men and women over the Alps into Italy, arriving in Rome in Holy Week. As the hotels had been filled in advance, Cook, a genial, patient, farseeing man, moved his charges into a palazzo. An Italian journalist who saw this Roman contingent noted that the tourists were neither well-heeled milords nor artists, but plain bourgeoisie who had paid the Cook agency thirty-six pounds sterling for first-class accommodations and thirty-one pounds for second class, sums that covered transportation, food, and lodging. Five years later, in 1871, tourism was helped along when the eight-mile Monte Cenis Alpine Railroad Tunnel opened, removing the necessity of making the uncomfortable and dramatic and sometimes perilous trip over the high carriage road Napoleon had built.

Cook took his people to Venice, Florence, Siena, Pisa, Naples, and Pompeii; and wherever they went they were resented by the resident English, who regarded Italy as their private preserve. (Some English even resented the Italians, an attitude that gave rise to the saying that Italy was too good for the Italians.) A rumor circulated that the new invaders were inmates of English lunatic asylums who were being treated to travel as a cure. The novelist Charles Lever, who was to spend the last five years of his life (1867-1872) as the British consul at Trieste, wrote in *Blackwood's Magazine* that Italy was being flooded with these new visitors. Using the name of Cornelius O'Dowd, he said the tours that Cook promoted were a government program to dispose of English convicts by dropping men and women here and there on the continent.

"I have already met three flocks," he wrote, "and anything as uncouth I never saw before—the men mostly elderly, dreary, sad-looking, evidently bored and tired, the women somewhat younger, travel tossed and crumpled, but intensely lively, wide awake and facetious. The cities of Italy are deluged with droves of these creatures, for they never separate, and you see them, forty in number, pouring along the street with their director, now in front, now in the rear, circling around them like a sheep dog, and really the process is as like herding as may be."

The new tourists picked up what souvenirs they could find; the *forestieri* who had more time pursued their shopping with what seemed to the Romans, however much they liked the profits, a kind of madness. The women spent large amounts of money on silks, velvets and woolens, while the men bought books, old prints, copies of antique busts, and pieces of broken marble which, following the Roman example, they affixed to garden walls and to the walls of country places at home.

Tourists and *forestieri* alike had their portraits painted with a recognizable monument in the background—a broken aqueduct, an arch, the Colosseum, a ruined temple. For seven *baiocchi*, a trifling sum, one could board a horse-driven omnibus at Piazza di Venezia and visit the antique sites and some of the churches in less haste than today's motorized groups. Experienced travelers went on foot when they could, stirring up the dust in the Forum Romanum and picnicking on the Palatine.

While Augustus Hare maintained that only through repeated visits could one come to know Rome, he knew that some visitors would never return and that some form of compromise was necessary. He therefore outlined tours of the city to cover a week's stay. He also offered a guide to the best time of day and season for painters and water colorists to work.

Some visitors went swimming in the Tiber. The river, which had carried sewage and the refuse of the streets—garbage, human waste, the manure of horses and cattle—down to the sea since ancient times, was polluted; but that had never discouraged Romans from drinking the water, nor bathing in it. The Cloaca Maxima, two thousand years old, had long ago lapsed through most of its regular course into a passage for underground marshland water. All Rome below its hills had been built on swampy ground; water sports had once been celebrated in the Campo Marzio, and unnumbered hidden springs and tiny rivers were a source of worry and annoyance, as they still are. The best Tiber bathing was from establishments north of the old Porta di Ripetta, where Memmo, the town's most puissant swimmer, challenged anybody worth challenging to a race downstream to Magliana, near the Church of San Paolo fuori le Mura.

A waterman more glamorous than Memmo turned up in Rome in January 1877. Captain Paul Boyton, a twenty-eight-year-old New York adventurer, who had journeyed down many of the long European and American rivers clad in an inflated rubber suit, arrived at Rome from Orte, forty miles by land to the north but 190 river miles, after a float of thirty-seven hours on the sinuous Tiber. (He propelled himself feet first with a double-bladed paddle and towed his belongings—tools, provisions, and a stove—in a small tin boat called the "Baby Mine," frequently frightening peasants with blasts on a bugle.) On the outskirts of the capital, he was welcomed by members of Rome's leading canoe clubs and escorted to a landing stage within sight of St. Peter's, while a band hired by the American consul played "Yankee Doodle" and crowds cheered along the low shore.

Boyton's coming was a pleasant diversion from the usual routine of Roman life: band concerts, opera, and theater attended by limited numbers, spectacles at St. Peter's and other churches, funeral processions, and the unrestrained revelry of the Carnival—ten days and nights of pre-Lenten collective *follia*, when the Corso was thronged with carriages and pedestrians and the windows of the palazzo were bright with candlelight.

The streets were always interesting. The most jaded traveler viewed sights not to be found elsewhere, such as the artists' models who gathered daily on the Spanish Steps in costume to hire themselves out as brigands, angels, gypsies, Biblical patriarchs, Madonnas, saints, courtiers, cutthroats, and more.

Public executions drew large crowds. Dr. Burney, trapped in one from which he could not escape, was pushed close to a scaffold where a poor wretch who had killed a woman was knocked on the head and stunned before his throat was slit and his hands and feet amputated. Byron went to a beheading; Dickens saw one in 1844—a procession of monks, a pale, submissive prisoner kneeling for the knife, the leather bag for the head, congealing blood, and flies. There were hangings and quarterings and other more horrible styles of capital punishment: In 1854, the Piazza del Popolo, under the Pincian Terrace, was jammed as six robbers were clubbed to death in an astonishing display of ferocity.

Behind the façade of religion and art, Rome was a confusion of virtue and corruption, arrogance and depravity, side by side with simple faith and piety. Yet there was also an alleviating charity, a tradition as old as the city itself. Nobody turned a beggar away, and nobody actually starved as people did in London and New York. There was always free medicine, there was food and shelter. Rome offered its poor good hospital care, as well as care for orphans, foundlings, fallen women, and lunatics.

Story was thirty-seven and going back to Rome—to his haunting, irresistible Rome—in December, 1856, when he landed in Italy with his family after a visit to Boston. The last leg of the trip, the forty miles from Civitavecchia, is described in the opening of *Roba di Roma*. He engages a yellow post-coach with three horses and a shabby, gaudy postilion, and, with a clatter of wheels and jingle-jangle of bells on the horses' backs, they make an early-morning start. They shake off a ragtag band of town beggars and go bowling down the Via Aurelia in sight of the glittering sea, past the ruins of Roman villas and vanished Pelasgic settlements that were old before the Etruscans came.

Half-way to Rome they change horses at Palo, a wretched little place of fishermen's huts, an inn, stables, and a desolate old fortress, now the restored Santa Severa, flanked by four towers. Eager to reach Rome before nightfall, the travelers strike inland over the Campagna, "dreary, weird, ghostly, the home of the winds, but its silence, sadness, and solitude are both soothing and impressive."

Mile after mile the coach lumbers on, the horses in a lather, steaming in the chill air; and suddenly at the crest of a hill they see the dome of St. Peter's hanging above the unseen city like a tethered balloon. The postilion covers the worn-out lace of his seedy livery with a heavy cloak that he flings over his shoulder to keep out the dampening air, gives a series of wild flourishes with his whip, breaks into guttural explosions of voice to urge along his horses, and they race at full gallop.

The loneliness of the countryside gives way to houses, to more houses, to groups of people at *osterie* sitting under the vine-covered arbors; and at last, toward sundown, they halt at Porta Cavalleggeri, a customs station, and over them rises the huge swelling dome of St. Peter's, golden in the last rays of sunset.

"The pillars of the gigantic colonnade of Bernini, as we jolted along, seemed to be marching in broad platoons," Story wrote. "The fountains piled their flexile columns of spray and waved them to and fro. The great bell clanged from the belfry. Groups wandered forth in the great piazza. The old Egyptian obelisk in the center pointed its lean finger to the sky. We were in Rome. This one moment of surprised sensation is worth the journey from Civitavecchia. Entered by no other gate is Rome so suddenly and completely possessed. Nowhere is the contrast as instantaneous as here, between the silent desolate Campagna and the splendor of St. Peter's—between the burrows of primitive Christianity and the gorgeousness of ecclesiastical Rome."

Twilight is deepening into dusk as they go through the Borgo. They see Castel Sant'Angelo and the rusty Tiber and plunge into deep, narrow streets, hearing all about them confused cries and loud voices, children screaming, men howling their wares for sale, bells ringing, priests, soldiers, peasants, and beggars thronging along.

"The *Trasteverini* were going home with their jackets hanging over one shoulder. Women in their rough woolen gowns stand in the doorways bareheaded, or looking out from windows and balconies, their black hair shining under the lanterns. Lights twinkle in the cavernous shops and under the Madonna shrines far within them.

"A funeral procession with its black banners, gilt with a death's head and crossbones, was passing by, its wavering candles born by the *confraternite* who marched along carelessly, shrouded from head to foot in white, with only two holes to glare through . . . It was dirty, but it was Rome; and to anyone who has lived long in Rome its very dirt has a charm which the neatness of no other place ever had."

Visitors like Dickens and many old residents did not think so. The execution Dickens witnessed was in a mean street near the Church of San Giovanni Decollato (the Beheaded)—"a street of rotten houses, which do not seem to belong to anybody, and do not seem ever to have been inhabited, and certainly have nothing in them . . . At the end of the street . . . a dust heap and piles of broken crockery, and mounds of vegetable refuse." The neighborhood, close to the Piazza della Verita and the Church of Santa Maria in Cosmedin, had hardly changed in the 1920s, when Mussolini's workmen pulled down the clotheslines at the so-called Temple of Vesta and cleared away the hovels that clung to the Temple of Fortuna Virilis.

To Story, the soil and stain which many call dirt was color. Thrift and cleanliness warred on the picturesque. Nothing was as prosaic as the rawly new. Time alone added a grace which man could never give a building.

"Fancy for a moment," he wrote, "the difference for the worse if all the grim, browned, rotted walls of Rome, with their peeling mortar, their thousand daubs of varying grays and yellows, their jutting brickwork and patched stonework, from whose intervals the cement has crumbled off, their waving weeds and grasses and flowers, now sparsely fringing their top, now thickly protruding from their sides, or clinging and making a home in the clefts and crevices of decay, were to be smoothed to a complete level, and whitewashed over into a uniform and monotonous tint. What a gain in cleanliness! What a loss in Beauty!"

He recalled a lovely old wall on the road between Grotta Ferrata and Frascati, a constant delight to his eyes until one day when the owner took it into his head to whitewash the wall. Story fumed. That man, he said, "was little better than a Vandal in taste."

Dirt and fleas. The dirt could be controlled; the fleas (*pulci*) were everywhere—in the churches, in the trains and carriages, in the houses of the poor, in the palazzo. Roman fleas were famous. "All Roman houses harbored them irremediably," wrote Mrs. Winthrop Chanler in *Roman Spring*. "They lived in the interstices of the brick floors and in the straw which lay under the carpets. There were methods of fighting the enemy, never of evicting him."

Frances Newman, a strong-minded Atlanta, Georgia, librarian, translator, and critic, wrote in the 1920s that no one who had read Walter Pater's essay on Leonardo da Vinci could look at the Mona Lisa in the Louvre without having a literary judgment affect the pure enjoyment of the painting. Not many people read Pater's little book of essays, *The Renaissance*, these days, and a large number have never even heard of Pater; but they have heard of Byron—it is likely that a good many may have read him or read about him, English and American tourists alike—and as they troop across Michelangelo's piazzetta on the Campidoglio and enter the Capitoline Museum, they are prepared to look without surprise at the Dying Gaul, which the poet, perpetuating an error of his day, called the Dying Gladiator. Praxiteles' Satyr, the Marble Faun of Hawthorne's novel, stands a few feet away. Byron's name may be uttered here by someone, but Hawthorne's rarely, since few people today can get through his novel and therefore have no idea how he made use of the statue and a monk from the Cappuchine church on Via Veneto and his other props to construct his absurd romance.

Byron's name may rise again among the literate, animated by a fragment of the poet's adaptation of the lines of the Venerable Bede—that while the Colosseum stands Rome and the world will endure—lines which annoyed James Joyce on a calm summer evening in 1906, when he and Nora visited the ruin and heard a London youth recite them aloud to his companion.

Considering Byron's brief association with Rome, the city has done well by him. During his 1817 visit, he posed for a small portrait bust by the Danish sculptor Thorwalden, whom he nettled by assuming an air of petulance. Nearly a century-and-a-half later, a copy of the head was attached to a body of white Carrera marble and unveiled in one of the shady avenues of the Villa Borghese.

Joyce, who worked as a bank clerk, left no mark on the city. He lived in Via Frattina, near the Spanish Steps, and Via de Monte Braziano, not far from the Tiber, in Renaissance Rome and close to the medieval house, the Albergo dell'Orso, where tradition says Dante lodged and Montaigne and Goethe were guests. The bank where Joyce worked, and wore out the seat of the trousers he had taken without permission

41

from his brother Stanislaus in Trieste, stood on the Via del Corso across from the Palazzo Chigi and Piazza Colonna. A department store now occupies the site.

Rome was too much for Joyce. After seven months, he went back to Trieste; and the ordeal of unheated lodgings and a hateful job might well have never been known to his readers if he had not unloaded his dissatisfaction on his brother. What a burden of complaints the mails carried across the Adriatic—with the usual requests for money. Yet Joyce was right about Rome—for Joyce. He was poor, shabby, almost penniless and unknown, and he made no intimate friends. The reality of the city oppressed him and gave him bad dreams. He was critical of Henry James, whom Stanislaus admired.

"What a beautiful country," Joyce wrote sarcastically to his brother. (Trieste at that time was Austrian.) "Your friend, H. J., ought to get a running kick in the arse for writing his tea-slop about it. I am damnably sick of Italy . . . and the Italians, outrageously, illogically sick. Every time a pupil asks me how I like Rome I vent some sneering remark." (Joyce gave some lessons in English while in Rome.) His behavior had a nightmarish aspect at the end, when he got drunk with two mailmen and went dancing with them on the Pincio; and a little later, having been paid off at the bank, he drank heavily and was robbed. He never returned to Rome.

The ruins that made Joyce uneasy were a restorative for Dickens, who returned to Rome in 1845, when he was thirty-three. He seems to have had little interest in Renaissance and Baroque Rome. One of his biographers, Una Pope-Hennessy, offered an explanation for his feelings.

"The measure of what one gets from sightseeing is governed by the amount one brings to sightseeing. Dickens brought very little. The educational and cultural background necessary to the understanding of the past was almost completely lacking and his reactions are sometimes silly and often shallow. In the paucity of his analogies the paucity of his general mental equipment is only too evident. Perhaps he could not comprehend great monuments in their majesty or integrity because there was nothing to link them up with human joys and human tears."

St. Peter's did not move him; the Colosseum did, and his description of his visit—the scene and his own feelings—gives us a better understanding of how the tourists of Dickens' day reacted.

"To see it crumbling there," he wrote, "an inch a year; its walls and arches overgrown with green; its corridors open to the day; the long grass growing in its porches; young trees of yesterday, springing up on its ragged parapets, and bearing fruit; chance produce of the seeds dropped there by the birds who build their nests within its chinks and crannies; to see its Pit of Fight filled up with earth, and the peaceful Cross planted in the centre; to climb into its upper halls, and look down on ruin, ruin, ruin, all about it; the triumphal arches of Constantine, Septimus Severus, and Titus; the Roman Forum; the Palace of the Caesars; the temples of the old religion, fallen down and gone; is to see the ghost of old Rome, wicked wonderful old city, haunting the very ground on which its people trod. It is the most impressive, the most stately, the most solemn, grand, majestic, mournful sight conceivable. Never, in its bloodiest prime, can the sight of the gigantic Colosseum, full and running over with the lustiest life, have moved one heart, as it must move all who look upon it now, a ruin. God be thanked: a ruin!"

CHAPTER 3

Awaking from the Long Dream

In 390 BC, three hundred and sixty years after its founding, Rome was destroyed by the Gauls. Livy tells us that when some of the homeless and destitute citizens advocated immigrating to the neighboring town of Veii, which they had conquered, Camillus, the general who had taken the city, opposed the move. Rome, he said, had been divinely ordained to be where it was. Rome had advantages not to be found elsewhere. The Tiber supplied good drinking water. It was excellent for bringing downstream on barges the grains and fruits of the fertile countryside, and good for floating up from Ostia cargoes from the outside world—the Mediterranean world. Rome was rebuilt and prospered.

How many times in the following centuries had the city undergone the agonies of pillage, fire, plague, and despair? Now, in 1870, Italian unification had thrown upon an amiable people and their city and their very lives the burden of changes which few desired—an upheaval with consequences nobody could foresee.

It was the speed of the changes—a revolution, archeologist Lanciani called it—as much as the changes themselves that angered and saddened so many people. It was as if the city authorities were bent on destroying Rome. Italians, someone remarked, were never so savage as when they cut down a tree; and in the emergent capital lovely gardens were uprooted and noble and venerable trees sacrificed by the hundreds. Scores of buildings were razed. The dust rose everywhere.

In the fourteen years between January 1, 1872 and the end of 1885, the municipal government opened, paved, drained, and built eight-two miles of streets. New residential quarters covered 1,158 acres; 3,094 houses were built or enlarged, bringing an addition of 95,260 rooms.

Paris had undergone a transformation earlier, losing its medieval aspect to become a bright new city; but that was surgery of a different order, and Paris was not Rome. Men like Story and Hare rejected the argument of a parallel. Rome was Rome, the Eternal City, unique and untouchable and not to be measured against other cities.

Rome was unique, certainly. It always had been and would go on being so, whatever changes were made. Its name alone conjured up a vision no other city could evoke. Its memory was the memory of man himself. No man who came to Rome felt himself a stranger, and no man left without leaving a part of himself behind.

Story and Hare were not testy old men: Hare was thirty-six in 1870 and Story fifty-one. Story eventually surrendered and went away. Hare was obdurate—and intemperate. A Roman by birth, like Lanciani, he could speak of "my city" with the fervor of Cola di Rienzo and quote with unaffected pride the lines Horace had written nineteen hundred years before: *Alme Sol! Possis nihil Urbe Roma vesere maius*—lines which Lanciani inscribed in 1903 in a friend's copy of his *Pagan and Christian Rome* and which he translated on the same flyleaf as: O genial Sun! May you not be able to behold anything greater than the City of Rome.

Hare regarded the new Rome as a personal affront. "There is not a single point in the entirely modern Rome which calls for anything but contempt," he wrote. Walking through the streets which branch off Via Venti Settembre west of Porta Pia, he was distressed by the Chicago-style structures, as he called them—"the ugliest buildings of the new town, wide shadeless streets of featureless, ill-built, stuccoed houses bearing foolish names connected with Piedmontese history."

Lanciani agreed that it was "impossible to imagine anything more commonplace and out of keeping and shabby and tasteless than the new quarters which encircle the city of 1870." The lovely regions crossed by Via Salaria and Via Nomentana, "formerly studded with patrician villas and gardens . . . have been transformed into an ugly city of five-storied anti-esthetic houses looking more like barracks than like dwellings for the cultivated inhabitants of the metropolis of a great kingdom."

Still, Lanciani was reluctant to blame the city government, which he felt had been taken by surprise, never dreaming of the rapid population increase, nor "that Italian and foreign speculation was ready to throw hundreds of millions [of dollars] on the Roman market." The value of land rose "from a few centimes the square metre to more than one thousand francs," and Lanciani blamed the greedy Roman aristocracy, "this degenerate race which sold the magnificent villas their forefathers had built and laid out for the comfort, health and welfare of their fellow-citizens."

But critical as he was of the disappearance of the gardens and charming lanes and the gradual encroachment of the city on the Campagna, Lanciani could praise some changes. "There were quarters like the Ghetto and the Regola" (a *rione* embracing an area near Palazzo Farnese), "the picturesqueness of which was the direct product of filth, and of a half-savage state of moral and material life," he wrote.

"There were the banks of the Tiber—the main sewer of the city—the poisonous effluvia of which, at low water, affected all the bordering districts. Can we honestly blame the city government for their efforts to improve this shameful state of things?"

The work of carving the wide avenue that was named the Via Vittorio Emanuele out of the solid body of Renaissance Rome demanded exquisite skill. The risks were great, the creation of a modern street through Campo Marzio was urgent; but just as urgent was the preservation of the quarter of the city extending from the Palazzo Farnese to the Palazzo Borghese. Such monuments as the Cancellaria, the Pantheon, Piazza Navona, and numerous churches and palaces remained untouched. It was this part of Rome that Marion Crawford, who had been away from the city and was disturbed at the changes, later examined in *Don Orsino*, a novel published with great success in 1891.

"Old Rome is gone," he wrote. "The narrow streets are broad thoroughfares, the Jews' quarter is a flat and dusty building lot, the fountain of Ponte Sisto is swept away . . . He who was born and bred in the Rome of twenty years ago comes back after a long absence to wander as a stranger in streets he never knew, among houses unfamiliar to him, amidst a population whose speech sounds strange to his ears . . . Where once he lingered in old days to glance at the river, or to dream of days yet older and long gone . . . he is hustled and jostled by an eager crowd, thrust to the wall by huge, grinding, creaking carts, threatened with modern death by the wheel of the modern omnibus, deafened by the yells of the modern news vendors, robbed, very likely by the light fingers of the modern inhabitants. And yet he feels Rome must be Rome still."

Brooding on the changes, he wanders off and climbs the Janiculum to the Church of Sant'Onofrio. As daylight falters, he looks out on the city—on Castel Sant'Angelo and the Pantheon and the dark web of old streets—and tells himself that Rome is still there, imperturbable, eternal.

Rome, as Lanciani reminded the world with scholarly forbearance, had always lived at the expense of the past. In a certain measure, he said, "every generation has absorbed or destroyed the works of the preceding one, and it is wonderful that so much should still be left of the works raised by the ancients after a process of destruction and transformation which has been going on for fourteen centuries."

The archeologists who cleared the Forum Romanum and delved where new streets and new houses were being built were justifiably proud of their achievements, but had to defend their industry and integrity against rude and senseless attacks by people who accused them of profaning the old city, suggesting they were no better than ghouls. Still, the work in the Forum was not universally criticized. Digging there had started as early as the Renaissance, when Raphael and his friends had done some exploratory work. In 1821 Valadier had restored the Arch of Titus, removing the excrescences of centuries. (The *Frangipani* had incorporated the arch in one of their strongholds in the Middle Ages.) The Dowager Duchess of Devonshire had privately financed excavations that uncovered the base of the column of Phocas; the French had contributed large sums for digging, and had brought to the work the archeological skills Napoleon had encouraged in Egypt. The Germans were active.

What really upset many people was the feeling that the whole city seemed to be under attack by pick and spade. Still, such criticism was hardly justified. New buildings required new foundations, and wherever one dug there was a temptation to dig deeper. Most of the land was held by the church and the titled rich, and for years the aristocrats had dug up their Campagna estates and sold statues outside the country, or had built up their own collections of antiquities in their villas and palazzi.

Lanciani, answering the criticism, said the views of most laymen were based on personal, political, or religious feelings that had little to do with reality. "It appears to me," he wrote, "that to satisfy our critics whose love for art and archeology goes beyond the limits of practical good sense, it would have been desirable to have had Rome annihilated with the empire at the end of the fifth century, so that we might excavate it now with the same ease and with the same freedom with which we excavate Ostia and Pompeii."

Much of what was now emerging would have lain close to the surface, and there would be no need to dig through seventy-two feet of soil, debris, and rubble, for example, to reach the inner courtyard of the House of the Vestals at the foot of the Palatine; or to go down fifty-three feet at the Piazza dell'Esquilino behind Santa Maria Maggiore to discover the remains of some baths with a precious collection of statues, busts, bronzes, vessels, inscriptions, and so on. Ancient Romans had been profligate and indifferent and sometimes, scared by earthquakes or fires or in emergencies real and imaginary, had abandoned their houses.

Amid all the upset, Rome, in 1870, had twenty thousand beggars and another twenty-two thousand mendicants, who wore the habits of various religious orders, *fratelli cercatori*, as they were called. But this and the fact that ninety percent of the population was illiterate were of no concern to the aristocracy and the fashionable *forestieri*.

Pio Nono's later loss of temporal power also hardly discommoded the Terrys and their friends; the teas, the balls, the dinner and receptions, the hunt meetings on the Campagna that had come into fashion, all went on. The nobility with close ties to the pope resented the new regime and sorrowed with Pio Nono when he moved from the Quirinale to the Vatican.

Mrs. Winthrop Chanler's youth and intellectual resilience made it easy for her to accept the changes that distressed so many older people. Her memories were as fresh as the early summer days she had loved in her girlhood, when the foreign visitors would leave Rome and the air was full of the scent of flowers and the sound of the fountains. Now a word, a place, the turning of a corner could start a flow of images: she had been taken to Liszt's sixty-sixth birthday party in 1877; she had heard him conduct a class in the Sala Dante of the Palazzo Poli; he had liked her and encouraged her pianistic talents; she had watched him at prayer in Santa Maria dell'Anima, the German church near Piazza Navona.

She had studied with Giovanni Sgambati; she had been a guest at the Thursday afternoon musicals at Madame Helbig's house on the Tarpein Rock. (Madame Helbig, born Princess Schachowakoia, had studied piano with Clara Schumann and Liszt and was married to Wolfgang Helbig, director of the German School of Archeology in Rome. The German government built him a house near the Palazzo Caffarelli, which was then the German embassy and is now one of the Capitoline museums.) Madame Helbig entertained the famous—Eleanora Duse was her friend. The historians Mommsen and Gregorovius came to the Helbigs' along with artists, diplomats, titled travelers.

The Rome of Mrs. Chanler's childhood thus had been the placid and picturesque city that had grown out of the seventeenth and eighteenth centuries, seedy but enchanting, an overpowering and humbling presence. The centuries jostled one another, yet never had come to a violent collision. The wisest scholars had confessed their limitation when trying to explain Rome. Gibbon had gone away from it to write of its glory and decline in London and Lausanne.

After 1870 the principal change in the structure of society was really its expansion, as a new set of diplomats arrived at the royal court to complement those assigned to the Holy See. The newcomers, like their counterparts, were witty and elegant—at any rate in their memoirs and in what others wrote about them. They had money and were at home in Paris, Vienna, London, Venice, and Brussels; they were of the noble class that owned castles and estates in Poland, Russia, Austria, Silesia,

Hungary, and Rumania. The new capital so annoyed journalists from
the north that one of them, Eraldo Baretti, proposed giving Rome back
to the pope and building a new capital elsewhere, an idea that city
planners of today think should have been adopted.

The arrival of "the Italians"—workers from Piedmont and
Lombardy and southern Italy, with little money but hopes for a better
life in Rome—provoked *un piccolo terremoto*, "a little earthquake," in
the tourist industry. *Forestieri*, one of the newspapers reported, were
prudently cutting the cord, leaving Rome while the Italians and the
Romans battled: the outsiders cried that the lodgings they could afford
for their families were dirty and cold; the landlords demanded high
rents for better quarters. As the population increased, so did the price
of food. Rome would be a new metropolis, but its birth pains would
be agonizing.

Living space had to be found for the new ambassadors, ministers,
senators, deputies, and hundreds of civil servants. Government
offices were needed. A bureaucracy such as no pope had ever
dreamed of was taking root. *Un piccolo terremoto* was too soft a
term. The Tiber, troublesome and dangerous for centuries, was to be
tamed—canalized—though it meant the destruction of the city's rustic
charm. The building of new streets and houses went on with great
haste, but the river still ran its willful course until Giuseppe Garibaldi,
Italian general and politician, came up from the south and expended
some of his smoldering fire. He even talked about straightening the
Tiber's loop; on that point he was ignored, but construction of the
high embankment was begun. No longer would the river flow inland
to make lakes of Piazza del Popolo and St. Peter's Square and render all
the city up to the foot of the Quirinal Hill a sinister waterway.

There were no protests when the Teatro Apollo, north of
Ponte Sant'Angelo on the left bank, was razed to make way for the

embankment. A plaque and a small drinking fountain mark the site where Verdi's *Il trovatore* and *Un ballo in maschera* had their premieres, the first on January 19, 1853 and *Un ballo* on February 17, 1859. The *Il trovatore* opening took place during one of the recurrent Tiber floods. The streets were full of water, and the impresario had raised the prices; but this was Verdi, and opera lovers began lining up at seven o'clock in the morning to buy tickets.

Now, attracted as much by the new city as by the ancient ruins and the later architectural wonders, the galleries and churches, tourists arrived in swelling numbers. Anthony Trollope, writing about tourists for the *Pall Mall Gazette* from his vantage point in Villina Trollope in Piazza Independenza in Florence, observed the people on their way to Rome.

He divided them into eight classes: first, those who came abroad to be educated but were worn out in the process of assimilating so much information; second, solitary travelers, homesick and dejected, who attached themselves to chance acquaintances; third, the Art Tourist, who raced from gallery to church to museum, guidebook in hand; fourth, the uninhibited foreigner, who asked strange and ludicrous questions; fifth, those who came for fun, were slovenly dressed, loud in manner, and saw everything as funny; sixth, the superior female, impatient with all who knew less than she did about Italian art, history, and literature; seventh, those who came because it was the thing to do and they wanted to boast at home; and eighth, husbands who were brought by devoted wives—for their own good.

Story, who had called it "a desecration" when Louis Napoleon "scraped the stained and venerable Notre Dame into cleanliness" in the rehabilitation of Paris, was saddened by Rome's transformation. Yet he acknowledged that, apart from the destruction of the great villas and gardens which formerly lent such a peculiar flavor to Rome, the city's material advantages had improved.

Hare was less tolerant. "Twelve years of Sardinian rule—1870-1882—have done more for the destruction of Rome, with its beauty and interest, than all the invasions of the Goths and Vandals," he wrote. "The whole aspect of the city is changed, and the picturesqueness of old days must now be sought in such obscure corners as have escaped the hands of the spoiler. The glorious gardens of the Villa Negroni and Villa Ludovisi have been annihilated; many precious street memorials of medieval history have been swept away; ancient convents have been leveled with the ground or turned into barracks; historic churches have been yellow-washed or modernized; the cloisters of Michelangelo have been walled up; the pagan ruins have been denuded of all that gave them picturesqueness or beauty; and several of the finest fountains have been pulled down or bereaved of half their waters.

"The Palace of the Caesars is stripped of all the flowers and shrubs which formerly adorned it. The glorious view from the Pincio has been destroyed by the hideous barracks built between the Tiber and St. Peter's. The Tiber itself has been diverted from its exquisitely picturesque course, to the destruction, amongst many other interesting memorials, of the lovely Farnesina gardens and the fatal injury of the inestimable frescoes in the palace."

He thought that in the general cleaning up the Baths of Caracalla had been turned from one of the world's most beautiful spots—like the Colosseum, the Baths had been covered with vegetation—into a place as unattractive as the ruins of a London warehouse. He was outraged by the government's seizure of the Quirinal Palace, where the king took up residence, and pointed out that, before he left Florence, Victor Emanuel had solemnly promised over and over again "that the property and privileges of Catholic institutions should be respected and secured." The confiscation of the Quirinale was followed by "the spoliation and ruin of the eight great convents—Santa Maria in Vallicella, Santi Apostoli, San Silvestro in Capite, San Silvestro in Monte Cavallo, Santa Maria della Vergine, Sant'Andrea della Valle, Santa Maria sopra Minerva, and Sant'Agostino."

The confiscation went on, and on May 27, 1873, "the insidious bill was passed which drove the monks and nuns from their homes, robbing them of their dowries by a process which was simply theft, making them dependent upon ill-paid pensions . . . and putting their lands and houses up to public auction."

In the preface to the eighth edition of *Roba di Roma*, written in St. Moritz, Switzerland, in 1886, when he was sixty-seven, Story conceded that some changes were inevitable, not merely minor ones such as Henry James observed in 1873 when he remarked that instead of *monsignori* in purple stockings with their large trains or servitors, the streets of Rome revealed the construction of new sidewalks, the widening of streets, and better drainage. To mourn the past—the already shrunken years of his own lifetime—was to squander decent emotions. Still, Story felt he could scarcely cast aside precious memories. For a moment he was nostalgic.

"It [Rome] is no longer the peaceful . . . place where the pilgrim might wander and muse over the past, far from the busy traffic of the world, and its worry and interests. The contemplative and almost monastic charm of retirement, which once made it a city apart from all others, is gone or going, and it is gradually drawing into line with all other cities. Life is astir in the crowded streets. It is awaking from its long dream. But one cannot but sigh in remembering how pleasant and soothing that dream of life was, and despite all reasoning there lingers a fond regret for the older time when Rome was sleeping."

Could it be only twenty-six years since Henry James, his fellow Bostonian, had thought the city medieval? Story died in 1895. In that year the touring club, Ciclistico Italiano, a band of stalwart young men, organized a caravan of bicycles in Milan and pedaled across the Apennines to Rome, to the astonishment of all Italy. In that year Michele Lancia made his first automobile. The Fiat was born four years later, in 1899, and a few years later still a new breed of tourists—*turisti Italiani a quarto ruote*—rolled into Rome, chugging along bravely at a maximum speed of eighteen miles an hour.

The discoveries and the changes continued to be talked about over the years, at all levels of society. Mrs. Mary King Waddington, daughter of Dr. Charles King, president of Columbia College in New York, who retired to Italy, where he died in 1867, had left Rome tearfully, never dreaming she would return in 1880 as the wife of William Henry Waddington, a retired French premier born of English parents in France. The new Rome pained her sensibilities, she wrote—"the new streets, an abomination, tall and ugly *maisons de location* and official buildings so new and regular—awful! . . . It wasn't until we got near the Piazza di Spagna that I really felt I was back in Rome."

Twenty-four years later, on another long visit to Rome, she writes home: "They tell me the present generation comes much less to the Villa Borghese and Pincio. They are much more sporting—ride, drive automobiles and play golf. There are two golf clubs now—one at Villa Doria Pamphili, the other at Aqua Santa. Every time we go out on the Campagna we meet men with golf clubs and rackets." And: "There are great changes—high buildings, quays, boats, carts with heavy stones and quantities of workmen—really quite an air of a busy port—busy of course in a modified sense, as no Roman ever looks as if he were working hard, and there are always two or three looking on, and talking, for every one who works—however, there is certainly much more life in the streets and the city looks prosperous."

Prince Colonna invites her to watch him carrying a cross at the head of an impressively solemn Easter Sunday procession. A friend advises her that summer is the best time to see a Roman fiesta, "when the whole population is out in the streets all day and all night in a frenzy of amusement—and no priests are in the streets."

Arthur Symons, the English poet and critic, who was much more at home in London and Paris than he ever was in Italy, thought the best time to see the Roman people was on St. Stephen's Day, December 26, when they went to San Stefano Rotondo on the Caelian, a fifth-century building and the largest circular church in the world, famous for its frescoes of martyrdom. "From early morning till late in the afternoon an incessant stream of people, mostly young people, out of all the alleys of Rome and from all the hills of the Campagna, surges in and out of the narrow doorway . . . Outside . . . there are lines of booths covered with sweets and toys, fruits and cakes." Not having known the old Rome—he was born in 1865—he can compare the new capital in 1896 and later, in 1904, only with what he has read and seen in pictures.

The racket of physical change, the hammering and sawing and pounding, the crushing traffic of drays and carts hauling marble, tufa, bricks, tiles, and glass, the endless burrowing to recover relics of the past, the movement of people—all these jarred the spirits of men like Symons, elated one day, dejected the next. He was displeased by the new Palazzo di Giustizia rising on the right bank of the Tiber north of Castel Sant'Angelo, and by the massive white marble monument to Victor Emanuel II, which was begun in 1885 and completed in 1911—the Vittoriana, as it was called or, jocosely by Americans, the Wedding Cake, which was slowly extending its dominance over Piazza Venezia and the skyline.

Symons was not singular in his resentment. The Italians, as the non-Roman people of Italy were called even when they settled in Rome—and even most Romans—may have been indifferent, but Symons was a foreigner, an Englishman, and foreigners—Englishmen in particular—had a proprietary interest in Rome, a possessiveness that was no less real because it happened to be emotional and intellectual.

The shrill outburst from Louise de Ramée, the novelist Ouida, at the time the Fountain of the Ponte Sisto was threatened by the building of the Tiber embankments was a typical reaction of a French citizen who loved Rome. The story of this fountain had really begun in 1612, when Paul V revived the second-century Trajan aqueduct and brought the water down from Lake Bracciano to the Janiculum. He was so proud of the achievement that he asked his architect, Giovanni Fontana, to carry the water across the river.

Fontana chose a spot opposite Ponte Sisto, which had been built 125 years earlier by Pope Sixtus IV. He sketched a lovely fountain but could find no proper site. The logical place, facing the bridge, was occupied by the Ospizio dei Mendicanti, a shelter housing two thousand beggars, which Giovanni's brother Domenico had built for Sixtus V at the river end of Via Giulia a quarter of a century earlier.

Giovanni solved the problem with admirable Italian ingenuity. He put the fountain into the wall of the hospice, and there for 265 years its bright waters were universally praised. But one day in 1879, the waters stopped running. The engineers were bringing the embankment southward, and the hospice and the fountain were to be demolished.

Among fountain lovers there was consternation. The loudest and most articulate voice was Ouida's. She had written about Rome's fountains in *Ariadne*, and La Fontana di Ponte Sisto was her favorite. She sent a passionate letter to *The Times* of London. Other people, Romans and foreigners, took up the cry: to destroy the fountain was a criminal act that must be prevented.

The protests were useless. In August the fountain was pulled down, but the agitation went on: the fountain was too beautiful to die. It must be brought back to life at a new location. Eighteen years later, in 1897, the municipal government acceded to the proposal and chose as the fountain's new home the Trastevere end of Ponte Sisto. A year passed before work began. The stones had been dispersed. Some were found in a municipal warehouse at Testaccio, some had been buried and had to be dug up; the epigraph was found in the warehouse of Volturno; other pieces were found in various yards and on the Janiculum. A lion's head that had been dredged out of the Tiber was in a museum. There existed old prints showing the fountain in the wall of the Beggar's Hospice, as well as a painting, a watercolor by Roesler Franz. Thus the old fountain was rebuilt.

Incidentally, Roesler Franz—who was born in 1845 into a German banking family—loved Rome to such an extraordinary degree that he spent his life painting it. He was not a very good painter, but his pictures had warmth and pictorial fidelity. He painted 120 watercolors and probably suspected for an instant that their antiquarian value would rise to such an eminence that they would be exhibited at the City of Rome Museum in the Palazzo Braschi. The collection was named *Roma Sparita* (Vanished Rome), and the title survives as the title of a book reproducing some of the paintings and is given to the thousands of postcard reproductions.

Crude as the paintings are, they convey a vitality that would be absent in the work of a more skillful artist. They suggest the smells and the dirt of Rome before its massive cleanup. Here is the Papal Rome of Hare and Story. Nuns in wide-winged snowy wimples trudging past a disengaged oxcart in the unpaved piazzetta of San Pietro in Vincoli; scabrous brown houses festooned with drying clothes; idlers lounging in grimy doorways; men hunching themselves on patient little donkeys or carrying back-breaking loads of firewood; Ghetto women in bright dresses of red and green and blue; small boys rowing and fishing in the yellow Tiber; houses with the melancholy air of condemned

59

tenements in the close streets of Trastevere, houses dangerously near the swirling river. Recognizable buildings are few: Santa Sabina on the Aventine; the so-called Temple of Vesta and the Campanile of Santa Maria in Cosmedin looming above the arched mouth of the Cloaca Maxima; Santi Quattro Coronati; a rosy fortress on a weedy hillock; a boy shepherd guiding a small flock up a muddy lane to San Nicolo da Tolentino beyond the stained Tritone Fountain; broom sellers, peddlers, gossips in Via dei Capellari near Campo de' Fiori; rain puddles in broken streets; glimpses of great churches towering above the poverty and squalor; a knife grinder at his machine under a corner shrine; a woman bearing on her kerchiefed head an enormous load; the crumbling steps of an old palazzo entrance; vegetable and fruit stands in Piazza Barberini; old arches linking old buildings—an air of decay everywhere—and everywhere life.

Since Italian unification, the show of ecclesiastical power, the proud processions of the clergy against the background of architectural beauty and demeaning poverty, had also vanished; and for many older people this was reckoned a loss. It was all the more poignant because it had been so commonplace in Papal Rome, especially in the eighteenth and early-nineteenth centuries. On fine afternoons the long street running from the Quirinale Palace to Porta Pia had been a favorite promenade for popes and cardinals and the aristocracy—a pleasant mile past the Bernini Church of Sant'Andrea al Quirinale, the Borromini Church of San Carlino at the intersection of Via Quatro Fontane; Santa Susanna and Santa Maria della Vittoria, and the Moses Fountain—the *mostra* of Aqua Felice.

It was a ceremonious stroll, all politeness, a sustained hum of gossip and news. Grand equipages could be seen there, sights for the stranger to turn into a lifetime of talk. Possibly the greatest of these spectacles was to be seen long before Story or Hare were born—the appearance of Cardinal de Bernis, French ambassador, who never made a public appearance without his usual retinue of thirty-eight footmen, eight couriers, ten Swiss Guards, four gentlemen, two chaplains, and eight valets-de-chambre, apart from his coachmen, grooms, and mounted equerries.

But while the pageantry was gone now from the streets of Rome, there was no lessening of splendor at the Vatican. Leo XIII, elected at the age of sixty-eight as Pio Nono's successor, reigned for twenty-five years, and the anniversaries of his coronation were big social affairs that jammed the Sistine Chapel and the Sala Regia with highly privileged men and women, both Italians and foreigners.

Twenty-two years after his irascible outburst against the transgressing monarchy, Augustus Hare still lived in Rome, partly on his earnings as a writer and on services for royal visitors, who paid him well. He guided the Duke of Connaught, Queen Victoria's youngest son, later Gustav V of Sweden, who gave him a decoration that pleased him so much that he loved to show it off. He boasted afterward that its brilliance enabled him to take two young friends to Leo's anniversary celebration, one as his chaplain, the other as his equerry.

Hare thought the pontiff looked like a dying man as he gave his benediction.

"Only his eyes lived," he wrote, "and lived only in his office; otherwise his perfectly spiritualized countenance seemed utterly unconscious of the thundering *evvivas* with which he was greeted, and which rose into a perfect roar as he was carried into the Sala Regia."

PART II

Scenes of the Twentieth Century

CHAPTER 4

Roman Twilights . . . Rambles and Cameos

*I*n the summer, thousands of tourists arrived by car, train, and bus. They came by air, on foot, and on noisy dirty motorcycles. They swarmed in and out of the dusty sun-scorched Colosseum and the Forum Romanum and along the sidewalks of Via Veneto, Via del Corso, Via Nazionale, and Via dei Fori Imperiali, and up and down the Spanish Steps, up and down the steps of the Vittoriana—the monument to Victor Emanuel II—around the Pantheon and Piazza Navona, and moved sluggishly, hundreds and hundreds of them, through the wide corridors of the Vatican Museums. The sound of voices in the Sistine Chapel was a low unbroken roar. The guides, gabbling in a dozen languages, could scarcely be heard.

On one of our early trips to Rome, within a few hours of our arrival, we had gone around the corner from our hotel, the charming old Continentale, to hear Bellini's *I puritani* at the Rome Opera. In those early spring weeks as we were settling down, neither Goethe nor

Stendhal could have been happier. Enchantment lay ahead in every step, and no grubby street was too grubby for us to walk through. Listening to the *vigili urbani* (city police) band playing its own arrangements of Verdi and Puccini on the Pincio on Sunday afternoons was heaven. Tourists jammed the Pincian Terrace; the short ones had to stand on tiptoe behind the front ranks to see the sunset.

When the flood of tourists was too great, we avoided the Spanish Steps and Piazza Navona and, at sunset, the Pincian Terrace. Late summer afternoons were the loveliest of times—enchanting, one could say, when an unnatural quiet settled over the city. Sometimes we strolled down to the Quirinale and sat in a small public garden across from the *manica lunga*, the long sleeve or flank of the palace. No one came to the garden at that hour, and we rested on one of the low benches behind the high equestrian statue of Carlo Alberto, King of Sardinia, until the base of the monument was in shadow and it was time to go to the piazza, past the sentries and the white figures of Castor and Pollux and their horses to the balustrade at the head of the fifty-two steps that go down to Via della Dataria. Here we stood gazing out on the city until the glow faded behind St. Peter's, the dome no longer was visible, and lights began to go on in the many windows of the Quirinale. By the time we descended the steps and the slope beyond and turned toward Trevi, the fountain was ablaze and tourists crowded the steps of Santi Vicenzo ed Anastasio.

To sit on the steps of Aracoeli was a conceit we managed, a little self-consciously, to support the illusion that we could retreat into a more desirable past. Our love of Rome bred such conceits, and our daily wanderings nourished them. Sometimes only the thickness of a wall separated us from another century. One day we went into a workshop near Campo de' Fiori and saw a man restoring an eighteenth-century sedan chair, patiently examining the shabby, brittle upholstery, a warped door, the faded armorial bearings. The man talked about the chair and the skill of the maker in the way a bookbinder we knew in a small inconspicuous shop in Via Torino spoke of the beautiful volumes in golden leather and crimson, azure and violet, yellow and green, that he had bound with his own hands and was loath to yield to their owners, so much of himself having gone into the work.

Aracoeli's 124 steps were too formidable a climb in the waning day to tempt weary sightseers from the Cordonata's easy ascent to the Campidoglio, and though we were never alone, the company on the steps rarely numbered more than eight or ten. The steps were fourteenth-century Rome, and a reminder of men's medieval faith; the Cordonata's graceful incline was Michelangelo's sixteenth century. Henry Adams had sat on the steps in the nineteenth century, and a hundred years before Adams, in 1764, when the steps already were four hundred years old, Edward Gibbon had loitered there, a plump, confident little Englishman of twenty-seven, equably facing, though he had no idea it would take so long, the labor of research and the fourteen and one-half years of writing the story of the Roman Empire's decline and fall.

The original steps were cut from white marble that one of the Colonna—Giovanni—had taken from the fallen Temple of the Sun in the Colonna gardens on the Quirinal Hill and given to the desolate city at the time of the plague, the *morbo nero* or black death in 1349. Dazzling white in the squalor and decay of the city, the steps had risen on the rocky slope up which bare-footed men and women with penitential ropes around their necks and ashes on their heads had crawled to pray to the Blessed Virgin for deliverance. The number of petitioners could not have been great, for the population of Rome had dwindled in the Middle Ages long before the first infected rat crept ashore at Genoa from the ship that carried the plague from the East. The popes, in 1349, were at Avignon in France, obstinately refusing to return to the true seat of Christendom. An earthquake that year collapsed part of the outer wall of the Colosseum.

We wondered often as we sat on Aracoeli's steps, watching the chimney swifts sweep and rise and circle in the pallid sky, why the crude façade of the church had never been sheathed in marble. Marble had lain everywhere in abundance—in the Forum, at the Colosseum, on the Palatine, in broken temples and baths—marbles from Africa, Greece, and Asia Minor, there for the taking, the precious marbles of many colors that afterwards went into the building of St. Peter's and the Renaissance and Baroque churches and palaces. Aracoeli, exquisite within, was bare outside on its lovely eminence.

In the years of Rome's stagnation, men had come down from Pisa and Orvieto to buy or steal the marbles of Rome, Ostia, and Porto for their new cathedrals. Nowhere else in the world was there so much marble of all kinds; yet the brick surface of Aracoeli's façade, which could have been made as handsome as that of any small church in Italy—San Miniato in Florence, for example—remained as drab as the garb of its owners, the Franciscans.

Pope Innocent IV had given Aracoeli to the order in 1250, taking it from the Benedictines, who had inherited it from some Greek monks. The Franciscans had joyfully rebuilt the basilica. They had scavenged through the vast quarry in their backyard for serpentine, porphyry, and various marbles, bright and dark, to pave the floor of the nave. They had placed in the nave, to separate it from the aisles, twenty-two columns, two of white marble, two of apollino, and eighteen of Egyptian granite—columns that had been cut seventeen hundred years earlier.

For the exterior they had done nothing. Was a lesson to be read in this: the plain, unattractive surface, the rightness within? No, that was too obvious. The monks had simply spent their extraordinary medieval energies on Aracoeli's interior and laid down their tools.

The contrast would always be there; that was Rome. Pius IX, an inveterate snuff user, carried a large cretonne red-and-blue-checked handkerchief like the ones used by Lorraine farmers. Francis Wey, the French traveler, had taken note of this "homely rag" and its humble place in the setting of imperial purple and gold that framed the papacy. Incense and snuff.

We had our own contrasts: the beautiful leather volumes in the binderies of Via Torino, Via della Scrofa, and other dull streets; the sedan chain *in restauro*, and outside, in the lumpy, oil-stained, narrow streets, a cheap little dented Fiat; the charming semi-circular porch of Santa Maria della Pace and—in the shadows at the side of the church—a rat feeding in a pile of garbage.

* * *

From the first, we were wanderers in a strange city, loving it, yet unable to define clearly its attraction, since it never seemed an alien place. In our early visits we favored the eastern end of Rome, far out Nomentana way, where we had found in Via Ajaccio the small palazzo turned *pensione* and, not far off, a tiny park where small children played under the restraining hands of grandmothers. This was Parco Paganini, named for the violinist.

The park was new, its trees were old. The land here was once remote from Rome. Nero had ridden along the ancient Via Nomentana with a servant to the lonely farmhouse just across the Aniene Bridge, to end his life with a dagger in his throat.

Rome revealed itself to us in pieces. Too often we blundered into places, as we did once when we found a portal open, entered an unfamiliar building, and found ourselves in the courtyard of the Palazzo della Sapienza; and, though we had heard much about Piazza

Navona, we saw it for the first time not at ground level, but from the back window of the Palazzo Braschi, the City of Rome Museum. It was vast, and its shape was perfect, a perfection formed in the first century of the Christian era when the pagan emperor Domitian built himself a circus, a stadium for athletic exhibitions.

The piazza had arrived in the twentieth century with two churches, Sant'Agnese in Agone and the Madonna del Sacro Cuore, several palazzi, three magnificent fountains, and tall buildings where people of good fortune dwelt. The wonder of it all was that the space had survived in a city where real-estate values had risen so dizzily after 1870.

And strange, too, as it now seems to us, we also went to the Forum Romanum and sat in front of Santo Lorenzo in Miranda. This had been the Temple of Antonius and Faustina, which had been converted into a church in the extravagance of Renaissance building. The huge marble steps had gone into the construction of St. Peter's and had been replaced here by wooden steps. Somehow the whole place seemed wrong.

*   *   *

Noon was the sacristans' time, the bully *sagrestani* who began clearing out their churches five, ten, fifteen minutes before noon, growling, thundering, threatening!

Once we were in San Vitale, thirty-five steps down from the sidewalk of Via Nazionale, when the *sagrestano* loomed in the shadows and said he was closing. My wife asked him a question, and he spun out a rapid answer about the antiquity of the building (which we knew) and its fourth-century heavy wooden doors.

My wife interrupted him. "What about the candle that you just blew out?" she asked. "I put one hundred lire in the box. Are you going to light that candle again at four o'clock?"

"Si, si, si, Signora," he replied quickly. "Si, si, si. Buon giorno."

With raised hands jerkily pushing the unresisting air, he impelled us silently into the sunlight.

*   *   *

Rome is a postcard city. It even exists as a postcard city for many people who have never been there, and for many other people who have been there and wish to keep reminders of Rome—the Colosseum, St. Peter's, the Forums, the arches, the fountains and piazzas, bridges, palaces, cloisters, cafes, and walls, both Aurelian and Servian. Over the years all of these have been engraved, etched, painted in oils and watercolors, and photographed. These images have been transferred to postcards. Medieval and Renaissance maps of the city, sometimes crudely drawn, as well as exquisitely delicate engravings of the Campagna, lovely *bozzette* (sketches) of broken walls and aqueducts, portraits of saints, emperors, and popes appear on postcards.

We saw them everywhere—every museum sells postcards that cover most of its important exhibits. Two of these museums, the Vatican and the Museo Nazional Romano, alone produce hundreds of postcards. Still more are turned out for palaces that have opened certain rooms to the public. Churches, chapels, and shrines, which number more than four hundred, are no less indefatigable in providing pictures of their exteriors, their noble facades, their campanili, and their contents—statues, paintings, mosaics, baldacchini, sarcophagi, the incised lids of floor tombs, altars, marble pavements, decorated ceilings, frescoes, baptismal fonts, pulpits, chapels, iron grills, candelabra, episcopal thrones, monstrances of gold and silver, and chalices, censers, and crucifixes, many of them studded with priceless jewels—everything, in fact, that seemed suitable for reproduction on a postcard.

Masses of postcards are on sale at newsstands, stationery stores, hotels, and in the museums and churches themselves. Street peddlers carry them in shoulder bags. They are stacked up at outdoor bookstalls. Even the flea market at Porta Portese sells postcards.

Books, though, were of more immediate concern to us, and in Via Carducci, behind a modest storefront with a window filled with books, we found the bookbindery (*legatorial*) where we were to have many books bound.

*   *   *

Our mornings were freshened by showers that came in from the sea. When summer passed, the days of October and early November were flawless—a fine white *nebbia* at dawn, and a chill in the air before the mist was dispelled by the bright burning sun. Once, when the weather was like this, it suddenly turned cold, dark, and blustery; and Ostia—when we went down to watch the eelers set their nets—was lashed by high waves and wind that hurled stinging particles of sand against our faces. The newspapers were furious; the weather was a treacherous beast.

There were other occasional escapes from Roman traffic. We went to Anzio, where the Allied troops landed in January, 1944; to the American military cemetery at Nettuno; and to the north, to Civitavecchia, and to the fourteenth-century castle at Santa Severa.

*   *   *

But Rome was full of enticements and ruined expectations. Given enough time—a lifetime, say—of unbroken pursuit, one might disprove Pio Nono's assertion that one could never see all of Rome; yet it was doubtful. Was there a way to remove the obstacles—a precise day and hour and minute, for instance, when one could knock with confidence at the low portal of Sant'Agata dei Goti at the corner of Via Mazzarino and Via Panisperna, and get a response and a chance to inquire for permission to enter?

Too many doors were secured from the inside; too many bells rang in silent, inaccessible interiors and were never answered. Unseen birds sang behind high garden walls; fountains splashed and dripped in courtyards no stranger ever entered. The bolt rusted, the moss thickened, new flowers took root on the broken roof. A sense of futility overcame the wanderer.

Even small successes were marred by a pervasive feeling of urgency or unwantedness. The patience of the nun who opened the door to the thirteenth-century cloistered garden of Santi Quattro Corinati, and waited there attentively in silence, embodied a prayer that we not stay too long. The nun who admitted one to San Sisto Vecchio in Piazza Numa Pompilio, opposite the Baths of Caracalla, shortened one's visit by her mute presence—one was aware of tension, of wasting the time of this humble servant of God by peering into dark interiors at unlighted frescoes.

Across the way at Santi Nereo e Achilleo, one stared at a fragment of San Gregorio's twenty-eighth homily carved on the bishop's throne in the apse and tried to stop up one's ears against the voice of the woman custodian. The unforeseeable was ahead in the fifth-century Santa Balbina on the pseudo-Aventine, where a fat, irreverent tourist in shorts posed for his picture in the Comatesque episcopal chair.

So we accepted all that Rome offered publicly, from the treasures of the Vatican Museums to the exhibitions of military skill and valor in the Museum of the Bersaglieri in the Porta Pia; from Bernini's David in the Villa Borghese Casina to the Roesler Franz watercolors of nineteenth-century Rome in Palazzo Braschi.

Scholars from the world over, armed with an authority we lacked, spent hours in private libraries, churches, convents, and palazzi. We had no special privileges, and we sought none. We were on our own, we had no goals, and while our interests were not limited, they sometimes were easily satisfied. We could contemplate the tomb of Antonio Tebaldo, poet and tutor to Isabella d'Este, in Santa Maria in Via Lata, and be unmoved. With the same rueful feeling that somehow we were less appreciative than we ought to be, we could look at two tombs of the Altieri family in Santa Maria in Campitelli and meditate on the utter sadness of the word NIHIL inscribed on one and, on the other, the word UMBRA.

As we rarely decided long in advance what our daily moves would be, much of what we did was impulsive. If we went to the roof of St. Peter's, we took coffee at the little shed once used by the Sampietrini; and if we felt we had enough energy that day, we went inside the dome and made the long climb to the top.

The sloping, winding passage was narrow, and the walls were penciled over with hundreds of names, hometowns, and dates. If we tired, we sat in the embrasure of one of the windows—in fact, one day, when we were hungry, we ate cheese and crackers while we rested. The final part of the ascent was always a laughing, groaning, desperate struggle up an almost vertical arrangement of marble blocks ten feet high, with the aid of a thick rope that hung like a bell pull at the side. Just when retreat seemed the only course, we heard cries of encouragement in the opening above and saw several out-stretched hands beckoning us to come on. We made it on the next try and were pulled through to a happy, breathless collapse.

We were all brothers up there, whatever the day, unified by the climb and the place. We exchanged names and addresses. On our first climb, we met two young Catholic college women from Chicago who were spending their senior year in Rome, a young Italian waiter who refreshed his body and spirit once a week by going to the top, a Frenchman, two young Canadians from Vancouver, and, wonder of all, a New York furrier who lived around the corner from us in lower Fifth Avenue.

We never stayed more than an hour, while earlier arrivals departed and newcomers came up through the hole, and the little ceremony of exchanging names went on. No place was more pleasant on a spring or autumn afternoon in Rome, no view more spectacular.

CHAPTER 5

The Adriano . . . A Renaissance Garden . . . The Pantheon

We spent one year at the Hotel Adriano in Campo Marzio on the northern edge of Renaissance Rome, near the Pantheon and the Palazzo Borghese, and only a block away from Hilda's Tower. The water that tinkled day and night in the small lobby fountain of the Adriano was Acqua Vergine Antica—the water that flowed at Trevi.

Our address was Via di Pallicorda 2, and every cabbie we ever engaged knew where it was; but just to make sure he did, we always added "Piazza Firenze." The hotel itself was said to have been built as a palazzo by Cardinal Ascanio Sforza, but nearby stood another large and more widely-known structure, the Palazzo Firenze, situated in Via dei Prefetti and forming most of the Piazza's northern side. Built in the sixteenth century for a cardinal, it had been acquired by Pope Pius IV, who then had presented it to the Grand Duke Cosimo. Galileo stayed there briefly in 1633, the year of his heresy trial. From the eighteenth

77

century until 1870, the palazzo had been the seat of the Florentine embassy to the Holy See.

The courtyard of the palazzo was porticoed and had a small formal garden circled by a wide path for carriages. We knew the courtyard long before we knew the Adriano, because the Dante Alighieri Society was housed in the palazzo and gave classes in Italian to foreigners. My wife was studying Italian, and I was waiting for her one forenoon at the foot of the broad staircase that led to the *primo piano* when a man came in from the street. He had a newspaper in one hand and, scarcely glancing at me, walked over to where two men were standing in front of a parked car. Without a word he opened the paper and spread it across the hood of the car. The man bent forward to see, and their silence and their rigid attention were so strange that I strolled over. The men made room for me to see. It was the story, fully illustrated, filling two pages, of two Russian cosmonauts who had returned to earth safely, it appeared, but were found to be dead when their capsule was opened.

Nobody spoke. After a while I went back to the stairs to wait in the cool shadows. I watched the three men; the man who brought the newspaper folded it carefully and suddenly looked upward at the blue sky. The others followed his gaze as if they would see something, a sign that would enlighten them. In a few seconds they lowered their heads and departed, two of the men going to a door on the far side of the courtyard. The man with the paper came towards me, our eyes met as he started up the steps, and we nodded as he passed, as if to acknowledge a fragile bond between us.

A faint scent of flowers pervaded the courtyard, and the sunlight seemed brighter when the men had gone. Red and gold, yellow, pink, and old rose. Unmoving flowers, unreal garden, a painted garden, touched that morning by death. I thought of the drowned man in Joyce's *Ulysses*, nine days gone in Dublin Bay, a swollen corpse, driven by a rising tide, bobbing upward, saltwhite face, saltblue eyes, from a green watery grave. Here I am.

And there were the two Russians in the capsule, brave men, space adventurers returning to earth. Here we are. On the low wide hood of an Italian sports car, faces turned upward, unseeing eyes in a Renaissance garden. Unreal.

*   *   *

The French brought tennis to Rome and played the game in the narrow land that ran along the western side of the Palazzo Firenze. Since it was an indoor game, it was necessary to put up a wooden building for the *pallacorda*, or tennis court. At some indefinite date in the later years, the game was discontinued, and the building was enlarged and turned into a theater called the Teatro Metastasio to honor the eighteenth-century Roman poet and librettist. The theater had a short life, but its memory endured; and when the papal authorities got around to giving names to all of Rome's thoroughfares, from wide street to meanest *vicolo*, or alley, Pallacorda and Metastasio seemed natural choices.

The naming of streets was a long time coming. The roads leading out of the city in ancient times bore names, such as Flaminia, Appia, Aurelia, or Salaria, and were known throughout the empire; and there were a few formal street names during the Renaissance. But it was not until 1744, when Pope Benedict XIV published a register of Rome's streets and squares, that anything like a serious undertaking was begun. Most of the names the pope listed were informal; but later, hallowed by tradition, they were given official recognition—streets, for example, popularly identified with the trades carried on there: Capellari (hat-makers), Falegnami (carpenters), Giubbonari (shirt-makers),

Funari (rope-makers), Coronari (where rosaries were sold to pilgrims heading for St. Peter's by way of Ponte Sant'Angelo), Coppelle (barrel-makers), Pettinari (comb-makers or carders of wool), Leutari (lute-makers), and Baullari (trunk-makers).

Benedict's collection included 271 streets and 185 squares. The register had little practical use, since no street signs were installed, and it was sixty years before the first of two hundred *tabelle stradele*, or road signs, were erected. These helped, but not much, because the white marble slabs were nothing more than boundary markers for the fourteen *rioni,* or districts, into which the city was then divided: Monti, Trevi, Colonna, Campo Marzio, Ponte, Parione, Regola, Sant'Eustachio, Pigna, Campitelli, Sant'Angelo, Ripa, Trastevere, and Borgo.

There were no house numbers, though some had been posted during the plague of 1657 as an aid to identifying the houses of the sick. This had been a stopgap measure and was abandoned as soon as it was no longer needed. The usual way to direct a stranger to a house, or for the owner or occupant to let a new acquaintance or an official know its location, was to describe the house in relation to some topographical feature or monument. For example: It is the building with the doorway next to the butcher's shop and nearly next to the Corsican guardhouse; it has green shutters and stands a few *metri* from the shrine of the Madonna near the barbershop.

Some devious thinking must have taken place before the names of Pallacorda and Metastasio were assigned. Pallacorda clearly had first rights to the lane, but Metastasio was a valuable name, not to be cast off without an argument. It undoubtedly occurred to someone that Metastasio could be honored by naming after him the street where he was born Pietro Trapassi in 1698. But that would have deprived the Palazzo Firenze neighborhood of its poet, so the western side of Piazza Firenze was called Via Metastasio, and the *via* where he was born retained the name of Cappellari. Metastasio died in 1782, and in good time a plaque was screwed to the front wall of his birthplace.

Names for other streets in the vicinity of Palazzo Firenze were readily adapted and registered. Via della Scrofa recalled an old fountain with the figure of a sow that once stood there. Via Cardelli memorialized the original owner of the Palazzo Firenze. Via Ascanio, which ran from Via della Scrofa to the piazza, took its name from Ascanio Sforza, the putative builder of the small elegant palazzo that had in 1965 become the Hotel Adriano. Vicolo del Divino Amore was named for a tiny oratory, and the Via dei Prefetti, the street of the Prefects, traced its name to the powerful De Vico family, hereditary prefects whose base of operations was the medieval Church of San Nicolo dei Prefetti.

Given our knowledge of the neighborhood, sketchy though it was, we felt an intimacy with Rome we had never known in any other part of the city: the joyful awareness of being in the right place, a contentment that over and over again suffused the spirit.

This warm feeling came over us on our first morning at the Adriano, when we opened wide the heavy slatted shutters of our single window and looked out on a jumble of squares and oblongs, the forms of houses, yellow, orange, brown, rose, pale green, and an irregular pattern of roof gardens, small trees, shrubs, potted plants, hanging plants, and ivy. It was quiet out there, a pretty stage-setting without actors; but at various times of the day, if we happened to be at home, we would see women at work, hosing, pruning, doing all the things that loving gardeners enjoy. The ceiling of our room was fifteen feet high, raftered, remote, and we wondered, though our speculation never went far, who had lived in this part of the palazza and what had gone on here.

It was easier to grasp reality at breakfast in the dining room, which had been the guard room, the common room for the cardinal's servitors. There we had our *colazione*, our breakfast, a pot of coffee and a few *cornetti* fetched from the coffee bar across the piazza; and there in the guard room we hoped, at the beginning of our stay, to find the soul of the palazzo.

Nothing of the sort happened. No ghosts dallied in the guard room; we heard no phantasmal echoes of boisterous sixteenth-century laughter. Reality was the crunching, crackling, breaking sound of hard rolls in the hands of two, three, or rarely, four businessmen, Dutch or German, and the low growling impatience of their voices.

The room was set below the level of the street, and its thick walls were pierced by three heavily-curtained windows through which we could see the feet and legs of people walking in Via d'Ascanio and hear a muffled babble of voices. The legs sometimes halted and were joined by other legs, and the babble grew more insistent, then died away as the legs departed. For the rest, we could find in these comings and goings only the banalities of daily living.

We were interested in our little palazzo, but of its history we knew nothing and could learn nothing. A tall, stately, white-haired woman in black, who moved through the room every morning for a brief visit to the kitchen, might have had the knowledge we sought, but she was unapproachable in her slow progress, never turning her head, never recognizing anyone in the room. She was the proprietor. Gino Pinna, the manager, told us this, and that was all he could or was willing to tell us. Was the Signora an aristocrat, a Sforza, perhaps, a contessa? Gino shrugged.

Gino was a Sardinian, a tactful man of thirty who spoke Italian, English, French, and German fluently and had a working knowledge of several other languages. He was married and had one son, whom he planned to send to a university outside Rome—Bologna or Padua, or possibly to Oxford or the Sorbonne. This, of course, was years away. Now he was intent on his career. His employer's life was private and clearly none of our business. Very likely he regarded the Adriano's past as of no consequence. Rome was full of romantic rubbish, though of course it was the foreigner's interest in this rubbish that brought people to the city and indeed was the heart of the hotel industry.

He could not overlook the past; it was important, but not as important as the present. In any case, I don't think Gino actually knew much about the palazzo's history. He spoke lightly about the little fountain and the murmurous Trevi water, and he said the lobby had been built in what had been a small courtyard, entered from Via di Pallacorda. On the question of the Signora—who she was, where she lived—he was respectfully silent.

Her demeanor reminded us of a gracious lady who had once invited us to share with her the small circular elevator in the Casina of the Villa Borghese. We had accepted gratefully, since it spared us the climb of the eighty-two shallow white marble steps of the curving stairway. We had stepped out at the *primo piano*, and she had continued to the living quarters above. We had assumed she was a Borghese princess.

The Adriano had eighty-five rooms and sixteen employees, and Gino managed everything down to the last tedious detail. He was interested in us because we were Americans but not American tourists. We were not going to leave in a few days or a few weeks, and we had come to the Adriano because an acquaintance whom Gino knew had recommended the place.

Most of the Italians we met in Italy were interested in Americans and in life in the United States. Many of them had relatives or friends in North America and doubtless saw in us a bond, however tenuous, with their kinsmen. Their ideas of that distant world, which an Italian had discovered and whose coasts Italians had explored, were formed by motion pictures, television, their own picture magazines, and the letters they received from abroad. Their view of all these sources was touched by a suspicion and skepticism. The movies distorted life, television and radio corrupted the truth—and could they believe everything that cousins Giuseppe and Rosa wrote? When they spoke to us, they wished to know the truth. Did we know a place called Brooklyn? Bridgeport? Buffalo? New Jersey? What were these places like? Were Italians respected in America? What did Americans eat? Did we know that Italy had a chewing gum called Brooklyn?

But Gino did not ask questions about America. He was curious about us. Gino was in a very good position to study people, but the people he saw every day offered him little for study. They were migratory birds, resting for a few days in a vacant field before moving on. They came down from the North—from France, Holland, Germany, and Scandinavia—and were disgorged from buses in Via di Pallacorda. They swarmed into the lobby, tired, relaxed, friendly. The sounds of their daily arrival, their exits for the long day's excursion, the sightseeing memories that never left them for the rest of their lives—nothing varied.

We were different. We were not like the young man on the fourth floor, an American who acted in small roles at Cinecitta and translated Italian dialogue and subtitles. We were not like the young American woman, the soprano who was a pupil of Tito Gobbi, the pretty girl who sent her sweet notes soaring over the roof gardens of Via della Scrofa. They were workaday practical Americans; we could tell Gino only that we had watched boys playing amid the broken stones and litter of the open ground next to the Teatro Marcello.

At first Gino questioned us in the casual way of hotel managers everywhere, politely, discreetly, showing decent concern for our safety in a strange city; but as it was gradually revealed that, having lived in Rome before, we knew the city, he grew more curious—and more interested. It was as if we were discovering Rome for Gino, who had had little time to make his own discoveries. We had gone to San Teodoro, the little circular church built in the waning days of the empire at the foot of the Palatine near the spot where the she-wolf had suckled Romulus and Remus, a church that was locked eleven months of the year and open only in October. We had found the doors ajar and gone in to watch a blue carpet being laid and fragile, toy-like chairs being placed for guests.

On another day we had climbed a broad staircase of many white marble steps leading from Via Giotto just inside the Aurelian Wall near Porta San Paolo to the pseudo-Aventine. Grass grew in the interstices of the marble, and children played noisily on the steps, as old people went up and down with great care. And another day, we told him, we had gone to Sunday Mass in the Barberini Chapel, Sant'Ivo, in the Palazzo della Sapienza, and had met a Bishop from Thailand. Gino's attention never flagged.

* * *

As we left the Adriano one morning, we saw three men close to the wall on the side of Via dei Prefetti. They had driven four metal rods into the ground and had joined the rods with white string, forming an enclosed square six feet by six. One of the men was pulling up the lava blocks of the paving, the others were making a neat pile outside the square.

We stopped to see what was going on. The men worked slowly and talked as they worked, and we thought of Taine watching idlers pulling up weeds in the stony courtyards of sad, discolored palazzi. What in the world were these old fellows up to? Was this the beginning of an archeological dig? Were they preparing the ground for experts who would bring into the light a new marble, fragmented or whole: a small boy struggling with a goose, perhaps (since ancient sculptors liked to portray tads in the act of strangling geese), or something breath-taking, a lovely Venus? A Venus would do very nicely—the Venus of Via dei Prefetti.

It was the Venus of Cyrene that came to mind, for we knew none livelier than this headless, armless girl found in the Libyan desert near the ancient Baths of Cyrene in 1913 and now on view in the Museo Nazionale Romano. She had a rival, the Venus of the Esquiline, dug out of the ruins of the Lamiani Gardens on the Esquiline and now in the Conservatory museum on the Campidoglio. Little excitement had attended the uncovering of the Esquiline Venus, because the gardens had yielded so many marble treasures in the 1870s, when every spade in Rome was active.

The story of the desert Venus, a fourth-century BC Greek work, was one of remarkable luck—and a storm. The setting itself was dramatic—the ruins of the Baths and the timeless wasteland—where a fierce *temporale*, a torrential thunderstorm of terrifying force, had come after nightfall. In the radiant sunshine of the following morning, two Italian army officers who were stationed nearby went walking in the desert. One carried a cane that he lightly swung, touching the ground at intervals as they sauntered along. Once his stick struck something hard, but he and his companion kept on walking for a hundred yards or more, when suddenly, overpowered by curiosity, he turned, ran back, and searched for the spot where the cane had hit the hard object.

He found it at last and, falling to his knees, delved furiously with his bare hands. The more he dug and flung away the sand, the more excited he became. The other man had returned at his call and joined him. What had lain hidden was plan to them now—something of white marble. It was too heavy to lift, or even to budge, so they went back to the barracks and picked a detail of men with shovels to finish the excavating. We reflected on this, as the men themselves must have reflected, and as so many others have done since 1913—how narrow the margin of discovery has been.

Once, many years ago, a section of Roman pavement had been uncovered seven feet under the street that comes up to Santa Maria in Campo Marzio. Recalling this, we watched the men a little longer before we realized they were merely mending the street. Via dei Prefetti was not about to give up a Venus, a boy with a goose, an old crone carrying a lamb, or, indeed, anything else. Via dei Prefetti was uneven, bumpy, and the men were making it a better street for the cars and small trucks that even now were squeezing past in both directions.

Meanwhile the work slowly progressed. When all the blocks had been taken up, the men smoothed the underlying soil with trowel and shovel until the square looked like a freshly-seeded backyard vegetable plot. Then, unhurriedly, the blocks were replaced and tamped down, each being gently struck with a hammer and brought to the level of its neighbors. When all were back in place, one of the men delivered some heavy blows with a rammer. The men removed most of the string and two of the rods, leaving two rods and the string between for the next enclosures.

We turned away and crossed the piazza and went down to the Pantheon. Since the authorities had banned motor traffic in the Piazza della Rotonda, the bordering restaurants had put out tables and chairs. They were damp this forenoon, and only a few customers were there drinking coffee and reading *Il Tempo*. The fountain had been turned off and looked lifeless. We skirted it and, passing between two large touring buses parked in front of the Pantheon, went inside. We noticed a small commotion at one side: an elderly man was scolding a youth for unseemly behavior. The boy had been laughing. You ought to remember that this is a church, the man was saying.

Yes, the Pantheon was a church, Santa Maria ad Martyres, consecrated in the year 609 by Pope Boniface IV; but it was also one of the greatest monuments of antiquity, and people who came to see it could never be sure if they should pray or simply admire its splendid architectural beauty and the skill of the Roman engineers.

After thirteen hundred years of Christian sanctification, it was still called by its pagan name. No stranger ever asked for directions to Santa Maria ad Martyres or to Santa Maria Rotonda, as it was also called. It was the Pantheon, and when men and women standing near the altar looked heavenward, it was likely they were moved more by curiosity than by any deep religious feeling. That opening in the dome through which rain and snow fell and the sun formed a shaft 141 feet long—that wonderful peephole up there—was twenty-eight feet in diameter, and the dome itself was wider than St. Peter's.

The Pantheon was also a tomb. Boniface had brought the first dead to this place—twenty-eight wagonloads of bones from the catacombs south of the city for interment within the nine-foot-thick walls. Nine hundred years later, Raphael's body had been brought to the Pantheon; four other Renaissance painters had followed. Four hundred years passed without further entombments before the House of Savoy, which had seized millions of dollars of church property for the new state, invaded the sacred precincts. The funeral of Vittorio Emanuele II in 1878 was so splendid that the Pie di Marmo, the famous Marble Foot that stood in the Piazza del Collegio Romano, had to be moved around the corner into Via San Stefano del Cacco to make room for the procession to the Pantheon. King Umberto I and Queen Margherita also found a last resting-place here.

CHAPTER 6

A Ride on ED

O ne of our enduring loves in Rome was a most unlikely convenience, a streetcar line of double trams that ran noisily around the city. Its official name was *Il circolare esterna destra*, but we called it ED, from the large block letters ED on the front of the cars.

ED sometimes seemed to wander aimlessly, as if it had lost its way, but the truth was that its route had been laid out with wonderful cunning by someone who wished ED to embrace all Rome; and when you studied the line, you were struck by its serious intentions, even if its darting movements here and there suggested a mischievous nature.

I took a small map of Rome one day and inked in the route of ED. The markings confirmed what I already knew, that ED was the best way to get around a good part of the older city if you weren't in a hurry. It was certainly the cheapest. For fifty lire, about eight cents, you could ride twelve miles. The official time for the run was an hour and fifteen minutes.

As public transportation, ED could hardly be overpraised. If you lived in Parioli and wished to go to St. Peter's or to the Sunday flea market at Porta Portese or to visit the Campo Verano cemetery, the best means of getting there, apart from your own car or a taxicab, would be ED; and it would be ED if you emerged from the Vatican Museums and decided to have a look at Palazzo Farnese or buy a hand-knitted shawl in Via Giubbonari or see the curious and somewhat pretentious Tomb of the Baker at Porta Maggiore—that is, if you didn't mind a long roundabout route.

The name of the line survived from the time when Rome was much smaller, and ED's tracks skirted the city limits. By the 1960s the population, which had been seven hundred thousand when Mussolini arrived in 1922, had grown to three million, and ED was more *interna* than *esterna*; but the famous landmarks, the monuments of antiquity and the Renaissance and Baroque periods, had not moved, and ED passed close to many of them, either within sight or within a few minutes' walk. As you passed Porta Capena, the original starting point of the Via Appia, for example, you could see St. Peter's in the west beyond the Circus Maximus and, in the other direction, the ruined Baths of Caracalla.

The "Destra" of ED meant that its course was clockwise from Viale delle Belle Arti near the Museum of Modern Art and Via Giulia in the northern part of Rome. (There was also a *Circolare Esterna Sinistra* that ran to the left, or counter-clockwise, but it was a bus line, and it ran in the boisterous manner of all Roman buses. I can't imagine anyone developing an attachment to it as one did for ED.)

Villa Giulia, built by Vasari, Vignola, and Bartalomeo Ammannati for Pope Julius III, houses one of the world's great collections of Etruscan art (Italy's other big collections are in the Vatican Museums and at Florence and Colterra), and my wife and I had spent an hour at the Villa Giulia one bright October day when she announced she was hungry. I suppose we would have found ED another day in another place, but I like to think it was all foreordained: A few minutes after we emerged from the museum, an ED tram turned out of Via Flaminia and headed our way.

When it stopped, the *conducente* (motorman) and the conductor got off to stretch their legs, and we asked them if they ran near Via Nomentana. They said they did, and we climbed aboard at the rear of the second tram and settled down in one of the hard wooden seats. The bell clanged, and we were off and up the hill, cruising past the back of the zoo in Villa Borghese and the elegant houses of Parioli and moving along Viale Rossini—the streets in that part of Rome are named for composers—to Piazza Ungheria and Viale Liegi, which shortly becomes Viale Regina Margherita and then Viale Regina Elena.

Traffic was heavy as we nosed into the wide, tree-lined Regina Margherita, but we forged ahead past automobile salesrooms, pet shops, *farmacie, macellerie,* and flower stalls, past villas and apartment houses—salmon-colored, faded orange, pink, yellow, red. The siesta had started, and at every *fermata* more people got on. All the seats filled, and the aisles were crowded. It was lively company, and the air was full of talk.

Roman buses lurch, pitch, and sway. They roll uphill and downhill at frightening speeds; they make dizzy turns, squeeze between lines of parked and moving cars where obviously no bus can go, and crawl through the traffic of narrow streets—and they are always jammed. ED moved rapidly, too, sometimes with the urgency of a fire engine; and, as we were to learn, it took the steep grade from the Colosseum to Porta Capena with bravura, rushing down in the spirit of a teenager riding his first motor scooter, then suddenly racing along the Lungotevere like a Ferrari.

We became so preoccupied with the movement, the street scene, and the people in the tram that we missed our stop at Via Nomentana and went on past the university and the Policlinico Hospital. We reached San Lorenzo fuori le Mura, one of Rome's seven pilgrimage churches, slowed down to turn into the broad Piazza San Lorenzo, crossed it, and went into Via Tiburtina, the ancient road to Tivoli.

We stayed on Tiburtina a few minutes before cutting through a poor neighborhood for several short blocks to turn into Viale Scalo San Lorenzo, where we ran past drab tenements and factories and warehouses beside street-level railroad tracks. We came to Porta Maggiore, the gate through which many of the first American troops entered Rome on June 4, 1944. It was a busy exchange point for trams and buses, and we lost a great many of our passengers as others got on. Some of our passengers were on business, but most of them were going home to have their *pranzo*, and in a couple of hours they would be beating their way back to work.

We left Porta Maggiore and headed toward Santa Croce in Gerusalemme, another of the pilgrimage churches; we turned again and ran smoothly along Via Carlo Felice to Piazza di Porta San Giovanni, where there was an almost general exodus while new riders came aboard. The piazza was another big transfer point. In the background were the Aurelian Wall and the Basilica of San Giovanni in Laterano. Here were incalculable riches: the church; the museums; the Scala Santa, the stunning red granite obelisk, 105 feet tall on a forty-nine-foot base, the biggest in the world, twenty-two feet higher than the one in St. Peter's Square, twice as tall as the Piazza Navona Obelisk.

We left the piazza and turned into Via Emanuele Filiberto, going past Villa Wolkonsky. A left turn brought us into Viale Manzoni, near the point where it becomes Via Labicana. We rumbled within a block or two of the churches of San Clemente and Santi Quattro Coronati and halted on the high ground above the Colosseum. Close to the tracks were the remains of the *Ludus Magnus*, the principal training school for gladiators, which, surprisingly, was not excavated until 1960-1961.

We swung left and started the long descent of the Caelian Hill to Porta Capena, rolling past San Gregorio Magno and the narrow Clivo di Scauro, which runs up under the flying buttresses of Santi Giovanni e Paolo. We had a view of the Circus Maximus as we crossed Porta Capena and passed the Obelisk of Axum, raised by Mussolini after he had taken it as a trophy of victory from Ethiopia's ancient capital in 1937.

In Viale Aventino we ran between the Aventine on our right and the pseudo-Aventine—the first, the site of Santa Prisca, Santa Sabina, Sant'Alessio, the church and Benedictine Monastery of Sant'Anselmo, the Priorata de Malta, the residence of the Grand Master of the Knights of Malta, and a piazza decorated by Piranesi. The churches of Santa Saba and Santa Balbina were steps away on the pseudo-Aventine.

At the end of Viale Aventino we reached Porta San Paolo and left the tram for a snack at an open-air café. Across the way was the Cestius Pyramid and behind it the Protestant Cemetery, where Keats is buried and Shelley's ashes are inurned. Half an hour later we were on another ED in full flight down the long Via Marmorata under the southern flank of the Aventine. We turned north at the Tiber and followed the embankment past Ponte Palatino, Ponte Rotto, and the other bridges. We sailed past the Piazza della Bocca della Verita, Santa Maria in Cosmedin, the so-called Temple of Vesta, the Temple of Fortuna Virilis, the Arch of Janus, and San Giorgio in Velabro—and a short walk away, but out of sight, the Theatre of Marcellus and, beyond that, the Campidoglio.

There were few of us aboard now as we sped past the Isola Tiberina and its famous hospital run by the Fatabenefratelli (the Do-good

Brothers), the opening of Via Giulia, and the rear of the Spado and Farnese palaces. Across the river on the Janiculum we saw the Lighthouse and Garibaldi astride his great horse. Traffic roared alongside us; the leaves of the embankment trees, dusty and dry, swished in the gusts of our passage. It was a ride for excited children.

We slowed down to cross Ponte Vittorio Emanuele and went past the opening of Via della Conciliazione, which was full of shoppers. At Viale Giulio Cesare we turned right and headed east to the river, past the long blocks of army barracks. At the Tiber, we ran a little distance north to Ponte Matteotti and crossed to the left bank, then ran another short distance and turned into Via Flaminia, a few blocks north of Piazza del Popolo. A final turn brought us into Viale delle Belle Arti, where we had started.

After that first ride, we began using ED whenever we had a chance to go its way. It was astonishing how often this happened. ED seemed always to be turning up, and it was a welcome sight indeed when it hove into view. It looked so true and dependable—so solid and reassuring—and we had the feeling that all the riders were as loyal as we were, capricious and cynical though Romans may be. If sometimes we were all bumped at San Giovanni or Porta Maggiore and lost our seats, there was no audible grumbling as we changed to the tram ahead; and the crews were always men of good humor.

We liked ED's homeliness, its air of confidence, and the changing moods of its interior as all the little verbal dramas and comedies of the people unfolded. The conductor, an amiable figure perched behind a counter at the rear of the second car, watched with benevolent eye the shifting cast of characters: women shoppers, nuns and priests, monks and seminarians, students and nurses and government employees, shopgirls and secretaries, elderly sweet-faced gentlewomen and grumpy old men who talked to themselves; businessmen, soldiers, sailors, children, and men with attaché cases who might be lawyers, teachers, or scholars, specialists in one of the numerous sub-classifications of art and archeology and history, who live in greater numbers in Rome than in any other city.

Romans talk—incessantly, animatedly, loudly, dramatically, angrily, tenderly. What they say is colored by a theatricality they themselves enjoy, as if it is quite natural to be overblown and bumptious, or openly despairing, even when the talk is trifling and the joys and woes of daily living are no more than an ordinary experience. Talk is a necessity, an outlet, and no place in Rome offered as much of it in such variety as ED. And in no other place in Rome was there such a feeling of unity in a crisis. If a bus or a truck or even the tiniest of Fiats came close to colliding with the tram, it was not only the *conducente* and the conductor who took offense. The passengers themselves rose in anger to shout at the enemy outside.

It was a good show. A mother scolded her small son, the chiding interspersed with terms of endearment—and if the kid wailed, the passengers regarded him indulgently for a while before crying out, "*Piano, piano! Basta!*" The mother smiled gratefully. Sometimes, when the company thinned out, there were stretches of silence, or as near silence as there ever is in Rome. But it took little—the explosive passing of a motorcycle, the sight of a fat cardinal in a chauffeured limousine—to restore the hubbub.

We rarely saw Americans on ED. Maybe the sight of the old tram pushing along so doggedly with clanging gong and clattering wheels scared off strangers. Our own long association with the line has endowed it with attributes that were fanciful, but real to us. ED was hospitable and safe and no more anachronistic than the San Francisco cable cars or the little fiery red trams that skittered to the outskirts of Innsbruck, Austria. It had the air of an old voyager.

We did not know, though we might have guessed, that ED could not go on forever. It was part of a public transportation system that had been in financial trouble a long time. Rome was building a new subway that cost billions of lire. The number of bus riders had fallen off, and the bus lines were losing money, as more and more people bought small cars they drove to work. At one point the authorities tried a corrective tactic that strained a New Yorker's credulity: The collecting of bus fares stopped, and all rides were free. It was hoped this would persuade people to leave their cars at home. Many workers did stop driving to work, but when the fareless experiment ended, the car owners went back to their little Fiats, the traffic jams were worse than ever, and the losses went on.

More economies were demanded. ED was doomed. In the hard times Rome faced, *Il circolare esterna destra* must have seemed an extravagance to the people who ran the system, but not to us and the other passengers who regarded it so affectionately.

We were away from Rome when the death sentence was executed, and so we missed the last ride around Rome. I think that if we had been there, we would have stayed on board for hours.

CHAPTER 7

Rossini, Cats, and a Candlestick

The story of the old Teatro Argentina is principally that of Rossini's *Il barbiere di Siviglia* and a cat; the story of the new Argentina is one of many cats. Rossini composed his opera in Rome in thirteen days, it was said, although long afterwards he said lightly that it may have been twelve days or fourteen. Rossini based the work on a play by Pierre Beaumarchais, *Le barbier de Seville*; and when Rossini started writing, he knew there already existed a comic opera, *Il barbiere di Siviglia*, by the Neapolitan Giovanni Paisiello. Paisiello had composed his opera in St. Petersburg, Russia, when he was living there under the patronage of Catherine the Great. It had its premiere in 1782, ten years before Rossini was born, and everyone in Europe and America knew it.

Rossini called his opera *Almaviva* in deference to Paisiello, and courteously wrote the composer that he did not wish to compete with him but merely desired to treat in his own way a subject that delighted him. He was twenty-four; Paisiello was seventy-six and had four months more to live. The old man's style already seemed mannered, even archaic, to the new generation of operagoers; but he still had many admirers, and it was these *Paisiellisti* who resented the upstart Rossini and set the tone of the February 20, 1816, opening-night disaster—with the unforeseen help of a cat.

The cast was excellent: Manuel Garcia, the tenor, played Almaviva. It was Rossini himself who started an uproar of catcalls, whistling, and laughter when he appeared in a hazel-colored Spanish-style habit with gold buttons, before an audience accustomed to seeing their *maestri* in black. Matters got worse when the basso, Zenobio Vitarelli (Basilio), entered in wonderfully comic makeup and tripped over a trapdoor. He fell heavily and nearly broke his nose; but he carried on bravely, staunching the flow of blood while the audience howled with pleasure, applauding, laughing, and demanding an encore, presumably of the fall.

As the finale of the scene approached and the ensemble began, a cat appeared, walking with upraised tail among the performers, rubbing against first one singer, then another. Luigi Zamboni (Figaro) chased it off to one side. It went behind the scenery, came out on the other side the stage, and threw itself in a wild leap into the arms of Bartolommeo Botticelli (Doctor Bartolo). When he threw the cat down, it jumped on another singer, clawing its way up his side. The singer knocked it over with a blow of the fist, but the cat, maddened by excitement, went on frisking, while the audience, completely out of control, meowed, screeched, and roared. Rossini stood it to the end and went home to sleep tranquilly.

Next night the Romans recovered their senses. The *Paisiellisti*, seemingly satisfied they had finished off Rossini, stayed away from the Argentina, and the evening was a success; but Rossini was not there. He had feigned illness, stayed home, and was in bed sleeping when a large part of his audience, lighting their way with torches, walked to

Via dei Leutari, 35, where the young composer lodged. There are two versions of what happened: one that he came forth and was borne off triumphantly to a banquet; the other that he fled from the house to a stable at the rear and stayed there while the crowd, led by Garcia, vainly implored him to come out.

Almaviva had a total of seven performances at the Argentina. The theater closed for the season on February 27, and the opera was not heard again in Rome for five years. In September, at Bologna, it dropped its name and was retitled *Il barbiere di Siviglia*. Paisiello had died, and though his work was still presented, Rossini's had outstripped it in popularity.

Two of Verdi's operas opened at the Argentina: *I due Foscari*, on November 3, 1844, was a *mezzo-fiasco*, a half-failure; *La battaglia di Legnano*, on January 27, 1849, was a big success, mainly because it related the story of the Lombard League's victory over Frederick Barbarossa at Legnano in 1176 and because Rome, in 1849, was about to declare itself a republic.

The Argentina's name had an interesting provenance, a corruption of Argentoratum, the Latin name for Strasbourg. In the middle of the fifteenth century, a man named Johann or Hans Burchard or Burckhardt was born at Haslach, an ancient town near Strasbourg, then part of Germany. Strasbourg had been established by the Romans and was the scene of a Roman victory over the Alemanni in 357. Burchard, or Burcardo, as the Romans called him, was an ambitious priest and highly respected administrator who moved to Rome in 1481 and two years later became a papal master of ceremonies. He was also named Bishop of Orte, a town about forty miles north of Rome; and he hoped, to no avail, to become a cardinal.

The failure of his scheming is rather curious, for he was at the seat of power so long—from the closing months of the pontificate of Sixtus

IV through the reigns of Innocent VIII, Alexander VI, and Pius III and the first years of Julius II. This was roughly ten years, and during that time Burchard kept a diary, mainly detailing his official duties in the papal government. The diary was half a million words long, and half of the intriguing narrative concerned the court of the Borgia pope, Alexander VI, elected August 11, 1492. (There is no connection between the two events, but that was one day before Columbus sailed from Palos, Spain on his first voyage of discovery.)

Burchard's industry as a writer assured him of some degree of literary immortality, for historians have found his work valuable as an original source and a corrective or counterbalance of other annalists and diplomats. He could not become a cardinal; but in 1503 he built himself a monument, a house befitting his position and importance, which he called Torre Argentina. Today it is Casa del Burcado, but Argentina is preserved in the name of the *largo* and in the Via di Torre Argentina, the little street that enters Largo Argentina from the north.

The popularity of the Teatro Argentina, which had opened in 1732, declined after 1880, when the Teatro Costanzi—now the Teatro dell'Opera—was built. In the 1920s Mussolini began pulling down some old buildings across from the Argentina and uncovered the remains of a group of four Republican temples dating from the third or fourth century BC. The excavated area was twelve feet lower than modern Rome at that point, and a low wall was built to prevent pedestrians from falling in; but this could not keep out stray cats, and the cats moved in.

In the 1950s, the Argentina was closed and put *in restauro*. The project, an important one, at once became the subject of a prolonged, windy controversy. Was it proper, the Communists asked, to use government funds on a theater, while the poor suffered from bad housing or no housing, no jobs, and insufficient food? Romans revered the Argentina as a monument as much as any place in Rome can be said to be revered, but the cost of the restoration had been estimated at two-and-a-half million dollars.

The Communists lost the argument, scaffolding rose in front of the theater, and the first wrecking crew went inside. This was to be a job that only Romans could do.

We had a look at the interior one summer when we went to a door in a side street and were allowed by a watchman to climb a long ramp and a temporary wooden stairway to an opening in the wall of the auditorium. The place had been gutted from basement to ceiling; nothing remained except the eighteenth-century shell. We went back two years later, when the restoration had been completed. There had been a brief run of Shakespeare's *Giulio Cesare* in a token celebration of the centennial of Italian unification; but there was no talk about opera. Instead, the plan was to present the work of repertory companies from Genova, Milano, Trieste, Torino, Catania, Bolzano, and Aquila. In the lobby a guard said nobody was permitted to enter, but he was easily persuaded to open a door and let us see the interior.

Il Messaggero had been right: the new Argentina must be the most beautiful theater in the world—elegant; chaste; incredibly, achingly appealing in its loveliness; a dream of old rose and gold, velvet and silk. The *platea* or orchestra had only 152 seats, and the circular arrangement of the *palchetti*, or boxes, allotted thirty-one boxes to each of the six floors—a total of 186. It was a jewel box, a perfect setting for *L'Elisir d'amore* or *Don Pasquale*—or even *Il barbiere di Siviglia*.

Spring and summer were hot, and the doors stayed closed and presumably locked. Traffic moved along the Corso Vittorio Emanuele and Largo Argentina and along Via Arenula and Via delle Botteghe Oscure.

Midway through that summer, rumors began to circulate in Rome that something was amiss at the Argentina, something too dreadful or too hilarious for words, depending on one's level of sanity. One day, as the story finally emerged, someone went inside the theater and discovered the ugly truth: cats from the ruins across the street had sneaked into the Argentina, or been lured inside, or carried there. They had caused unbelievable damage. It was an outrage, a sacrilege. The place stank. It was infested with fleas. The cats had propagated, fought, scratched the beautiful seats, clawed and torn down velvet and silk draperies, and fouled the seats and aisles.

Some people blamed the Communists. They said only Communists—Roman Communists—would think of such a revenge.

*   *   *

Via di Leutari, where Rossini lodged in 1816, starts at the Corso Vittorio Emanuele opposite the Cancellaria and runs a block to Piazza Pasquino. Another musical tradition is embedded a few steps away on the Corso at the Chiesa Nuova, or Santa Maria in Vallicella, the St. Phillip Neri church in whose Oratorio dei Filippini, rebuilt by Borromini, the saint instituted the musical gatherings that became known as oratorios and gave the name to a form of musical composition.

The Corso is broad and clean, and there is nothing in the Chiesa Nuova's appearance or in that of any of the relatively modern buildings along there to suggest what lies behind them. It was there in the crooked little streets of Campo Marzio that I experienced one of the most frustrating times of my life as I walked north, south, east, and west in dogged search of a shop where I had bought a brass candlestick.

For a decade or longer, we had collected old single brass candlesticks, neither large nor elaborate. We had found them in Liffey Street in Dublin, in Paris, Rotterdam, Luxembourg, Innsbruck, and Alicante, Spain, and in half a dozen Italian cities—Rome, Lucca, Pisa, Vicenza, Padua, Perugia. There are hundreds of variations of these, but there is no literature to speak of on brass candlesticks, and sellers usually are cunningly, or agreeably, ignorant on the subject.

I bought a simple candlestick once in Via della Palombella, the short street behind the Pantheon, in a store whose owner repaired and sold furniture. It was a pleasant transaction, and whenever I passed his place and looked in at the doorway, he always greeted me cordially and, in anticipation of any inquiry, shook his head: *nulla, niente*. Rome's antiques stores have fancy and decorated candlesticks, but they are overpriced—nevertheless, the one that set me off on my idiotic search was priced fairly. I had wandered along Via del Coronari looking at the small fine antiques shops, and coming to a corner, I had turned off. Afterward, when I tried to reconstruct that day, I was never sure where I had made the turn, or how far I had gone, when suddenly, in a widening of the *vicolo*, I saw a man sitting outside a store, reading a newspaper. He looked up, nodded, and said, "Buon giorno." I nodded and smiled and looked through his shop window at some odd pieces of cheap furniture and, heaven be praised, two candlesticks.

He put down his paper, followed me into the store, and waited politely as I pretended to examine the furniture and then, as casually as I could, turned to the candlesticks. They were lovely, and there was no price on them. I picked them up, inspected them, and asked the question with my eyes. Fifteen thousand lire ($25), he said, adding that was for both.

I shook my head: too much. I offered five thousand lire ($8) for one.

Instead of haggling, he went to a chest of drawers, withdrew an old issue of *Il Tempo*, and quickly wrapped the candlestick I held out. He was pleased. I was pleased. He thought I should take the second candlestick at the same price. I said no, I would be back another day.

I didn't think I could explain to him the pleasure of discovery and purchase. In Perugia once, the owner of a smart antiques shop, on being asked if he had any brass candlesticks, had opened a drawer and taken out seven or eight. Such abundance diminished the plain joy of collecting. Here in Rome, I had spent many hours looking for candlesticks; and now that I had found one, I could renew my pleasure by returning the next day. The man resumed his post outside and said, "Ciao"; and I was so happy, I hurried away without asking him for a business card, assuming he had such a thing, or noting the street. I knew old Rome so well that it never occurred to me what trouble lay ahead.

The quarter is fairly small in area—Via dei Coronari on the north, Corso Vittorio Emanuele on the south, all to the west of Piazza Navona. By the time I had passed through the open-air fruit and vegetable market near Santa Maria della Pace, I had forgotten the way I had come. I crossed Piazza Navona and went into the Church of the Madonna del Sacro Cuore, originally San Giacomo degli Spagnoli, to cool off as I listened to organ music. I opened the newspaper wrapping to admire the candlestick and was tempted to go back to the store for the second one. But it was so warm.

The next day I set out for the store by way of Santa Maria della Pace. I was in no hurry, and I thought I might get inside the church, which was *in restauro*. I was admiring Bramante's cloister when a German tourist and two girls appeared with the sacristan. He opened a small door, and I followed them inside. The place was dark and dusty and stuffy, and our feet stirred up tiny clouds of pulverized plaster. As the German and his companions were looking at Raphael's Four Prophets, I made my way out as we had come in, through the sacristy, and happily thought of my second candlestick. There was no point in delay.

I went along Via dei Coronari and turned the corner at a store filled with handsome furniture and statuary, confidently expecting to see my friend sunning himself and reading *Il Tempo*. He was not in sight. The store was not there. I walked more slowly, deeply puzzled. Obviously I had made a mistake, a miscalculation. I went on and came out to Corso Vittorio Emanuele near the Chiesa Nuova, the church of Santa Maria in Navicella, and went back into the maze. I walked to the vegetable market and idled there, watching the women shoppers, listening to the noisy talk, the scraps of gossip and news. Tiring of this, I started walking again.

In one of his plans to modernize old Rome, Mussolini had considered destroying Via dei Coronari or widening it. It is an old street, once called Via Recta. In the early Renaissance, it was lined with shops which sold devotional goods, especially rosaries, to the hundreds of pilgrims who came down from the north. Coronari derives from rosaries. Today's pilgrims are not bound for St. Peter's but usually are looking for antiques. Some non-Romans live in the street—a friend of ours lived on the top floor of a palazzo—but strangers rarely are seen in Rossini's Vin dei Leutari or the other offshoots of Coronari. When I had walked around for a while, I began to feel I was attracting attention.

The idea that I was conspicuous in tie and seersucker jacket was not to be dislodged. Traffic, except for early morning deliveries to coffee bars and food stores, had recently been banned in Coronari, and I had the sensation that I was being watched. Yet I knew it wasn't so, or not to any great extent, while I minded my own business. And that was to find the store and the second candlestick. I might even forego the candlestick, but I must find that store.

Nobody openly paid the slightest attention to me. If the owner of an antiques shop looked up as I peered through his window, I pretended to myself that I really was looking inside at his stock. If he looked up half an hour later as my shadow fell across him, I inwardly shrugged and told myself to be calm. I didn't look like a bill collector, a policeman, a revenue agent, or a spy.

I passed a couple of mechanics working on a car. I halted to watch several men polishing furniture outside one of the ground-level caves that serve as shops and small factories. Nobody looked at me with curiosity or hostility, or asked what I was doing in those parts and did I need help. Still my discomfiture persisted.

It was easy to rationalize. In the beginning, I told myself, anyone seeing me walking along Vicolo della Vetrina or Via di Panico or through the market might assume I was lost and, as I would be gone by afternoon, that I had found my way out. On the other hand, why should a man who is lost walk through Vicolo delle Vache three times in twenty minutes, when he could easily ask for directions? And why should a man who is lost and finds his way home return the next day to get lost again—and the next day and the next?

Hatless, with shirt drenched, I tramped through the poor streets under the walls of faded brown and yellow and gray with their old bracketed lamps, soiled political posters, chalked slogans and other defacings, the bitter Communist pronouncements, the obscene graffiti. I passed the same wool carders and the masons who were patching a broken lintel. I went into narrow courtyards under high lines of wash, not to find anything but to vary the monotony. I saw children at strident play, listened to two shrill old women at a running street hydrant, saw a priest, a barber, a one-legged man crutching himself along the cruel uneven lava blocks, threading his way in alleys built for an age of horsemen and sedan chairs.

I recognized my enemy on the second day: the *saracinesca*. Two fears have governed Romans since their city was founded—fire and robbers. People who set fires or carelessly allowed them to start were severely punished in the Empire. Burglars got short shrift; but, as the fear of punishment was not a reliable deterrent, householders protected themselves with iron bars at lower windows, and they hired watchmen.

Janitors sometimes were chained to the entrance, lest they be tempted to stray or be lured away.

The windows of palazzi and lesser residences are still protected by bars in the old districts, but the most common means of protecting a store is to install a *saracinesca* or steel shutter. The *saracinesca* is rolled up in the morning or whenever the shop opens. It comes down for the *pranzo*; it goes up after the siesta and comes down at closing time, which may be seven or eight o'clock. If your ears can somehow shut out the noise of traffic in Rome, you will hear the clank and rattle of *saracinesche* start shortly after the noon gun booms on the Janiculum.

The *saracinesca* is more than a formidable barrier; it is a mask. The sound of a *saracinesca's* steely ring on a travertine sill has a finality few other sounds can match. The little world of the shopkeeper vanishes in an instant from the sight of outsiders—the pale golden light on mellowed walnut, *gesso* picture frames, silver teapots; the ropes of dried figs, pendant hams and cheeses, salami, fish; gleaming glass and bright ceramics, women's dresses, men's suits; books, displays of phonograph records, radios and television sets—all that is so tempting is shut out from public gaze. In a street like Via dei Coronari this withdrawal is eerie in its effects: Life suddenly has been cut off.

Most of the little shops have no business signs, nothing to indicate what is behind the *saracinesca*—*formaggio* or flowers, a fifteenth-century chest, precious jewels, or children's clothes. And there is no orderly process in the rise and fall of the shutters. Shopkeepers open at will; some take the day off without notice. Some open early and close after two hours. As for the caves where men and women may be stuffing mattresses or polishing buttons or doing all the mean and profitless jobs the poor necessarily do for the other poor—these are dark mysteries. Guarded by *saracinesche*, they could be dens of wild beasts, kidnappers' lairs, the plants of counterfeiters. All look alike.

On my third or fourth day, I went farther afield—to the palazzo del Governo Vecchio, to the Piazza dell'Orologio, along Via degli Orsini and Via di Monte Giordano. I went into the cloister of San Salvatore in Lauro—and so on and so on. One morning I was in Via di Panico shortly after a woman rolled up the *saracinesca* of her small antiques store. I watched her as she made for a coffee bar—on her return she unlocked the door and welcomed me. She had a candlestick I liked. She wanted so much for it; I offered her less, and we compromised. It was a bargain, and I was tempted to go home and abandon my search.

But the day was young, and I took up my plodding once more, though I was sick of the whole business. It was not the candlestick that drove me now; it was the store. Where was it? It was there in one of those little streets. It had to be there. The man had been real. The deal had been made in daylight. We had come out of the store together and saluted each other, and he had picked up his newspaper and sat down again. The *saracinesca* was the only logical explanation. The store was there; the man was away or he opened after *pranzo*.

I tried entering the quarter from the Chiesa Nuova. Not very convincingly, I pretended this was my first walk through these squalid streets so choked with the past: Rossini, Orsini, Pasquino, Cellini. I tried going through the market to Via dei Lautari. I went to a short street called Piazza Fiametta and walked through a narrow arched alley called Via dei Tre Archi, which is six feet wide and has been called the shortest street in Rome. It is no more a street than Piazza Fiametta is a piazza; it leads to Via dei Coronari, is usually littered, and stinks from stale urine.

At the end of my fifth day of searching, I went home in disgust. I had walked miles in the hot sun. I felt foolish. But the weekend refreshed me, and on Monday I returned to the neighborhood. My wife gave me no encouragement. She had a hundred reasons for the man's disappearance: He had added my eight dollars to twenty dollars of his own money and made a down payment on a car; he was at Fregene lying on the beach, or at Ostia Lido, or visiting relatives in Viterbo or Rocca di Papa. I had never known her to give her fertile imagination such free play.

In the end I gave up. I was certain now that people must have put me down as a crank or a lunatic to spend hours strolling through byways that were never meant for such relaxing pleasure as a stroll, with their humpy paving, puddles, and smells. We took the two candlesticks to a friend, an expert in *ottone* (brass), and he cleaned and polished them.

Since then we have gone along Via dei Coronari and through Via di Panico when it has been necessary, and if a shop interested us and we intended to return, we have made a note of it. In one case we found on our return to a shop about eight months later that it had closed. As for the man who involuntarily sent me on my absurd sweaty search, I wonder. He was such a gentle, accommodating man that I hope he thrives.

CHAPTER 8

The Vasari Room

*I*t was a dreary Sunday. The cold rain that began falling at daybreak had let up in midmorning, but the low gray clouds that hung over the city did not go away, and showers still fell from time to time. People who had no business outdoors hurried home after Mass and stayed there.

All Rome dripped. Water ran everywhere, and the fountains overflowed. Water stained the scarred columns of the Temple of Neptune and formed little beads that broke and ran down the bronze head of Giordano Bruno in Campo de' Fiori and flowed in tiny rivulets along the folds of his bronze cloak. The frayed posters on the face of Sant'Andrea della Valle were sodden.

Water ran over the roof tiles into the rain gutters and into the gurgling rainspouts of tenement courtyards; and where trees had shed their leaves, the leaves lay in thick soggy masses or were flattened and plastered, leaf by leaf, on the footpaths of the little parks and the Lungotevere. After every shower a puddle lay on the pavement of the Pantheon until an attendant came with mop and plastic pail and dried the spot.

The rain fell on the house in Piazza di Spagna where John Keats died, and on his poor grave behind the Cestius Pyramid. From the spongy ground under San Giorgio in Velabro, the water seeped upward through the marble floor and spread in a thin sheet along the edges of a fine blue carpet, installed two days earlier for a wedding.

The Tiber, swollen to a yellow flood by downpours north of Rome and the tributary burden of the Aniene, swirled seaward, rocking crazily the boathouses moored along the embankment. Throwing high its muddy waters above the railings of the low bridges, it raced in two unequal parts past the Isola Tiberina where the Fatebenefratelli nursed the sick and dying and a medieval tower, once part of the Pierleoni fortress, still held its ground as firmly as when it sheltered Matilda, Countess of Canossa.

Gino may have wondered, as we left our room key at the desk of the Adriano, why we were going out in such unfriendly weather; but he said nothing, and we surmised—correctly, I think—that his thoughts were on a group of new guests, Scandinavians by their looks, who stood in a glum, silent huddle near the fountain. How would he explain this ferocious Roman wetness?

We walked up Via dei Prefetti past San Nicolo and farther along the house where Samuel F. B. Morse, Yale graduate, painter, and inventor of the electric telegraph, had lived in his Roman days. By Palazzo Chigi we reached the shelter of the Galleria Colonna just as a new shower began. When the rain had spent itself, we walked down Via del Corso past the bank that was established in 1492, past Santa Maria in Via Lata and Palazzo Doria, to Piazza di Venezia and, rounding the corner of the palace, crossed to the park and stood under the rain-laden trees.

Since leaving the Adriano we had seen very few people, no more than six or seven. Two or three empty buses had rolled routinely along the Corso, and several cars had sped past us, but Centro, the mid-point of Rome, was desolate. We had it all to ourselves and could hardly forbear smiling when we remembered how often we had sat there, opposite San Marco, watching hot, thirsty boys and men eagerly turn their heads sidewise to catch a mouthful of water from the fountain's curving stream. We went on, and as we passed the Gesu, another shower descended and we dashed inside.

The rain held off as we walked down Corso Vittorio Emanuele, and we had come to the Palazzo Massimo when the first drops of a new shower pelted us and we went into the porch. A girl sat on one of the stone benches, her hands folded, her head slightly bowed. She looked at us as our feet touched the gritty paving, but she said nothing; and when my wife spoke about the rawness of the damp air, she was silent. We sat down on a bench on the other side of the doorway to wait for the shower to pass.

The palace was closed—we had read somewhere that the prince had gone away—and it looked dark and lifeless behind its lovely black columns; but we suspected someone would be inside, the caretaker and his wife and their bright little boy. I said aloud to my wife, "Remember?" for I felt she would be thinking, as I was at that moment, of a summer day once when we walked by the palazzo and, seeing the door open and the small front court beyond, crossed the threshold for a better look. The caretaker's cry that the place was not open to the public had halted us; but when we explained that we merely wished for a brief look, he had allowed us to go in with his son, a small spirited child of nine or ten, who identified a few of the busts for us and ascribed everything he did not know to "antichita." We had tipped him and praised him lavishly, telling his father he was a fine little cicerone.

The shower eased off and the skies seemed to brighten, but a new hard rain began, and when it slackened a slow drizzle filled the air. The girl's presence was disquieting. What was she doing, sitting there? We could justify our own presence: We had found a temporary refuge. But the girl had been there before the shower started. My own thoughts about her annoyed me. There was no way of defining even her posture. She was calm; she seemed indifferent to us and to everything about her. We had fallen into a waiting silence ourselves.

The scene suddenly appeared absurd. It was natural enough to get out of the rain, even to stand in a strange doorway. We were not in a strange doorway. We were sitting in the porch of a private place, an historic palace familiar to St. Philip Neri. We were sitting on a stone bench as if we had every right to sit there. How ridiculous we would have looked if the day was clear and people were passing. Romans and tourists sat on church steps and on the Spanish Steps but, as many times as we had passed the Palazzo Massimo, we had never seen anyone sit on the stone benches.

It seemed certain the girl was not going to speak. I gave up my fruitless train of thoughts, and when at last the drizzle stopped, we got up and left without a word. The girl did not look up.

As we turned off the Corso and headed for a trattoria where we frequently lunched, we heard the noisy putt-putt-putt of a gas engine coming from the courtyard of the Cancellaria—the *cortile* once falsely attributed to Bramante, the handsomest in Rome. We crossed the narrow piazza and walked to the palace gateway, and what we beheld shocked even as it amused us. A teenager was riding a motorbike around the sides of the courtyard. Who was this fearless intruder? A youngster who had seen the open gate and had dared trespass so boldly? A boy who probably didn't know it was the Cancellaria and who was now racing around that lovely interior, so satisfying in its beauty that people seeing it for the first—or the hundredth—time marveled?

We stood there watching and wondering why nobody came out to stop this profanation, but nobody appeared, and after a few minutes the rider came close to the gate and dismounted. It was a girl of twelve or thirteen, a pretty little thing in dark jeans and a snug zippered windbreaker. She ignored us and, grasping the handlebars of the bike, wheeled it through a doorway at our right. So that was it: she belonged to the Cancellaria—the daughter, probably, of one of the maintenance staff.

I was about to leave when my wife tugged at my sleeve and said, "Vasari!" in an excited voice.

For a moment, I had no idea what she was talking about. Vasari was the name of the establishment in Piazza della Republica where we had our films developed and printed. Then I remembered, and knew that she was thinking about the Vasari room in the Cancellaria, the great *salone* that Giorgio Vasari, art historian, architect, and painter, had painted with the help of two assistants, most likely his pupils. She had tried at various times for several years to see the room and had been turned away, chiefly because the *salone* was not open to the public and required special permission to visit.

Now I was suddenly aware of what she had instinctively felt when she saw the girl take her bike inside. The Cancellaria was vulnerable. If the person in charge at the porter's lodge could allow a motorbike to be ridden in the courtyard, it was possible that another regulation could be lifted and we would be permitted to go inside. Thus my wife had perceived the possibility at once; she started walking toward the open doorway, and I followed her into a room where two men were on the floor working over a television set under the eyes of a priest in a black cassock.

All three looked at us when we came in, and my wife, excusing our intrusion, asked if we could see the Vasari room. Without waiting for an answer, she added that we had tried several times to see the room; we loved Vasari; we had visited his little house in Arezzo, admired his piazza in Arezzo and all that he wrote. We were leaving soon for New York and: "Could you for once, please, make an exception and let us go in?"

It worked. It was as if she had cast a spell over them.

It was that television set, too. The priest had not been distracted by the motorbike. His thoughts must have been on getting the TV in good working order for the afternoon *calico* game somewhere. And we were strangers, Americans who came thousands of miles to see things that most Italians never troubled to look at, or regarded with indifference. For once, could not a rule be broken?

The priest nodded, and one of the men—the father of the girl, I assumed—called her from the adjoining room and told her to take us to the Vasari room. She detached from the wall a bunch of keys and beckoned us to follow her.

We crossed the courtyard to a door that she unlocked. We followed her inside to a hall and stopped at a self-service elevator, which she also unlocked. We all entered, rode up one flight, got out, went through another door to the portico, followed the girl to still another door, and went in.

We now walked down a long hall and through a door into a big room. We thought this would be the room, but our guide shook her head and led us across the room and through a doorway into a larger room.

"Ecco," she said.

She went to a light switch and then hoisted herself up onto a flat-topped desk and sat there, swinging her short legs sideways and snapping a wad of chewing gum, as we looked at the walls and ceiling in the brilliant light. Heavy draperies hung from the windows and, peering out once, we saw rain falling.

We studied the scenes Vasari had painted—events in the life of Pope Paul III, Farnese—but we did not stay long. The murals had not overwhelmed us. There was too much to be seen in the brief time we could spend in the room; and I'm afraid that we could not forget as we looked at them what Michelangelo was reported to have said when he saw the work and was told that Vasari and two pupils had done the job in a hundred days: "It looks it."

In the elevator, my wife thanked our patient little guide and tipped her, and we went back to the office to thank the priest and the two men.

Only a thin rain was falling as we dashed across the piazza to the trattoria. The owner's wife and two children were watching an American western film on TV. I recognized the setting—the Red Rocks, near Sedona, Arizona. Unlike the ground beyond the trattoria door, the ground in the film was very dry and hard, and the cowboys' horses were kicking up clouds of dust.

CHAPTER 9

The Torlonias, Nobles by Purchase

A fight, in Italian, may be a *lite*, a *rissa*, a *mischia*, a *zuffa*, or a *tafferuglio*.

A *lite* is not much of a fight—maybe no more than two women screaming at each other, or a man and his brother-in-law angrily trading insults. I never understood the difference between a *rissa* and a *mischia*, and Italian friends of mine, while warmly assuring me that they would let the light of day shine on the darkness of my perplexity, had their own difficulties distinguishing a *rissa* from a *mischia* and a *zuffa* from a *tafferuglio*.

An uproar or riot is a *gazzarra*, but *Il Messaggero* seemed to shy away from the word. If several hundred youths battled the police all the way from Piazza di Venezia, I mentally tabbed it as a *gazzarra*, but *Messaggero* stuck to *tafferuglio*. Cars might be upset, shop windows smashed, buses and trams halted, and dozens of participants and spectators hurt by thrown stones, but to call such an occurrence a riot was plainly provocative; it was a *tafferuglio*.

Il Messaggero had two other word for violent action. One was a *match*, a word taken from the paper's sports department; the second (for street fights) was *un Western*.

Since the editors and reporters clearly relished fights, they were in a happy, boisterous mood one August night when the Torlonia family had a private brawl. The newspaper used a three-column headline to alert its readers:

> *A palazzo Torlonia*
> *match tra zia e nipote*

That is to say: there was a fight at the Palazzo Torlonia between aunt and nephew. *Il Messaggero* had a special style for action stories—a staccato style. Short sentences, crisp phrases. Blows of every kind, it said, were struck in the courtyard of the Palazzo Torlonia in Via Bocca di Leone, 78. Protagonists of the *zuffa* between relations were the thirty-four-year-old Prince Marco Alfonso Torlonia and his Aunt Cristiana, fifty-three years old, sister of Prince Alessandro. The *lite* exploded shortly before ten o'clock in the courtyard of the big palace that faces on Via Bocca di Leone, Via Condotti, Via Borgognona, and Via Mario de'Fiori. At the outset it was simply a discussion between *nipote* and *zia*, but the *diverbio* quickly degenerated into a *rissa*.

Heads and fists (the account went on) were freely used by the two noble combatants, without regard for their close kinship or the difference in their ages. Marco Alfonso was wounded in the head, the face, and the right arm. La Zia Cristiana suffered contusions on the back of her head, on one eyebrow, a cheekbone, and her lower lip. Someone telephoned the police, and the two battlers were taken to San Giacomo Hospital a few blocks away for repairs. They freely admitted they had slugged each other but declined to tell the police the cause of the original argument or whether other members of the family had participated.

Il Messaggero, while scarcely containing its scorn, reminded its readers that this was not the first time the Torlonia family had had a *zuffa* in that same *cortile*. Only six months earlier, in January, Marco had stood shoulder to shoulder with his father, Prince Alessandro, and his (Marco's) brother Marino and Conte Clemente Lecquio, against the *advocate* Giovanni D'Onofrio, a Torlonia relative by marriage. That *diverbio* had ended in court.

The angry screechings in the Torlonia *cortile* that moved *Il Messaggero* to muffled laughter were not echoes from a heroic past. The Torlonia family is immensely rich, but it has always worn robes of borrowed glory. No military adventurer or naval hero, saint, cardinal, artist, or explorer ever bore the name of Torlonia. The Torlonia position in Roman society came from wealth, and the wealth came from shrewd land speculation and money-lending. The Torlonias were latecomers, but not so late as to miss the market in titles.

Giovanni Torlonia, founder of the fortune, was born in 1754. His parents were domestic servants or second-hand dealers, and Giovanni started his swift climb in the money market as a lackey who became the agent for Prince Furstenberg at the Holy See. A man with the instincts and talents of a Figaro for intrigue, his financial dealings with Pius VI and Pius VII were richly rewarding. Pius VII made him Marquis of Romavecchia and Prince of Civitella-Cesi. Real estate, banking, and titles were the old man's dominant passions. (His son, Prince Alessandro, bought the old sixteenth-century estate of Bracciano for nine thousand crowns and for an extra fifty crowns picked up the ducal title.)

Torlonia money bought alliances with the old feudal families. A Torlonia married into the house of Sforza-Cesarini. Other Torlonia members took Chigi, Colonna, Borghese, and Ruspoli brides. The wealth was fabulous. The old prince and Alessandro bought numerous farms, small country estates, and city properties. In 1870, when the capital was established at Rome, the price of land skyrocketed. At one time the first prince, Giovanni, owned the Teatro Apollo on the Tiberbank, and in 1821 brought the Teatro Argentina; he also had a stable of the finest horses and carriages in Rome.

And still the Torlonia wealth grew, until all Italy and eventually all Europe knew the family and spoke of the sons as people spoke of the Rothschilds. Macaulay patronized the Torlonia bank; Stendhal was an intimate of the old prince; and Thackeray went to a Torlonia reception in the historic palazzo in what is now the Via della Conciliazione, the wide avenue that leads to Bernini's Colonnades and St. Peter's.

The first Torlonia palace was at the southern end of the Corso, in Piazza di Venezia, across the way from the Palazzo Venezia. It was razed in 1902. It was here that Torlonia told Stendhal how he had gone to Paris to buy the great gilt-framed mirrors that everybody admired. The old man had dressed poorly and explained to the dealers he met that he was an agent for the greedy old Roman banker, Torlonia. In that way, Torlonia boasted, he bought the mirrors at a discount of five percent.

He was, in fact, an extraordinary money-maker and, outwardly at least, a pious and ambitious Catholic who hoped that the wife of his oldest son, Alessandro, would bear a son who would become pope. She had a child, a daughter. A second baby, a girl, was stillborn, and she herself died soon afterward.

The old Roman nobility—the Colonna, Santacroce, Orsini—bred numerous bastards and much violence. They were the stuff of romance and adventure. They had their own small armies of *bravi* and bloodletters, no better than the *banditti* who infested the city and the countryside. In the Middle Ages they fortified buildings, oddly enough helping to preserve structures which otherwise might have fallen into ruin. They were a mettlesome, murderous lot. One day in September, 1332, they staged a rousing bullfight in the Colosseum. It was a crude, ugly, worthless exhibition in which eighteen young patricians were killed, and nine were badly mangled.

Nobody can imagine a Torlonia taking part in such pleasures. The Torlonias were always proper—and dull. They had safe marriages and added a second-hand luster to the Torlonia name. But they built no new palaces or churches, and when Prince Alessandro bought the Villa Albani out on Via Salaria, where Winckelmann had originally assembled the sculpture that Napoleon coveted and stole, the place became virtually off bounds to the public, admission being granted sparingly and grudgingly.

Prince Alessandro, born in 1800, died in 1886. He added a tiny footnote to archeological history when he became interested in the ancient Claudian port at Ostia, which Trajan had enlarged. "We can see with our own eyes the perfection of Trajan's dock," Lanciani wrote, "and I, better than anyone else, because I have been the only archeologist allowed to follow the excavations which Prince Alessandro Torlonia, the owner of the ruins, has carried on for five consecutive years, doing more harm to the place in this short time than had been done in fifteen centuries of abandonment and desolation."

The Palazzo Torlonia near St. Peter's, where Thackeray attended a big party, was originally called Palazzo Giraud. It was built at the end of the fifteenth century for Cardinal Adriana da Corneto as a smaller copy of the Cancellaria. Thackeray knew Rome as well as most Englishmen of his day and, as an inveterate gadabout, he made cool appraisals of foreigners and Italians alike. The Torlonia affair was brought shortly to the readers of *Vanity Fair* where, in the final pages, we attend Becky Sharp and Major Loder on their evening of entertainment.

"It happened in Rome once," the novel says, "that Mrs. De Rawdon's half-year's salary had just been paid into the principal banker's there, and, as everybody who had a balance of above five hundred scudi was invited to the balls which this prince of merchants gave during the winter, Becky had the honor of a card, and appeared at one of the Prince and Princess Polonia's splendid evening entertainments. The Princess was of the family of Pompili, lineally descended from the second king of Rome, and Egeria of the house of Olympus, while the Prince's grandfather, Alessandro Polonia, sold wash-balls, essences, tobacco, and pocket-handkerchiefs, ran errands for gentlemen, and lent money in a small way. All the great company in Rome thronged to his saloons—Princes, Dukes, Ambassadors, artists, fiddlers, monsignori, young bears with their leaders—every rank and condition of man. His halls blazed with light and magnificence; were resplendent with gilt frames (containing pictures) and dubious antiques; and the enormous gilt crown and arms of the princely owner, a gold mushroom on a crimson field (the colour of the pocket-handkerchiefs which he sold), and the silver fountain of the Pompili family shone all over the roof, doors, and panels of the house, and over the grand velvet baldaquins prepared to receive Popes and Emperors.

"So Becky, who had arrived in the diligence from Florence, and was lodged at an inn in a very modest way, got a card for Prince Polonia's entertainment . . . and went to this fine ball leaning on the arm of Major Loder . . . Major Loder knew a great number of foreigners, keen-looking whiskered men with dirty striped ribbons in their button-holes, and a very small display of linen . . . Becky, too, knew some ladies here and there—French widows, dubious Italian countesses . . ."

The Palazzo Torlonia in Via Bocca di Leone is not a Roman landmark, and most strangers and Romans as well don't recognize it. The ground floor is occupied by shops. It was in this palazzo, in

1949, that Princess Margaret of England was guest of honor at a ball attended by three hundred men and women. The lighting was brilliant that night, especially in the *cortile* where Prince Marco Alfonso would one day punch his aunt in the face.

CHAPTER 10

Il mostro . . . Regina Coeli . . . Janiculum's Roses

The Tiber frees itself from its high stone embankments downstream and runs placidly to the sea through a sparsely settled countryside. When the flow diminishes in the summer months, low sandbanks and shallow pools appear, and small boys play at piracy and other games in the water and among the reefs. Moviegoers who saw *The Bicycle Thief* may remember this part of the river and the anguish of the poor father who thinks his little son, whom he has scolded harshly, has fallen into the water and drowned.

On one of these sandbanks, three boys made a grisly discovery in the glaring sunlight of a June day. An old torn plaster sack they had dragged from the water held parts of a woman's dismembered body. The police came and searched the river for days. Through diligence and accident—a fisherman found a head—they recovered the rest of the body in another sack and parts of a second body, a man's, farther downstream. The two were identified: she was a poor prostitute, the man was her husband and pimp. They had two children.

The woman had carried on her trade on a road south of the city, taking her customers to a mattress she kept in a dry culvert. A second man, who had shared the couple's lodgings and the woman's wretched earnings, was arrested in a small hotel in a street behind Sant'Andrea della Valle, near the site of the Theater of Pompey, where Caesar was murdered. The newspapers promptly named the prisoner *Il mostro* (The Monster). There was talk about the dangers of roadside prostitution, but, as it happened, this *puttana* and her husband had been slain in their own rooms.

Il Messaggero's account was a ghastly romp. Curious neighbors told the police that around the time when the murders were believed to have been committed, they had seen *Il mostro* carry some old empty plaster bags into the tenement. Later they had seen him carrying the bags out to his little car. The bags looked lumpy. They bulged. Naturally, a woman said, we suspected nothing. *O, povera donna.* That poor unfortunate soul. What if she did do the things they say she did? She worked for her children and that vile husband.

Amid all the excitement, *Il mostro* appeared to be unruffled, behaving as if he wished to separate himself from the whole mess. He had not tried to run away. He had taken a room in the Albergo Paradiso, where the police found him in the company of a young woman who apparently knew nothing of the crime. The newspapers might call him *Il mostro*, but he seemed reluctant to fill the role, and in his appalling reticence and absurd detachment he emerged, in *Il Messaggero's* stories, more lout than monster.

The awful stupidity of the murders disqualified the crime from serious public consideration. There was simply nothing to talk about: no ground for arguments about innocence or guilt, no questions about a reasonably interesting motive. There had been no honor here, nor lust, nor greed; no wounded love. And in these circumstances, given the low character of the principals, Rome rejected the butchery of *Il mostro* as little more than a rude interruption in an uneventful summer. *Il mostro* had removed two poor people from their empty existence.

His own existence henceforth would be barren. The newspapers, having led their readers so far, felt obliged to go on and dutifully report the final public action: the judicial process. He had committed a revolting crime, but he was not to be put to death as he would have been in former times. Italy had abolished capital punishment. *Il mostro* would spend the rest of his life in prison.

Something about this swift and easy disposition of the case vaguely disturbed me. There was a demonic levity about it. Overnight the populace had accepted *Il mostro* as a public figure, as it accepted every new rising cinema star and *calico* player. There was no longer any need to call him by his right name. It was in fact forgotten, living now only in the archives of crime.

One more thing disquieted me: *Il mostro* was going to Regina Coeli Prison, and Regina Coeli struck me as a sorry place to repent. A crime like *Il mostro's* called for a prison more chilling. As it happened, we knew more about Regina Coeli than we had ever expected to know, more indeed than we had a right to know.

Outsiders had always found Regina Coeli to be a strange name for a prison, and I had been no exception to the common reaction; but residence in Rome and a better knowledge of the city's quirky history had attuned me to reality. Regina Coeli had been named after an ancient church that stood on the right bank of the Tiber about midway between the Santo Spirito Hospital and Porta Settimiana—a small, undistinguished place of worship built when the land and materials were cheap and men asked little or nothing for their labor and skills, considering such work an act of love and faith.

When the church was pulled down, its name was bestowed on the new prison. It was quite likely that nothing would have been said if the church had been called Santi Apostoli or San Cristoforo and the prison had taken one of these names; but Regina Coeli was the title of Rome's most revered saint. Still, in the unregulated and therefore sometimes inconsistent usage of names, nobody had thought it odd that a theater had been named the Tordinona when it was built on ground lately occupied by the Tor di Nona prison, where men in deep dungeons drowned whenever the Tiber overflowed its banks, while rats were allowed to escape to the safety of the Viminale.

When Innocent I built his Caceri Nuove in Via Giulia in the sixteenth century, Romans probably were amused to learn that a short, rough passageway that led to the prison had long been named Via del Malpasso (Street of the Misstep). Rome was willful, a city where vestal virgins had once been buried alive, where medieval Franciscans, living at Aracoeli, publicly yanked the bad teeth of the city's poor without charge; a city where, in the days before Michelangelo transformed the Capitoline, the authorities, from time to time, set up a gallows, *una forca*, for public hangings.

Nothing really was strange in Rome, or, in any case, stranger than man himself. To question the name of Regina Coeli was to quibble; yet that was exactly what American newspapers did when Regina Coeli appeared in news stories from Rome. They scorned the Latin for English, as if afraid readers would not understand and therefore would miss a chance to snicker. It was a tasteless, unnecessary, journalistic barb.

Regina Coeli's appearance disappointed me. It lacked the sinister aspect of such penal strongholds as the Tower of London, the Bastille, and other such places, most of all the Eastern Penitentiary in

Philadelphia, where I grew up. Regina Coeli's builders, of course, had no way of knowing that an American would one day judge it from that viewpoint. But that momentous boyhood encounter—my first sight of the Penitentiary—had filled me with excitement. I was twelve years old. My heart raced, and I trembled, but my fear passed almost instantly, and I felt unaccountably elated. The place was colossal! The dwellings that, from the width of a street, enclosed it on four sides were dwarfed by its immensity. I stared in awe at the massive crenellated entrance towers. It was a fortress, a vast silent monumental pile. I was thankful that I could stand safely on the far side of Fairmont Avenue, and look at the great somber gate, and know I was free.

Eastern Penitentiary covered eleven acres and was a short walk from the heart of the city. Its hard stone walls were eight or ten feel thick and thirty feet high. Huge round towers fifty feet tall and manned by armed keepers protected the corners and the entrance. Charles Dickens had toured the prison and written in praise of its humanitarian treatment of inmates, an innovation in mid-century prisons.

I knew nothing of Dickens and his interest in prison reform, and my ideas of what went on behind those frightening walls arose, as I grew older, from agreeably-written magazine stories. I read about inveterate criminals, men of terribly bloody misdeeds transformed by years of incarceration into passive creatures; lifers who, bereft of human companionship, made friends of mice and even rats; men softened by daily submission to discipline. It was all punishment and no talk of rehabilitation.

The waiter at the café on the Via Arenula end of Ponte Garibaldi thought we were joking, making sport of him in some way he did not understand, when I asked him about Regina Coeli. He held against his heart like a shield the small tray on which he had carried our gelati while he considered a reply.

"We're serious," my wife said. "We've heard so much about Regina Coeli that we'd like to see it."

"Well," he said, brightening, "there's not much to see."

But he suggested that we walk along the river embankment to Ponte Mazzini and cross. It occurred to me then that, as many times as we had gone that way on ED, we had never looked for the prison. We finished our gelati and set off. It was October, and we walked under the trees and kicked the dry leaves, and every car that passed whirled them around our feet. The bridge was quiet, and half-way over we stopped, in no haste to go on. I had looked across the Tiber as we approached Ponte Mazzini and foreseen my disappointment,

There were no dark menacing high walls over there, no stern towers, nothing to frighten even a timid child: nothing but a long, low box with windows, as harmless in appearance as a shoe polish factory. No wonder we had never noticed it before. We had even driven past it without realizing that this mean construction was the famous Regina Coeli.

We leaned against the bridge railing, gazing at the wide, unhurried flow beneath us. Downstream at Ponte Sisto the river, reflecting the sky, was blue; but here was the Tiber's true color, yellow, a bright, smooth surface broken only by playful eddies. The land on the Regina Coeli side had an ill-favored look. Romans always seemed indifferent about the embankment, allowing tufts of grass and weeds to lodge in the crevices. Graffiti had begun to appear. Upstream near Ponte Margharita someone had painted in foot-high letters, VIVA L'ASSASSINO.

We walked on, holding back our words until we were close to the end of the bridge, when we halted again. I was chagrined; I had expected too much.

But my wife was smiling. "You're always telling me you like the surprises Rome gives us," she said in a tone of sympathy. "How many times . . ."

When we reached the Lungotevere, we stopped until we had a chance to dart across. We walked to the northern end of the building and turned the corner, expecting to be confronted by a prison guard; but nobody was there, and we went forward, cautiously, then with curiosity, past a door and, father on, a discolored yellow-washed concrete entry box under the high prison wall. The wall ran a short way to the blank face of another wall that formed the rear end of the blind alley or courtyard where we stood.

In wonder, we loitered. The place was unswept, lightly strewn with litter, dead yellow leaves, wind-blown newspapers. Someone had dumped a pile of trash in the sentry box. Squalor and desolation. We were about to go away when, on a sudden impulse, I went to the door, followed by my wife, and grasped the knob. I turned it and pushed, and the door opened slightly. I pushed harder, and it swung open, and in that instant our forward movement impelled us over the threshold.

We were inside Regina Coeli, and Regina Coeli, so like a forsaken warehouse as we had stood on Ponte Mazzini, was a bedlam. We were engulfed without warning in a deafening uproar of voices. We were stunned. With no idea of what we were getting into, we had blundered into a prison on visitors' day.

We were in a long narrow room full of men, women, and children. One side of the room was screened heavily from floor to ceiling, and on the other side of the screen were men: prisoners. No one spoke to us, and the guards who did notice us were too polite or indifferent to ask us what we were doing there. The authorities apparently felt there was no danger in allowing the families and friends of prisoners to visit them in this fashion. Women with children held the little ones aloft to let the caged men see them. Everybody pressed forward, but as it was impossible to dislodge the visitors who had seized the space along the screen, the others had to be satisfied with waving and shouting.

I took my wife's arm. We had not been able to move far, and now we looked toward the door. On reaching it, I pulled it inward and, allowing my wife to pass, followed her outside.

Oddly enough, we did not remember that *Il mostro* was living in Regina Coeli.

*   *   *

One day at the bus station across from Teatro Argentina, we boarded Number 45 for the Janiculum; and as we rolled down Via Arenula toward Ponte Garibaldi and Trastevere, we felt as if we were going on a picnic. My wife carried her enduring cheese bag, into which she had stowed the usual rolls and cheese, a vacuum bottle of coffee, and, for this late October outing, a dozen precious strawberries encased in a plastic box.

The Janiculum was Rome, but it was always a remote part, accessible yet distant. If you stood at the head of Via Basilio, not far from the American Embassy in Via Veneto, you could see the Janiculum against the western sky and, in a break of the trees, Garibaldi astride his horse. In the dark of moonless nights, the red, white, and green beams of the Argentinean lighthouse cut through the gloom, a lonely beacon on a lonely hill.

The bus dropped us in Via Quattro Venti, the first stop over the crest, close to Salvator Mundi Hospital; and when we walked back to reach the Janiculum's Passeggiata, we heard a man shouting. It was impossible to understand his words or why anyone would be so noise on such a lovely day, harder still to guess his purpose. He was standing across from the San Pancrazio Gate, and when we came near it was clear what he was up to. He was no haranguer. He was not a dangerous man shouting insults and threats. He was selling roses, and we thought how silly and desperate he must be to try to see red roses when not a soul except ourselves was there to hear him. Then a car came through the thin passage from Via Aurelia and stopped, and since we knew the Italian weakness for flowers, we were not surprised when the driver bought a few roses.

We walked past the roses and went on out of the sunlight into the tranquil shadows of the pines, and when we paused by the roadside we heard, below the whispering and rustling of the trees, faint sounds of music. Then we remembered there was a children's playground or amusement park somewhere over there. The music was coming from a miniature merry-go-round, and small children, submissive tots held in check by the disapproving looks and cries of loving grandmothers, would be riding primly round and round, smiling.

We dawdled along, relishing the sweetness of the air and our indolence. The music stopped, and we saw coming toward us down the avenue a large bulky shape and heard a soft thudding on the paving. When the strange form had drawn nearer, we saw that it was a small caravan of a dozen children on ponies and in pony carts, attended by four men on foot. The solemn procession moved past us in silence and, going as far as the San Pancrazio Gate, swung around and headed back.

The music was playing again as we approached Garibaldi, and we walked into laughter and childish shouts and clapping and the general hilarity of a puppet show. Gathered in front of a tall, curtained booth was a small audience of boys and girls and a few adults. We listened to the loud thwackings and the players' voices, and when the performance ended and a man emerged from the back of the booth and moved among the people, thrusting a collection box at the adults, we contributed our *lire* and were profusely thanked.

On the far side of the piazza, away from the monument and the puppetry stand, sat half a dozen elderly men and women taking their

ease where a gap in the pines let in the sun. They smiled and spoke
to us as we moved over to look down on the roadway cut out of the
western side of the hill. The dome of St. Peter's, sunwashed, serene,
rose beyond the dark trees.

We took a bench near the old people and listened to their talk,
timeless gabble on the ancient land where Martial, countryman and
friend of Trajan, had dwelt and gibed at the fair city across the river.
The noisy chatter of the puppet show had started up anew, but when it
stopped we heard again, borne on wayward currents of air, the rollicking
tunes of the playground. The loveliness of the day possessed us, and
we would have been content to sit there in a drift of lazy thought;
but the obtrusive throbbing of a tour bus coming toward us shattered
the peace. The bus rolled to a stop on the far side of Garibaldi, and,
rising from our bench, we nodded good-day to the elderly company
and went across the piazza to watch the tourists alight near the souvenir
and postcard stands.

We knew them by their voices and laughter even before we saw their
bright cottons and polyesters. Americans. Their presence brought unease:
voices calling across the breakfast tables at Heidelberg, overblown jollity
in the Munich beerhall, irreverent jests in the Colosseum, tasteless quips
in Pisa at the Torre Pendente, the tour guide's forced smile, browsers
among the Florentine leather stands at the Uffizi, and, in Venice,
buying from duplicitous shopkeepers the beribboned straw boaters and
striped shirts of *gondolieri*. Women and men came in equal numbers, in
their middle years and younger and, as a token of invincible old age, a
few spry oldsters. Who could measure their endurance and the tedium
and weariness of their journeyings? The boredom and bewilderment?
Carrying the burden of heartburn and constipation, they trudged
through the bazaars of Cairo, Istanbul, and Rhodes and climbed to the
Acropolis with a bellyful of Hellenic cuisine.

We turned away and our feet carried us beyond the piazza to a rough path that ran behind a low wall along the top of the cliff. We had escaped from the rising clamor and now walked on in silence, restored in spirit by the day. When we stopped to rest, we heard only the scratching of birds and their soft peeping in the undergrowth and, in the trees, the sound of gently moving air.

A day of murmurous stillness. Stendhal had come to the Janiculum on such an October day, crossing Ponte Sisto to make his lonely way up the roadway that was to be named Via Garibaldi. He was fifty years of age in 1833 and had less than a decade to live. The thought of Stendhal always filled us with sadness, so much did we admire him. He had stood at San Pietro in Montorio gazing at the far-off Alban Hills. His heart was full of love, and I think we loved him because he loved Rome as few had loved her.

San Pietro was back there on the hillside below Garibaldi and the Ossuary and the monumental fountain, the *mostra* of Aqua Paola, and the amber and red jumble of Trastevere rooftops. The shape of the Janiculum changed toward the north. The long pleasant slope where cars raced round the tight curves of the snakey Via Garibaldi gave way to a precipitous cliff, and the Tiber ran closer. Even so, I was not prepared for the shock when, on a sudden impulse, I got to my feet and walked to the wall and looked down. There in all its yellow ugliness was the Regina Coeli.

A Roman trick. Once when I was new to Rome, I had asked a man why the walls of churches were not washed clean of black streaks and blotches. That dirt, he replied, was the dirt of *antichita*, and to destroy it would mar *antichita*. Nonsense, of course. Baroque churches were not ancient. Legitimate dirt lay elsewhere, seventeen hundred years of it on the exquisitely carved *sarcophagi* the visitor to the Museo

Nazionale Romano passed as he plodded through heavy gritty soil to reach the Venus of Cyrene.

Afterward, when we had left the Janiculum, I remembered the disappointment I had felt early one morning when we saw a troop of Caribinieri riding back from their early morning exercises at the Galoppatoio in the Villa Borghese. We were living at the Residence Tevere at the corner of Via Isonzo and Via Tevere, just above Piazza Fiume, and had been wakened several times by the sound of hoofbeats from not a few horses, but many.

Rising early one day, I went down to Via Isonzo in time to see the troop coming toward me, two by two, on their handsome well-curried mounts. But the horsemen who cut such striking figures in St. Peter's Square and before the War Memorial, and when they clattered past the United States Embassy in Via Veneto, were now quite informal—hatless men in soiled, faded khaki riding breeches and sweaty short-sleeved undershirts. They slouched in the saddle. Some appeared to be sleeping. Only a few seemed alive and, with their incurable politeness, responded to my salute with a cheerful "Buon giorno!"

Rome was to be forgiven, but Regina Coeli was not. It lay down there, an alien form embedded in the earth, most of it shielded by the trees and wild shrubbery of the hillside. The embankment trees hid the river and Ponte Mazzini, and I could see nothing of the building on the Lungotevere. My wife had joined me at the wall, and we stared down long and steadily, but we could see only a part of the pitched roofs of the prison wings and the twin round turrets where armed keepers watched by day and by night. When we raised our eyes to the city, we found Villa Medici and Trinita de Monti, and the long sleeve of the Quirinale Palace and Borromini's campaniles, Sant'Andrea della Fratte and Sant'Ivo, and the flattened dome of the Pantheon. City of unspeakable traffic and unstilled voices.

We looked down again, hoping to discover some movement in the turrets or at one of the narrow windows in the wings. We searched in vain. Regina Coeli was secure from snoopers, even innocent ones like us. We were not the first to come this way, treading a path many a wayfarer had trudged in centuries past. A guard who looked aloft would see us as remote beings of unknown age and race. Idlers. We were nothing to him. He knew all that was withheld from us, what went on in the dreary corridors and cages under his feet, the loneliness and emptiness, the quiet despair and the hope. It was all very sad, no doubt, and it was sad to think of it on such a serenely beautiful October day.

I left off this maundering and at that moment my wife, as she often did, picked up a thought that had crossed my mind.

"*Il mostro,*" she said.

I nodded. Of course. *Il mostro* was down there.

CHAPTER 11

Freddo and Il radio

To many Romans winter is a stab in the back, an unforgivable blow not to be averted by prayer or thick underwear. The warnings are never lacking. In late October and November, the stalls in the street markets offer long drawers for the men, stylish union suits for the ladies. Roving peddlers drape themselves in the garments; the smart women's shops display sleeveless vests and woolen panties; and in the stores that supply such religious articles as chalices, missals, vestments, crucifixes, monstrances, and other church goods, room is made in the windows for tasteful showings of heavy-duty clerical undershirts and sturdy drawers that surely must keep out the penetrating cold of the heatless Roman churches.

The winter population of Rome is thus heavier by hundreds of thousands of kilos when December comes, but winter is still resented. Winter is a betrayal, a *trucco*, a colossal swindle of nature, a piece of treachery underlined by the fact that weather forecasts in Italy are usually vague or cast in terms so general as to be worthless. The word for cold in Italian is *freddo*, and I can give only an inadequate idea of its effect on the Eternal City by recalling an early December account in *Il Messaggero* announcing that *il freddo* had arrived with an "F maiuscolo"—that is, a capital "F."

What had happened that had so vexed the newspaper? Well, in twenty-four hours, as it told its readers, the thermometer had suddenly descended and the temperature was severe, stinging, *da mozzare l'orecchie*, biting the ears, as one would say. The streets were deserted, *Il Messaggero* declared, and when offices and stores closed, everybody hurried home to a hot supper and a good rest in an armchair with eyes fixed on the television screen.

(I turned aside for a moment the day I read this to look at the demographic figures for the previous day: Born—males, sixty-one; females, fifty-five; died—males, thirty-one; females, thirty-eight; married—twenty-nine. Males had won the day.)

Back to *il freddo*: *Il Messaggero* confessed there was little to say. "We Romans do not love *il freddo*," it said, "perhaps because we are not used to it, perhaps because one can count on the fingers of one hand the rigidly cold days, so that when the thermometer drops we prefer to suffer the television rather than go outside."

And what of the days ahead? *Messaggero* had consulted the meteorologists, a move that struck me as naïve. "*Siamo in inverno* (we are in winter)," responded the weather bureau. "Certainly one cannot hope to have in the cold months the tepidity of October." It would be cold for a few days, *Messaggero* concluded. The cold must be endured. It will be necessary to suffer. Summer bathings are still far away.

I looked at the meteorological bulletin for all of Italy: Weather was slowly improving in the north, in central Italy, and on Sardinia. The south was getting *maltempo*, bad weather, the temperature was diminishing. The seas were agitated.

There is another way of looking at the weather: that is to say, it is never cold in Rome. Or in Florence. It is not cold even when the temperature goes down to thirty-five degrees Fahrenheit and women clutch the collars of their fur coats. To be cold is to be *freddo*, and *freddo*, as I have said, is an unpleasant word. *Freddino* is the word one uses—*freddino*, with a waggling deprecatory motion of the gloved hand—coldish, chilly, but not cold.

Americans boast about their weather. They talk about record lows and record highs, blizzards, freezing rains, deep snows and windstorms, as if they personally created such conditions. I prefer the Italian attitude of indifference or cynical resignation or outraged feelings. Through September and October, when the weather may be a happy succession of sunny days, the Romans warn visitors that *Il Tempo* gets *brutto* in November. It is then, they say, that the rain comes; but when *la pioggia* does come, they act as if they had been betrayed. It is not the fault of Italy, they cry; it is the Mediterranean, the treacherous Adriatic, the Alps, North Africa. Waves lash at the shores, and the newspapers, which had been reporting all along that *il mare* was *tranquillo*, now report a *movimento* of the waters.

Movimento indeed! You drive along a road near the coast toward Civitavecchia, gripping the wheel as the car shudders and behaves as if it is about to leap a ditch. Cypresses bend before the gale, doves and barnyard fowl huddle behind the farmhouses, and sheep stand motionless in the fields. At a café where you stop for coffee, you say it is a miserably cold, wretched day. The owner smiles.

"It is the wind and rain," he says. "Tomorrow will be a fine day, *una bella giornata*, and if not *domani* then the next day or the day after. It is the sea. It is turbulent."

* * *

The radio in Rome was always a diversion. News was delivered by two and sometimes three persons who spelled one another. The changes were necessary, since each speaker read the news at breakneck speed. We liked this: The speed conveyed a sense of urgency, and even when we did not listen attentively to the words, we had the feeling that we were keeping abreast of everything that was happening.

The commercials were trashy, perhaps trashier than American commercials; but whereas American commercials were irredeemably bad, their counterparts in Rome were full of incredible bravura. We can't remember the products—coffee, butter, pasta, soap powder, shoes, sweets, cars—and there is no need to. We remember that, whatever the products, they were always sold by the same two people, a man and a woman, who engaged in a rapid-fire dialogue, trying to outdo each other in extolling the merits of the product and ending with an exultant, triumphant shout of "*Fantastico!*" The fact that they sometimes promoted a soap powder called "*Fantastico*" and a cigarette called "Stop" didn't bother them in the slightest. Let one of them merely mention a new brand of sneakers named "*Fantastico,*" and the other bawled out the adjectives; the first responded.

This display of enthusiasm sometimes wearied us, but we never tired of the sound effects of the westerns and melodramas that supported the commercials. Never outside Italian radio have we heard such clatters of hooves, never such neighing and whinnying. At times it was hard to hear the cowboys and the sheriff speak, with all the whinnying that went on; and in the Christmas season, when a band played "Jingle Bells" on the radio, the clatter of reindeer sounded like the finish of the third race at the Aqueduct on Long Island.

Older people who grew up in America will remember the sound effects: the crash when Fibber McGee opened his closet door; the creaking doors of haunted houses, and the swish of spectres, the lonely hoot of an owl; Jack Benny's agonizingly painful descent to his money vault to withdraw three dollars; the fast cars and screech of brakes; the rain and thunder.

The Italians took all these sounds and developed them until, in my case at any rate, I became quite content to listen to the sound effects and forget the story. The story, indeed, often impeded the sound effects. We knew that when the telephone rang, it would sound like an alarm, that every knock on the outside door spelled trouble, and that whoever answered the door would run down a hallway half a block long. If the visitor came in a raging storm, as was usually the case, he would sound half drowned and be led to a room full of men, all of whom talked at the same time before a great roaring log fire.

The arrival of a stagecoach in a western was always a joy to hear, as everybody alighted and went into the bar, followed by all the cowboys who had been loitering outside at the hitching posts. They entered with a mighty stamping of boots and cries of "Wheesky, ragazzo, wheesky!" And in no time at all, a poker game was going, the noisiest you can imagine, and the shooting began. The cowboys would scatter, the sheriff would form a posse, and off they would go.

Television has spoiled a lot of this radio pleasure. The horses in the TV westerns don't know how to whinny; or, if they do, they won't.

CHAPTER 12

San Tommaso in Formis
and a Green Door

We were walking along Via San Gregorio Magno one Sunday forenoon in early May when suddenly, and not unhappily, we were caught up in a wedding party that came down the steps of San Gregorio and flowed like a bright tide over the rough paving to the curbside. All Roman brides are pretty on their wedding day and all the bridegrooms gallant, and we lingered, savoring the laughter and the exuberant chatter until the principals had gone and the guests began thinning out. Instead of going on to Porta Capena, we turned aside to the Clivo di Scauro, the narrow road that goes up the Caelian Hill.

Mild spring air softly moved the higher pines and cypresses on the hillside above us, but where we walked among the young trees, the air was still and warm and smelled of freshly dug earth; and when we came to the old garden that was planted year after year, we saw the first vegetable sprouts, tiny greens no larger than a child's finger in long rows, neatly spaced. A strong wire fence rose by the roadside to block trespassers. We looked through and saw an old man dozing in the sun in the far corner. A clutter of small gardening tools was arranged outside a rude shed: a wheelbarrow, a watering can, spades, hoes, a rake, a hose, something piled up under a dirty tarpaulin, ancient bricks, a bundle of beanpoles tilted against the side of the shed.

We could not see his face clearly, but the little we could make of his features reminded us of the elderly man, not the *sagrestano*, surely, but another employee of San Gregorio who once had shown us the three outside chapels. He had been pleasantly informative and without the glib assertiveness of a mannered guide, and we had listened with pleasure to the story we already knew—how Gregory had fed twelve paupers every day on the long marble table in the middle of the room. The table was dusty now, and the chapel itself had a bleak air.

Our narrator had been shabby, a poor man reciting the tale of Gregory and Augustine's mission to England. He was diffident of speech, and we felt guilty, as if we were taking too much of his time. He seemed wistful, a naturally reticent man, tired perhaps of his own voice and his role as guide; and suddenly yielding to some unaccountable urge, he had said like one confessing his faults that he was an American by birth. He had seemed to ask for our understanding. His parents were Italians who had settled in Wilmington, Delaware, where he was born and had grown up.

He had come to Rome as a visitor and now could not remember why he had decided to stay. He had ignored the entreaties of his father and mother to return, not because he was stubborn but from feelings he was unable to explain, even to himself. Rome, not Italy, had imprisoned his spirit, and his irresolution or will to escape had kept him here, a humble servant of a church whose history and legend were more English than Italian.

We stared now at the man in the garden on the Caelian Hill, hoping he would look our way. We waved, but he did not move. We would have liked to say, "Una bella giornata!" But finding no way of getting his attention, we moved away from the fence. The gate to the police barracks across the road was closed.

We breathed deeply the garden fragrance and stopped again, this time to admire the high Lombard Gothic apse of Santi Giovanni e Paolo before going on under the low flying buttresses and past the antique wall lanterns to the church piazza. Another lively wedding party was assembled, but we did not tarry.

Across the piazza, the back gate of the Villa Celimontana was open, and we were tempted to enter and dawdle along the yellow gravel paths of the broad lawns. Instead of going in, we took the Via San Paolo della Croce and walked toward the Arch of Dolabella and Silvanus and the Trinitarian Hospice of San Tommaso in Formis. If the arch, erected in the year 10 AD, had had any esthetic value, it was soon lost, for Nero, on becoming emperor, had used it as part of the aqueduct he built to carry water to the Palatine from the Claudian aqueduct. The Trinitarians, having no regard for pagan remains, had further disfigured the arch.

The roadway, hard and dusty, ran between two walls. The one on our left, a rise of dark stone, hid from our eyes the monastery and lovely campanile of the Passionist Fathers and a field of scattered stones and clumps of shrubbery. The other wall, enclosing the garden of the Villa Celimontana, was stuccoed. Its rosy wash had faded to pink, and its flat monotony was broken at intervals by blind windows framed in white marble. Thick weeds, clotted with dried mud, grew along the base, and the lower pink was stained with muddy splashes. Tough old vines climbing up the inside wall from the rich soil of the garden hung loose masses of leaves and dangling tendrils over the top.

The wall abutted on San Tommaso, close to the arch, and we would not have stopped here had we not been puzzled by a little door in the hospice. The door was painted green—a bright green—and had a metal doorknob and a modern lock, a shiny brass disc. Just above the lock, on the doorjamb, was a push-button that we assumed was attached to a bell inside. I pressed it. We heard nothing. I pressed it again. Silence. Either the bell was broken, or nobody was inside; or if someone *was* inside, he did not care to answer. I rapped on the door; I pounded it with my fist. This had happened several times before when we had come this way.

We walked under the arch and stood close to the hospice. Augustus Hare, writing a hundred years before, had described the place as deserted. It had a strange look. From where we stood we could see the roof of San Stefano Rotondo above the treetops. A lane wound out of that side of the piazza and stretched all the way to the Lateran district, past San Stefano, past the hospital of the Blue Nuns where C. Scott Moncrieff, translator of Proust, had died in 1929 and George Santayana, Spanish-born philosopher and Harvard professor who died in 1952, had spent some time in the last years of his life.

Every minute or so a car darted out of Via Claudia or raced down Via Celimontana, sped past us, and went swiftly down the hill toward the Baths of Caracalla and, we supposed, on to Porta San Sebastiano. We waited for our chance to run to the other side and, when we got there, stood our ground and looked back. We had a good view of an odd assortment of structures. They were certainly unlike, yet they were not incompatible. They were, in fact, the kind of Roman huddle that we liked. The arch was first-century, the hospice was from the thirteenth, and the Church of Santa Maria in Domnica (or Navicella) and its exquisite interior and perfect measurements were Renaissance, built on an ancient foundation. Finally, the front gate of the Villa

Celimontana was modern; and no one would ever guess that, not far from the gate, archeologists had once uncovered the second-century station of a Battalion of Vigiles—the police.

The hospice could not have changed much, if at all, since Hare's day. The windows were irregularly placed; the cable protruding above the façade at one side seemed intrusive. We stared at that faintly derelict exterior, the great arch above the heavy portal and the Comatesque work over the arch, the patchy stucco, dull red brickwork, and weathered marble—a homely face, venerable and worn and somehow wonderfully right. It had been there on the high airy Caelian for 750 years. Behind it was a small house of God, a poor little chapel, consecrated in the fragrance of burning gum and spices from the East by Pope Innocent III when he presented it to John of Matha and Felix of Valois and their new order of Trinitarians.

For a moment, I think, we expected a response of some sort, a signal that our long scrutiny had been observed and our presence was being judged. After a while we went over for a closer look. I touched the wall. Then I went to the door and rapped loudly. Silence.

People were everywhere on the Caelian that day. They were there as they were every Sunday in spring and summer, when so many Italians marry. Since couples were free to be married in churches other than those they regularly attended, the romantic notion of taking their matrimonial vows in one of the churches of the Caelian or the neighboring Aventine had become increasingly popular. The Aventine, once shunned because it was thought to be malarial, now had the air of a small suburban community. The Caelian, so rich and desirable in antiquity, was still sparsely peopled and seemed unlikely to change. Considering how near it was to downtown Rome, this was strange, but the Caelian was a strange hill. Part of it didn't even look like a hill.

In earliest times the Caelian was Mons Querquetulanus, the heavily-forested Hill of Oaks. It got the name Caelian or Coelian from Coelius Vibenna, a noble Etruscan, who came to the aid of Romulus in his war against the Sabine king Tatius and then established himself on the hill and transported hither the Latin population of Alba Longa.

In imperial years the northern part of the hill was an aristocratic quarter, a pleasant stroll from the Forum Romanum and the Colosseum. Fire, more than likely set by an incendiary, ravaged the hill in the third century. The area was rebuilt and was destroyed in 1084 by Robert Guiscard. The ancient churches of San Gregorio and Santi Giovanni e Paolo were demolished and later reconstructed and renovated over the centuries until they appeared as they do today, but the stricken northern part never fully recovered. Hare, writing eight hundred years after Guiscard's savage excesses, found the hill almost uninhabited except by monks of the Camaldolses, Passionist, and Trinitarian orders. The Romans showed little interest in the hill, but visitors from the British Isles thought the Caelian enchanted. From the Palatine, across Via di San Gregorio, the Caelian and its old trees and wild vines seemed remote.

John of Matha and Felix of Valois were young French priests who had come to Rome from Paris in 1198 to tell the pope about a strange vision John had beheld while celebrating his first mass. Over the altar an angel had appeared standing between two kneeling men, one white, one black. The angel wore a white robe with a cross of red and blue on his breast, and his hands rested in benediction on the heads of the two men. The pope, a famous interpreter of dreams and visions, read the vision with unconcealed pleasure, for he had seen the same vision, at the main altar in the Lateran, at the moment of John's enlightenment. The kneeling men, His Holiness said, were Christian slaves of the infidels, and the command from heaven was clear: John was to organize a society of men to ransom prisoners of war and piracy from their captors along the Barbary Coast.

The monastic garb, chosen by John, was copied from the robe worn by the angel of his vision. The men he enrolled for the rescue missions were men of strong faith and resolution, tactful and brave. The Mediterranean and its African shores were full of dangers—robbery, murder, disease, and bondage—and not all of the Trinitarians who set forth hoping God and their blue and red cross would protect them returned to Europe. Despite the perils, volunteers were never lacking, and stories of courage and extraordinary adventures strengthened the reputation of the Trinitarians, or Redemptorists, as they were also known. (Among the slaves they brought home to Spain were the novelist Cervantes and his brother.)

Miracles were attributed to John. One of these heavenly interventions took place when John was about to set sail from an African port with 120 slaves he had freed. The infidels, suddenly angered, tore up his sails and broke his rudder. Dismayed, John spread his mantle to catch the faintly stirring air, and the men he had liberated did likewise. Then all knelt in prayer, and the ship was borne gently over the sea to Ostia.

In the towering ruin above the Arch of Dolabella and Silvanus, the brothers built a small cell as John's hermitage, and it was here that he died. After his death a mosaic portraying the vision of the angel and the two men was installed above the main door of the hospice.

And so the work of redemption went on for 650 years, until piracy was put down. The monks, relieved of their hazardous duties, locked the convent door, came down the hill, and went across the river to a new home at the fifth-century Church of San Crisogono in Viale Trastevere.

In June we went back to the Caelian for another look at San Tomasso and the little green door, but there were no signs of life, and I pressed the button with no expectation that my ring might be answered. It was not. At this point we could have gone away and put San Tomasso out of mind, to wonder now and then what lay on the other side of the door without allowing the question to nag us.

Rome had many doors but only one San Tomasso, and the hospice, lonely and forlorn, was unlike anything we had ever seen in the city. It had been built at a time when the Romanesque was in full flower and all Italy, outside Rome, challenged by the new style and spurred on by monastic fervor, was creating fresh architectural beauty. Rome was almost, but not quite, indifferent. It raised the Campanile of Santa Maria in Cosmedin; it mended some churches and neglected others; and it built, out of old bricks and pieces of marble salvaged from the ruins, the hospice of San Tommaso—a poor little house of no pretensions; an architectural scrawl. But San Tommaso served its purpose, and in the final reckoning the awkward gable and the plain windows and wide arch that framed the front door mattered little.

The odd part of all this is that Innocent III does not appear to have had any interest in the shaping of the hospice. A nobleman by birth, Lotario dei Conti di Segni of Anagni, who had studied theology at Paris and canon law at Bologna, was only thirty-seven at his election on January 8, 1198. He was a fearless pontiff—some historians have called him the greatest pope—who assembled the Papal States and got clear title to them from the Emperor Otto IV.

Innocent dwelt in the Lateran Palace, a short mule-jog from the Caelian, and might have constructed a monastery of granite and marble for John of Matha. It is idle to ask why he did not. He died in 1216 in Perugia after a reign of eighteen years, and it was not until 1891, 675 years after his death, that his body was brought to Rome for entombment in San Giovanni in Laterno.

I took many pictures of the hospice, usually from the same angle, and in their enlarged state studied them as if I could discover the secrets it concealed; for we felt something was hidden within those walls, something we would know if we could get through the little green door. Secrets: pieces of the past moldering in unlit chambers; a pair of ratskin mittens that warmed the chapped fingers of a Moldavian peasant; the stub of a candle. What else? A worm-eaten table, threadbare chasuble, broken incense boat, withered husks of dead insects, desiccated beetles, flies, mildew, and cobwebs. My wife scoffed.

We saw the moon rise above *Aida* at Caracalla, more radiant than the Pharaoh's court at Memphis, and, rising, turn from orange to yellow to silver as it moved up the Roman sky. Before the Tomb Scene's end, we were on our way; we found a taxi and shot up the Caelian to San Tommaso.

Moonlight softened the rude outlines of the hospice, and softened, too, the rugged face. It laid shadows under the gable and deepened the gloom of the dead windows. All was quiet, and in the stillness a muffled iron clapper began telling the hour: bong, bong, bong, to twelve. Mezzanotte. The Passionate Monastery. When I turned for a moment, I saw the cabbie watching us curiously.

I had hoped that a night visit might explain my obsession with this strange building, but nothing of the sort happened. I still wondered what lay behind the little green door.

We told the driver to go along Via Claudia so that we could see the Colosseum as we rolled downhill to the Via dei Fori Imperiali; and when we were home again in our high-ceilinged room at the Adriano, we opened wide the shutters and gazed on the shadowy unlighted houses around us denied the moonlight by houses in Via d'Ascanio. But the rooftop gardens of Via della Scrofa were all light and shadow.

The moon was shining on all Rome: on the terrace of Castel Sant'Angelo and St. Peter's Square, on Aracoeli, the Campidoglio and Navona; shining among the ruined tombs of the Via Appia and the mutilated marbles of the Forum Romanum, on the Tiber bridges and the Quirinale garden, on Garibaldi and the Ossuary of his men who fell in 1849 on the Janiculum, on all the obelisks, arches, and fountains, the mean tenements, and on the Palatine and the ghostly Circus Maximum.

The mystery of the green door came to an unexpected end as summer was drawing to its conclusion. We had hardly noticed the passing, so like other summers was this one. *Il Messaggero* had wakened us, reminding us that the Ferragosto (the August 15 holiday) was over, that it was time to think again of *lavoro* and to be thankful the holiday had caused no serious disruptions in the lives of Romans. As for our mystery, we were resigned to let it go. We had not invented it. The door was there.

We had hardly settled into the mood when a different decision was fixed for us. One Sunday morning, on one of our walks around noon, as we came to the green door we saw a small card pinned to the jamb. Neatly typed was the message that Mass was celebrated there every Sunday and Holy Days at 9 AM. That was it. It was incredible. Was this new, something the Trinitarians were initiating to give life to the old hospice, or had Masses been celebrated here through the years? We had never been on the Caelian as early as nine o'clock and had never seen anything to suggest that a chapel actually was there. Next Sunday we would see. The long wait would be over, and we would know the truth.

We took no chance of being late. A taxi hailed by Gino brought us to Santi Giovanni e Paolo at 8:30, and we strolled toward San Tomasso in the cool of a lovely Roman morning. The door was closed, and there was nobody in sight. As usual, we were alone. Where were the worshippers, and where would they come from? From the neighborhoods of Quattro Coronati and San Clemente? We waited, and turned again to speculating about what was inside.

We looked at our watches. Why were Romans so afraid of bring on time; and when they were late—as they invariably were—why did they act as if they were on time?

Nine o'clock came. A minute passed. I pressed the bell, as I had on our arrival. No answer. We waited a few more minutes and were about to turn, when a small Fiat darted under the arch and nearly hit us. The driver—a plump priest wearing a long black coat over his robe of white with a square pectoral cross of blue and red—allowed the car to scrape the wall.

My wife addressed him: "We were hoping to attend Mass here," she said. "Is it possible?"

"Certo, certo," he said cheerfully. Smiling benignly on us, he introduced himself as Father Bernardino Frattini. He seemed amused. He was not used to seeing strangers at San Tomasso, although they were common enough at San Crisogono.

We walked to the little green door, but Father Frattini was in no hurry. He faced us again and smiled. His right hand sank into the right-hand pocket of his coat and came up with a heavy bunch of keys, from which he selected one. No go; wrong key. He found the right one on the third try while we waited, controlling our excitement. The moment of revelation was here; in seconds the truth would be known.

Father Frattini turned the key in the lock and pushed the door slightly ajar. Through the crack we saw sunlight.

I was stunned. I touched my wife's arm as if I wished to assure myself that the sunlight was real.

It was all too real. The door swung inward and Father Frattini crossed the worn threshold—and I saw no medieval room—no remnants of the past—only a bright, fresh, flourishing garden of flowers, with shrubbery set at random in the black moist earth, shaded by lofty old trees. The mysterious little green door I had wondered about for so many months was a thick, solid, wooden garden gate.

I could not think clearly. I could not comprehend fully my feelings, nor find in them any sensible order. Fragmentary images beset me; my conjectures now seemed wild and absurd: frayed chasuble, ratskin mittens, desiccated beetles. I was glad nobody could read my thoughts.

But my dismay slowly passed, and I became calm as we followed Father Frattini down the path to the low building that I now assumed must be the old chapel with a new façade. This time I was prepared for disillusionment.

Father Frattini unlocked the door and preceded us into a windowless room. We waited while his hand groped for an electric switch. When he found it, the room was flooded with light, and all around us I saw walls of chaste white and two frescoes, whose faded colors had lately been brushed to new life. There were five or six rows of pews on each side of a center aisle, and a small confessional. Shortly after we sat down, the people began coming in—ten or twelve, no more—as Father Frattini prepared for the Mass.

Our minds were still too numb to try to work through the wreckage of our shattered expectations. We could not even reconstruct San Tomasso as it stood in its original state. Now, indeed, that shabby aged exterior standing in Piazza della Navicella could be a stage setting, a wall that had charmed us by its homely rectitude.

But what actually lay behind the wall? In the garden we had no way of telling, since an inner wall, obviously new, rose above the shrubs. We were confused.

Father Frattini said Mass quickly and offered communion to a few people who came forward. After the Mass he took us into a small room and bade us follow him up an iron spiral stairway. At the top we stood in a room with a door leading to an outside terrace. A conventional stairway rose to a room, or cell, built into the tower above. St. John of Matha had passed his last years and had died here. The vision at that Paris Mass—the vision that Innocent III had shared—had led here. But, like so much in Rome, it had suffered change. The ascetic's bare cell had become, in the restoration, a shiny new chapel.

The following Sunday, when we went back again to Mass at San Tommaso, Father Frattini invited us to drive with him to Trastevere, where he would lend me a history of the Trinitarians. He was treasurer of the Trinitarians and had a small car at his disposal.

As we had suspected, Father Frattini was a spirited driver. We made our river crossing at Ponte Palatino, moved bravely through the Sunday traffic, and parked at the side of the church with a gentle bump.

Father Frattini remained imperturbable. We went into the convent—Italians use the term convent for both men and women—attached to San Crisogono and, while my wife and I waited in a room set apart for visitors, Father Frattini went off to get the history. But after ten minutes he returned empty-handed and explained that the book had been misplaced. It would turn up, he promised.

We became very fond of Father Frattini. His hair was white, and we judged him to be about sixty. We could not imagine him ever in a state of anger or loud laughter. He smiled easily. He had a good sense of humor. He had traveled a great deal, from America to Madagascar. He had crossed the North Atlantic by steamship and had played bingo. He looked amused as he told us this. He liked Americans and American cigarettes.

Early in November, he moved to a convent on Monte Mario, and we saw less of him then. He invited us to come up for dinner, but we never made it, and it was not until the week before we were going home that we saw him again. We would have coffee together, he said, and we suggested that he name a meeting place. He chose St. Peter's, close to the *edicola*, the busy newsstand behind the Colonnade.

Daylight was going and a chill coming down on the city when we arrived. A great many people were about, furtive figures moving in the murky light or sitting along the Colonnade, neighborhood people from the poor little houses of the Borgo. They were always here taking the sun, the breeze, talking, watching the crowds. We were early, and we walked around a little before heading for the *edicola*. A light shown within, and against its warm glow we saw Father Frattini. I think he saw us at the same time we saw him: black coat, pectoral cross. Plump. A smiling face.

As we came up to him, I noticed a young man standing near him, regarding us. A tourist, I thought, an eavesdropper on the lookout for local color, something to tell his friends about back in the States. *"When I was in Rome . . . one day around dusk loitering in St. Peter's Square. You know . . . over there behind that newsstand behind Bernini's Colonnade . . . a priest lurking, waiting for someone . . . you know, there are Vatican spies and counterspies . . . Well, as I stood there these two people . . . English they were. . ."*

The young man could scarcely mask his feelings. He was smiling. His light brown hair and short beard were fashionably shaped; he wore a turtleneck sweater and an expensive tweed jacket, and I was about to be rude to him if I could think of something to shake that smile from his face, when Father Frattini turned slightly aside and the young man extended his hand.

Father Frattinii introduced him as Brother Roland. Brother Roland? A Trinitarian? He was smiling; Father Frattini was smiling. I don't think they were aware of our surprise. They weren't joking. This young man—who could have been the model for a television commercial for wine or after-shave lotion—was a monk. He lived in a convent with other monks, and wore a white habit with a pectoral cross. We had seen pictures of Franciscans kicking a football in a Tuscan mountain pasture, but they wore their monastic garb and were bare-footed. Many seminarians went about Rome in Borghese—civvies—but they were indistinguishable from other young men—we didn't know they were seminarians. Our image of a monk was a man in the uniform of his order, recognizable for what he was. Wearing a heavy girdled habit of black or white with a long skirt could be irksome, but young men ought to know that and accept it as Dominic and Loyola and Francis of Assisi had done. The religious orders gave color to Rome. Squads of seminarians in the vivid sashes that denoted their nationality, nuns marching two by two across St. Peter's Square to the Basilica, cardinals and monsignors—all these were part of our Roman picture, and the least change was a loss.

Father Frattini led us out of the square and steered us along to the narrow sidewalk, past the Fountain of the Four Tiaras and through the street opening of the Passeta, the hallowed wall that is the escape route from the Papal Palace to Castel Sant'Angelo. Walking on to the next block, we turned into a Borgo street and entered a coffee bar. The front of the place was full and noisy, and we went to the back room.

Father Frattini was familiar here. He ordered coffees laced with his favorite liqueur—he thought we would like the taste. Brother Roland looked around warily and in a low voice said the people in the Borgo were all Communists and hostile to the clergy and to tourists. A dangerous place, he said. He spoke in English, which Father Frattini did not understanbd.

Brother Roland was from Chester, Pennsylvania—a few miles south of Philadelphia, on the Delaware River. He had been in Rome for two years and was a courier, a motorcycle rider. The spiritual heir of John of Matha speeding down the Rome-Naples highway, helmeted, muffled, encased in thick woolens and leather, buffeted by the wind that came in from the mischievous sea, nearly eight hundred years of Trinitarian history riding on his back. His duties at the convent and his trips to Naples left him little time to see Rome, but he was slowly taking possession. He spoke Italian very well. We could not ask many questions, and what we learned of his past and his activities among the Trinitarians was volunteered.

Father Frattini talked. He was sorry we were going to leave, but he knew we would be back, and he told me, as he had told me before, that I could never really know Rome until I had been in a catacomb. I laughed at that, and he smiled. A most amiable man. We were grateful for his friendship.

On December 8, the Feast of the Immaculate Conception, a church holy day, we took Bus 85 as far as San Clemente and walked over to San Tommaso. The day was raw and the streets we walked had a sodden, dismal look. We came down Via Celemontana to the piazza and went under the Arch of Dolabella. The little green door was wide open, and we went down the unswept path to the chapel. It was cold.

A small girl knelt at the corner confessional, and we retreated to the garden. A man who was standing there nodded, and we remarked about *Il Tempo. Brutto.* The man smiled and said, "Si." He was waiting there, he said, for his daughter, the little girl we had seen inside confessing her sins.

CHAPTER 13

Old Bookshops and Roman Fever . . . The Laocoon

A white-haired woman of genteel manners kept a junk shop in Via Labicana, not far from San Clemente, and we went there from time to time to look for books, a candlestick, and possibly a small fragment of marble, a mislaid piece of antiquity, among the heaps of discarded clothes and badly-worn household goods. The only book we ever found worth buying was Michelet's *Roman Republic*, translated by William Hazlitt and published in London in 1847. The paper was as fresh as it was on the publication day, good quality rag, and the type was excellent. The *legatorio* in Via Carducci was pleased to give the book a red binding.

Via Labicana yielded nothing else, and neither did the open-air dealers who sold old books, prints, ugly brass lamps, nicked china, chainless censers, and what they called bric-a-brac in the Piazza Borghese. The few second-hand bookstores we knew invariably over-priced English books and dealt in French and Italian works that didn't interest us.

Where were those aged barrows and bookstalls, loaded with treasures for eighteenth—and nineteenth-century booklovers—the books, the dusty sheets of parchment, letters in spidery script, bundles of commercial documents, unsorted records of parish births and deaths, testaments of the long dead, diaries, translations of Virgil and Catallus, the scourings of remote castles, monasteries, and looted villas, carted to Rome to be sold for pennies? All gone now, lost forever, or locked up in private libraries.

The fact, of course—and on this point we could not deceive ourselves—was that much of the stuff was plain trash, or for tastes so refined they could get pleasure in the writings of now almost-forgotten polemicists, wranglers over Jansenism and regalism, Josephism and illuminism, straining intellectual strivings, tortured arguments, and unresolved disputes. When these matters arose in books we occasionally scanned, we passed over them, both humbled and annoyed by our ignorance and our disinclination to overcome it by study. There was no help for it. Rome was all we desired; and if we chose a change and there was no opera or concert worth attending, we spent the evening reading.

We read books we should have read at home; we read them in Rome, because we found them in new inexpensive small editions: George Barrow's *Wild Wales*; Jerome K. Jerome's *Three Men in a Boat*; Dinah Maria Mulock's *John Halifax, Gentleman*; George Eliot's *Felix Holt*; Maria Edgeworth's *Castle Rackrent*; Mrs. Afra Behn's *Oroonoko* (a seventeenth-century English curiosity); and many more, including Italian translations of Hemingway's *A Farewell to Arms* (*Addio alle Armi*) and Joyce's *Dubliners* (*Gente di Dublino*).

Rome had many stores that sold new books, and more stores opened every year. Most of them sold Italian or French books—the classics, art books, late fiction. Rizzoli's in the Galleria Colonna carried a good assortment of English-language books. Our friend Mrs. Edna Goldfield sold paperbacks at her Economy Bookstore, Piazza di Spagna, 29, almost next to the Keats house. The Lion Bookshop in Via del Babuino was run by an English woman who spoke beautiful Italian. The one thing we missed was a good second-hand bookstore where we could look and hope to find good books for the Via Carducci man, Tauchnitz editions in mint condition—a pleasant dream and nothing more.

But we did make a discovery. In many churches—in Santa Sabina on the Aventine, Sant'Andrea al Quirinale, Santa Maria Maddelena, for example—we found histories of the churches, monographs of sixty-five to ninety pages generously illustrated with photographs of exteriors and interiors, with architectural drawings of ground plans and lateral sections. These booklets, measuring about seven inches by four, were paperbound and printed on good paper. They were placed on a table or desk at the rear of the church near a slotted box into which money could be dropped in payment. A church sold only its own book.

We bought all we could find, but unfortunately the publishing project had ended, and some churches no longer had copies for sale. We went to the editorial office across from Santa Maria sopra Minerva, but it was closed and, not surprisingly, none of the people in the street knew where the printer had gone. Eventually we tracked what was left of the establishment to a small shop in the western part of the city, so far west that the area was printed on one of the subsidiary maps of Verdesi's *Nuova Pianta di Roma*. We bought the monographs we lacked and had them bound in small, compact fawn-colored volumes, three or four churches to a book.

One of the small churches we collected was Santa Maria della Quercia, the Church of the Butchers' Guild, an old and honored structure restored in 1727 by Filippo Raguzzini. We first saw it, yellow-washed and squeezed between two buildings in a narrow piazzetta, one Sunday morning as we were taking a short—cut from Piazza Farnese. Just ahead of us we heard a woman berating a boy for making noise while Mass was going on, and it struck us as very funny that the woman, shrill and angry, was probably making more of an uproar than the boy had caused.

We caught up with her and watched; the boy walked off in silence, and the woman disappeared through a side door of a curiously-shaped building. It was evidently a church, but it was unlike anything we had ever seen in Rome. The Butchers' Guild dated from antiquity, its members proud men who, as good Catholics, wished for the best—a church to be respected and praised—when they replaced their old church with a new one. They had papal support, and they hired a good architect.

Raguzzini could have given Santa Maria della Quercia (Saint Mary of the Oak) a complacent façade—Renaissance or Baroque—two columns, a porch, something compatible with the cramped quarters. He designed instead a front with a bulge, a ridge around the middle, a low street-level portal, and a high square central window. It reminded me vaguely of—what? It wasn't until I saw the façade in a black-and-white picture that I recognized it: Raguzzini's eighteenth-century confection looked like a nineteenth-century American wood-burning stove.

*　　*　　*

A Frenchman, reproached by a friend for lingering so long in Rome when his interests presumably were in Paris, replied amiably: "You must learn never to believe people who say they are leaving Rome." William Dean Howells spoke of the Roman fever—not the malaria that killed Henry James's pretty Daisy Miller, but the obsessive love of Rome that entered the soul and mind and never died.

We had it, this love that made us overlook so many of Rome's faults. The poor custodial worker at San Gregorio Magno had yielded to it, though he would never be able to explain it or know its meaning, any more than Seroux d'Agincourt, the French nobleman famous among biibliophiles for the *Fermier generaux* edition of the *Contes* of La Fontaine, could define the Roman fever. He had come to Rome as a pilgrim, but Rome had seduced him, and he had never left.

If Roman fever was hard to analyze, or even worth the effort to try to do so, its signs were easily recognizable—a tolerance, for instance, of Via Panisperna, a dull, slatternly street that we were required to walk through occasionally; and the kind of curiosity that made us look up the derivation of the name of Via Scellerata, an Italian word that means "wicked." That ancient street had borne its unhappy name since Tullia, daughter of Tullius Servius, builder of the first wall, had driven her chariot over the dead body of her father more than five centuries before the Christian era.

The more we read about Rome, the more our appetite grew. The most trivial bits of information—something about Candlemas Day at San Biagio in Via Giulia, or an old tobacco factory in Trastevere—became a part of us, simply because they were Roman.

There was danger in this pursuit: the knowledge we were amassing could easily become oppressive, too intrusive, possibly boring. Yet we could not stop, though we might ask: What did it matter that we remembered, in passing across Porta Capena, that the Aqua Marcia Aqueduct once rose there and that Juvenal and Martial had complained of the leaks that wet their togas? But it was undeniably amusing to recall young Luigi Braschi, who lived in princely luxury in the Palazzo Braschi on the wealth bestowed on him by his uncle, Pope Pius VI (Angelo Braschi, who reigned from 1775-1800).

The outward symbol of riches in that period was the carriage. The best of these were magnificent vehicles. Three of them, sent to the French ambassador by Louis XV, were so heavy that, on being landed at Civitavecchia after a sail from Marseilles, they had to be dragged to Rome by oxen. The Roman nobles competed in numbers of carriages: the Prince of Gallicano had sixty beautiful ones, the Constable Colonna had eighty.

Braschi had only twenty but tried to give the impression that he owned many more. One day he showed the French Marquis de Breteuil around his stables, and, as they finished the inspection, Braschi said to his visitor, "Well, how did you like my hundred carriages?"

"These twenty," the diplomat replied, "are absolutely splendid, and we can see the rest another time."

The old Marchese Altieri was no competitor: She had only one carriage. It was drawn by six horses and attended by richly liveried servants. To Romans who happened to be in the Via del Plebiscito, it was a grand occasion to see the lady, primly erect in the cushioned interior, transported from the palazzo to the Church of the Gesu across the street.

History in anecdotes, in small illuminating pieces about unusual people . . .

*   *   *

For lovers of art and antiquity, and also those at the court of Julius II, the most memorable event of 1506 may have been the accidental discovery of the Laocoön in the hillside vineyard of Fella de Fredie behind the Colosseum. It was a day of rejoicing for all, from pope to kitchen scullion, and a good part of the feeling that spread through Rome was due to the simplicity of the happenings.

All those years when Rome was going through so many violent changes, all those years of pillage, fire, and bloodshed, those dreadful years of persecution, plague, murder, and destruction, this priceless statue of concentrated agony—a man and his two sons in the grip of serpents—had rested peacefully where it had fallen centuries ago under the ruins of the Baths of Titus. The masses of marble, as well as those of the Baths of Trajan that had stood nearby, had been carted away, but somehow the Laocoön had been buried. Now by sheer chance, the unexpected had occurred. Scores of other statues, or parts of them—busts, torsos, headless figures that once adorned temples and other public places—would be recovered; but the Laocoön was unique and of singular workmanship.

Literate Romans knew the Laocoön myth from Virgil's *Aeneid*, and the marble statue, attributed to three Rhodian sculptors, Agesander and his two sons, Polydorus and Athenodorus, had been described in detail by Pliny the Elder. All that was needed when the statue was freed from the imprisoning earth was verification of its identity. Julius II called in his friend and favorite architect, Giuliano da Sangallo, and told him to go over to the Edquilline and have a look.

The charm of the story remains with us today because Da Sangallo did not go alone. The sixty-three-year-old architect had two companions—his son, Francesco, who was twelve, and Michelangelo, who was thirty-one and already famous, since he had carved his *David* in Florence when he was only twenty-four and his *Pieta* in Rome when he was twenty-six. Francesco has told us something of that day, but not enough to satisfy our craving. What did the two men talk about as they trudged along the rough, unpaved streets and lane and open spaces where pigs and cattle roamed, through narrow passages where carts lacked wheels and men brawled and women screamed?

Francesco grows tired, and his father pats him affectionately, kisses his cheek, and hoists him to his shoulder. In this fashion the three arrive at the vineyard where a few people stand watching. Francesco tells us his father and Michelangelo instantly recognize the Laocoön and, after another look and some talk about the digging with the owner of the land, they go back to the Vatican and tell the pope the good news. Only then do they have breakfast.

The news of the discovery created great excitement throughout Europe, and scores of eager buyers sought out de Fredie; but he rejected all the offers and gave the statue to Julius II, who, in gratitude, gave the landowner and his son an annual charge of six hundred gold ducats upon the tolls of Porta San Sebastiano. De Fredie was further rewarded by being given a pavement tomb in Santa Maria in Aracoeli.

A bronze copy of the Laocoön was made for Francis I of France. This was a fortunate move, because we can see the statue now as it appeared when unearthed. Its missing right arm was "restored," but experts suspected the restoration was faulty, and indeed it was.

But again good luck attended the Laocoön. In 1905 the missing right arm was found in a marble cutter's workshop in Via Labicana, not far from the spot where one day a genteel white-haired lady would keep a junk shop that we sometimes visited in the hope of finding books, a candlestick, and possibly a small fragment of marble, a mislaid piece of antiquity.

CHAPTER 14

At Home in Prati

$\mathcal{S}$uetonius tells us that Julius Caesar, confronting the mutinous Tenth Legion, whose leaders were demanding the legion's discharge from the wars, addressed the men as *Quirites* (civilians) instead of *Milites* (soldiers), so deeply wounding their martial pride that they fell at once in line and swore anew their allegiance. Eighteen hundred years after Suetonius wrote his history of the Twelve Caesars, Mussolini's Fascist government dedicated, in 1928, a fountain in a small piazza in Prati, the district of Rome on the right bank of the Tiber north of Castel Sant'Angelo. It was called Prati from the wide expanse of open fields (*prati*) that lay there before 1870.

For reasons never publicly disclosed, the piazza was called Piazza del Quiriti, and the fountain the Quiriti. Everybody seems to have been puzzled by the choice of the name, and to this day no reasonable explanation has been forthcoming. The principal feature of the fountain is four naked girls—pretty girls, if they were not pouting. They are seated on a large lotus leaf above the wide cup of a flower, and support over their heads a smaller leaf that projects, not as incongruously as it would seem, a pine cone. Water jets upward from the cone, falls on the leaf held by the petulant maidens, and veils them thinly as it tumbles below.

We came many times to the Piazza dei Quiriti to look at the doleful girls under their lotus petal umbrella. That was the summer we lived in Prati in a rented studio, so-called, behind the Pakistani Embassy on the Lungotevere delle Armee above Ponte Matteotti. We had come down to Italy after an extended stay in Trier and Innsbruck and further delayed our arrival in Rome by taking long drives to Naples, Salerno, and Paestum, and Nola, Casserta, and Benevento before turning north to Perugia, Lucca, Viareggio, and the stout German ladies with the enormous handbags on the beach at Pietrasanta.

We liked Prati. It was new and spacious and airy and good for walking. The streets were wide and level and the sidewalks broad and uncluttered, and in the general area of Piazza Mazzini the streets were so haphazardly designed that strolling through them at any hour was a pleasure.

Prati was convenient. We could walk a few blocks and board a bus that crossed Ponte Matteotti, pushed on to Via Flaminia, and, turning south, went through Piazza del Popolo and ran smoothly down the Corso. We could walk down the embankment under the trees as far as the decaying Palazzo di Giustizia and cross Ponte Umberto to Renaissance Rome.

It was said of Prati that the streets in one whole section had been paid out by Masonic engineers at an angle that cut off from the long perspective any view of St. Peter's dome. Prati had another interesting distinction: someone, having noted that the city had exhausted some obvious groupings of street names—Torino, Napoli, Milano, for example, among cities; Isonzo, Piave, and Tevere among rivers; and the names of composers—had turned to the past, to Rome's own history, and had finally honored a very old Roman, Julius Caesar—Giulio Cesare. Other grand names were chosen from antiquity—Scipioni, Gracchi, Crescenzio, Pompeo Magno—and at least one, Cola di Rienzo, from the Middle Ages.

A poor banana tree had somehow found root in the wild greenery where our rented studio, so-called, stood. The place was not without charm, though the door key did not always work, and when it failed us it was necessary for me to enter by a window left unlocked for these emergencies.

Tommaso gave Delia's place, as we called our quarters, the only authentic charm we were willing to grant it. We were there four months, and in going regretted only that we would miss Tommaso. He was a turtle of quick intelligence, and he lived in the garden, a small, damp, weedy space enclosed by a high wall where savage Roman cats gathered at daybreak for a handout. The studio, so-called, had been made out of a converted carriage house or stable. The garden was revealed to us when we opened the French doors of the living room. Tommaso's dominion out there was explained to us by Delia, the middle-aged New York woman from whom we sublet the place.

We saw Delia only once, on the day we made arrangements to move in when she left for New York to attend to some complicated business relating to the unexpected death of her father. In her company that day was another American, a Southern male, a painter. He painted the head of Marilyn Monroe. He painted it over and over again. The color of her hair and eyes and lips never varied. One of his larger canvases contained fourteen heads of Marilyn Monroe. There were smaller canvases of three of four heads. On the day we moved in, the painter, at my request, hauled out thirty-three heads of the lady he admired.

Marilyn was gone, but Tommaso was there. He was there when we called to him, and he ate without fear from our hands.

"Tommaso," my wife would say, "where are you? Where is the best little turtle in Rome? What are you up to in the shadows back there?"

We would see the movement of something among the ferns and wild greens, and Tommaso would emerge, head and thin neck protruding from his carapace. He liked bread and a tiny piece of raw chopped meat. On an impulse to waggery, someone had once carved on his underside the letters SPQR (Senatus Populusque Romanus), a legend to be found in high and low places in Rome, from the Campidoglio to manhole covers in Via Montebello.

It was very easy to get sentimental over Tommaso when we thought of him all by himself down there in his corner of the garden in that humming, stridulous world of aphids, crickets, ants, worms, ladybugs, and fluttering butterflies. Who had brought him to this scruffy yard? We never knew.

The top of a handsome white apartment house in Via Nicotera was visible above the patch of trees and tangled undergrowth behind the garden wall. The fierce hungry cats came that way, sneaking through the thorny bushes, prickly vines, and coarse thick roots. The neighborhood cat population was large. Cats prowled along the rough, untidy bank of the Tiber, dirty, unwanted scavengers.

I had a fair chance of judging one day how many homeless, famished cats there were along the river and in the backyards of Prati when I carried out a meatloaf to give the flea-ridden strays. It was a very good meatloaf, weighing about two pounds, prepared for us by Agnese, the cleaning lady and cook (our *donna di servizio*), who had come to us through the kindness of Gemma, the vegetable and fruit lady.

The day following the day that Agnese made the meatloaf was too warm for meatloaf. Agnese was not coming that morning, and I decided to dispose of the dish at once. Wrapping it in yesterday's *Il Messaggero*, I went out through the long driveway, past the Pakistani Embassy, and into the Lungotevere. Two or three cats picked up my scent as I emerged through the front gate. It was a highly spiced meatloaf—Agnese was a natural cook. I crossed the wide street to the path under the trees and walked toward Ponte Matteotti, but the cats suddenly were too numerous and clamorous. I opened *Il Messaggero* and dropped it and its burden and retreated as the cats fell to in a snarling, scratching, biting mass. For days thereafter I dared not go out through the front gate, lest the cats trail me. I used the back way.

The back way, through somebody's courtyard, was more convenient and far more pleasant than the Lungotevere delle Armee entrance, but in using the back way we lived for four months as neighbors of the Pakistanis without ever meeting them. The embassy was a big white villa that had been erected when this area was still rural. Trees screened it on three sides, but the front was open to view. The building and the land were owned by two elderly Italian women whom we rarely saw. They were cranky, revealing in words and manner of speech a shrewish temper. I always thought they regarded us with contempt. My wife encountered one of the women one day in the mass of trees that lined the driveway. La Signora was looking for a marble head that was there on the grounds, she wasn't sure where. She had looked at my wife as if she suspected her of stealing it.

Our floors were marble, because marble was cheaper in Rome than wood. White marble was good, because the ants that came in from the garden were easier to see. We fought them and the gnats and mosquitoes with spray guns, and doused the cats with water. The leader of the cats was an overgrown tom, a formidable beast, originally white but gray in his present state. His face was large and hideously scarred. One of his eyes was missing, scratched out probably in the battle that had left him with a cruelly comical twisted grin. I threw a bucket of water at the ugly tom the first day, but he was too quick for me and simply leaped backward. I caught him the next day with a shot of cold water from the hose, and that was the only time I did catch him. He was on the wall every morning.

We had three neighbors, all in their early twenties—two women, one a velvety light brown, the other white; and a man, an American named Paul, who was in Rome to study piano. The girls lived next to us in rooms patterned like ours. The brown girl, Peggy, spoke English with a British West Indian accent and called herself a model. Harriet, who shared her lodgings, was English and worked in a Roman business establishment. Her boss took her one weekend to Sardinia. They sailed in one of the small liners that made weekly or semi-weekly runs from Civitavecchia. Harriet returned from the outing with arms and legs covered with mosquito bites. Paul lived on the second floor of a small two-story building that abutted on Peggy's quarters. He played in the afternoon: Chopin, Liszt, and Schumann mostly; a little Mozart and Debussy. A narrow spiral iron stairway mounted in a single half curve from his rooms to the roof. Sometimes he went up there to sunbathe.

We saw Peggy one day away from home. We were sitting at a table on the sidewalk of Via Cesare Battista near the Corso when our eyes were drawn to something that was going on across the street. People at the other tables were staring, and some pedestrians on the opposite sidewalk, finding their passage partially blocked, had stopped. Others joined them and quickly formed a small crowd. We expected the police to intervene, but nothing happened.

We had no clear view while the traffic was moving, but when it halted momentarily we saw two figures, a man and a woman, splashes of bright color, and in the woman my wife recognized Peggy. She wore white shoes, pale green shorts, and an orange shirt, and her long black hair hung to her shoulders. The man wore red trousers and a multi-colored shirt and a large round straw hat.

Peggy and the man were oblivious to the growing number of bystanders. They gesticulated wildly and appeared to be screaming at each other. They were unable to stand still. They moved forward seven or eight steps, turned, came back. The onlookers seemed spellbound.

We sat there with our gelati melting in the warm sunshine, hearing nothing, seeing only Peggy and the stranger. It was not a day for arguments or violence. The weather was too fine for even the mildest disturbance, and here in the center of Rome, the true center only yards from the Campidoglio, no one was upset—only curious, as we were. Beyond Peggy and the man, we could see Mussolini's old balcony on Palazzo Venezia, empty, no longer funny. Black dots, tourists, moved up and down the broad staircases of the War Memorial, the Vittoriana: Germans and Americans and Italians from the South—Bari, Lecce, Campobasso, Reggio Calabria—and soldiers on leave, Alpinists, Bersaglieri in hot brown uniforms through which sweat seeped in large dark blotches, people who found the monument irresistible.

For ten minutes we watched Peggy, wondering what it was all about and how it would end. Then, abruptly, she and the man were still—and, indifferent to the crowd, went off together, walking up the Via Cesare Battista.

PART III

Echoes and Re-Echoes

CHAPTER 15

Trevi Water and the Aqueducts

e came this way many times, walking through the morning sounds that shaped the day's beginning, hearing with quiet joy the voices all about us and the fresh laughter: the twitter of caged birds, the gurgle of a broken watering hose, the clank and grind of an ascending *saracinesca* and farther off another; everywhere the beeping vans, somewhere church bells—Santa Maria della Pace, Santa'Eustachio?

We moved through these narrow treeless streets as if they were our streets, and the people our people, so happy were we to be there in Rome, though we had no ancestral connection with the city. We felt an innate empathy with all that we found about us.

Augustus Hare, remembering all that he had read of the pale marble beauty of the ancient Campus Martius, had recoiled in his middle years from the Campo Marzio, which he found a maze of dirty streets "seldom sought out except by those who make a long stay in Rome and care for everything connected with its history and architecture." That clearly defined us.

Hare's scorn and disaffection were implicit in much that he wrote—in his description, for example, of the area once covered by the Baths of Diocletian, where, in the 1880s, he was offended by the sight of a prison for women and an institution for the deaf, dumb, and blind close to Michelangelo's Santa Maria degli Angeli. What ugly disorder! But that part of the city would shortly change as the Fountain of the Nereids rose and Koch's handsome hemicycle emerged to frame the western side of the Piazza Esedra, now the Piazza della Repubblica.

Changes that Hare could not envision also would come to Campo Marzio, and we would see no squalor in the curious antique stones in the porch of San Lorenzo in Lucina, where Browning's Pompilia and her parents had worshipped, and none in the pleasant little shops. If we turned to the left when we came out of the Adriano Hotel and walked back through Via di Pallacorda to the Palazzo Borghese, we could look up Via Borghese-Fontanella and see, in the distance, Trinità dei Monti and the Spanish Steps.

Young people, mostly Americans, would be sitting at the Barcaccio Fountain, dipping their hands in the water—Trevi water—and we would smile, because it was Trevi water that tinkled so lightly in the lobby of the Adriano and shot so ferociously from the rigid showerhead in our bathroom. At home in New York, it never seemed strange to us that the water in our bathroom was the same water that leaped and fell mechanically in the fountain at Lincoln Center, ran so freely in the stalls at Fulton Fish Market, and dripped from every leaky pipe in the unwholesome slums of the city. Croton water. All Croton.

Rome had not one source of water supply, but nine, four of them papal gifts—reconstructions, that is, of ancient aqueducts. Trevi water was one of these, and the one we found most appealing. Trevi water was famous for its purity and taste, and a *cappuccino* made of Trevi water was said to be the best in Rome.

Trevi water was Acqua Vergine Antica, and Acqua Vergine Antica was the old Aqua Virgo, brought to Rome in 13 BC by the soldier and statesman Marcus Agrippa and restored by Pope Nicholas V nine hundred years after the invading Goths had broken the city's eleven aqueducts. Trevi, or Aqua Virgo, to be exact, had served the city for 550 years, then had been cut off for nine hundred years, and now had been flowing again for over five hundred years. Two thousand years altogether.

And Trevi had a story as simple as a Roman myth that might, in fact, easily have been invented had it been necessary. Agrippa, having completed the Pantheon in 19 BC, needed water for the new baths taking form under the eye of his old schoolfellow and father-in-law, Augustus. Agrippa sent a detachment of military engineers out to the wild Campagna to find a source of water. They searched and searched; and one day, fourteen miles east of the city, a young girl saw them and led them to springs shielded on all sides by shrubbery—to water that had come from the heavens as rain and snow, falling on the Alban Hills and coursing through the volcanic purifying rock before surfacing. The water was named Aqua Virgo, not because of the girl but for its own purity.

Agrippa was a builder and water engineer of extraordinary talent and energy, who opened five hundred new fountains in one year. Later the breaking of the ancient aqueducts by the invading Goths had depopulated the Campagna, and the people who came down to the flat ground below the hills had to depend on the Tiber and some wells. Waterless and neglected after the Gothic sack, Agrippa's Baths fell into ruin. The Pantheon, badly damaged and structurally weakened by fire when it was less than a century old, was razed by Hadrian in the first century AD and replaced by the one we know today.

With the passing of the Middle Ages and the new growth of the Renaissance city, water again became a critical problem. The aqueducts lay out there on the Campagna, the paths of some unknown, the whereabouts of others sketchy at best.

I cannot remember a time when the aqueducts seemed strange to me. In my boyhood the aqueducts were always there in the schoolbooks—lofty stone arches striding across the Campagna, abandoned monuments to Roman genius—reminders, like the chariots, the gladiators, the Colosseum, the dilapidated tombs of the Appian Way, and the pictorial reconstruction of the Circus Maximus, of Rome's grandeur.

Nicholas V, a man of strong resolution elected pope in 1447 at the age of forty-two, served only eight years. A realist and a good organizer and builder, he encouraged artists and artisans to come to Rome and gave them employment. He knew the difficulties of bringing to life an aqueduct that had lain dormant so many centuries, seven miles of it underground and seven miles on arches; but he went ahead.

It was not an easy undertaking. Virtually everything once known about the construction and maintenance of the aqueducts and the distribution of the water along the routes of the conduits and in the city itself had been forgotten. But fortunately for the old world, there lived in the fifteenth century a scholar and humanist who liked nothing so much as settling himself in an old library or storeroom and examining ancient Latin and Greek manuscripts, some almost indecipherable, some palimpsests, but all of them, whatever their state, of interest to him. His name was Poggio Bracciolini. In 1429 he found, in the library of the Benedictine monastery at Monte Cassino, a priceless treasure—a copy of *De aquis Romae*, a scrupulously-written account of the aqueducts of the imperial city.

The author of this remarkable work was Sextus Julius Frontinus, a Roman patrician born about 35 AD and educated, it is thought, in Alexandria. He entered the service of the state and advanced rapidly, becoming *praetor* of Rome in the year 70 and consul in 73, 98, and 100. In 76 he was sent to Britain as governor and distinguished himself by building strong forts and roads. He tried to placate and Romanize the Silures, a troublesome warlike people who lived on the border of Wales; and when reason and compassion failed him, he defeated the tribes in battle. (His successor, Agricola, a less humane governor, massacred the Silures.) In 84 Frontinus wrote a book about warfare. He called it *The Strategems* and filled it with examples of fighting drawn from Greek and Roman history.

In 97 Frontinus was named *curator aquarum*, or water commissioner, a post conferred on the most eminent men. Agrippa himself had held it at the request of Augustus long enough to rid the office of corruption; but that was a century ago, and corruption had returned. The department was being wretchedly mismanaged.

Trajan and Nerva, both reformers, knew they had in Frontinus a man of sturdy honesty under whose direction the *Statio Aquarum*, as the water department was called, could be restored to health. Frontinus knew nothing about water supply, and he set out to learn. As he learned, he wrote, and it was this compelling necessity to know and to say what he was learning that brought forth the book.

He had two assistants, both of senatorial rank. One bore the title of *procurator aquarum*; the other, *tribunis aquarum*. There was a staff of scribes, technical advisors, and architects. The *Statio Aquarum* employed seven hundred workers—water inspectors, plumbers, plasterers, stone-masons, bricklayers, and other artisans, as well as two groups of slaves—*aquarii*, or watermen, several hundred strong, who patrolled the aqueducts.

The terminus of the aqueduct was the *castellum*, the settling tank and the distribution point. Private users were licensed and taxed for

185

fixed amounts of water. The outward sign of the *castellum*, a *mostra*, was a showpiece, usually a fountain. The Trevi Fountain is such a *mostra*.

For Nicholas and his advisors, reading Frontinus must have been like going into a dark room with a lamp and seeing it for the first time—its walls and floor and furnishings. Frontinus was the indispensable guide, chatty and abundantly informed: Through his eyes the fifteenth-century Roman, aghast at the ruinous state of his city, could see how it had been in the time of Augustus.

Frontinus located the sources of the water and described the quality, sparkling bright in one case, discolored by mud in another. He revealed that the total length of the aqueduct was 270 miles, and the fact, astonishing to his readers, that only forty miles of the system were on arches, the rest being underground in tunnels modeled on the Roman sewers and large enough for men to enter, as they did at certain inspection points to make repairs. Stoutly built as they were, the tunnels still suffered from rainwater seepage and from incrustations of lime from the water they carried. This lime had to be cleaned out. (In the nineteenth century it occurred to archeologist Lanciani that he could trace the route of one of these lost underground passageways by searching out and following the piles of discarded lime deposits—and he did.)

Arches were used in crossing ravines or long valleys and in the approaches to the city. The arches, parts of which were badly constructed by dishonest contractors, were subjected to storm damage. The water ran in channels nine feet wide, covered to reduce the loss from evaporation.

One of the first things Frontinus did on taking office was to measure the quantity of water entering the aqueducts at the source, and the amount that reached Rome. He was thus able to know how much was lost in transit. His inquiry disclosed the extent of leakage, and it also brought into the open the widespread practice of bribe-taking by the *aquarii*. These men were supposed to report leaks to the head office, which dispatched masons and plasterers to make repairs; but the *aquaria* were slaves, and slaves could buy their freedom. Large land-owners on the Campagna had no trouble paying off the *aquaria* to overlook a leak.

Stealing water inside the city, where it was distributed through an intricate system of pipes, called for cunning and stealth; but the *aquaria* freely tampered with the pipes, inserting illegal pipes into the legal pipes to draw off water, substituting pipes that carried less water for larger ones, and selling water through pipes whose grantee had moved away. Frontinus found one whole section of Rome where the flow of water was illicit.

Having confirmed his suspicions, Frontinus had all the pipes of the city exposed. Illegal pipes were removed, and all pipes henceforth were to be stamped with the owner's name and the amount of the water allowance. The water supply, Frontinus happily reported, doubled.

Nicholas V did not call his water Trevi. Three hundred years passed before Acqua Vergine Antica got that name from the massive Baroque Fontana di Trevi at the rear of the Palazzo Poli. It is now widely accepted that the word Trevi is derived from *tre vie*—three ways or roads that met there.

The first *mostra* of Acqua Vergine was a wall fountain in the Piazza dei Crociferi. It was esthetically pleasing and the flow of water generous; but Rome had always been a restless, changing city, emperors and popes constantly looking for ways to improve the city and enhance their own reputation. By the middle of the seventeenth century, Rome was becoming more and more sumptuous. It was evident that Acqua Vergine's *mostra* would no longer do.

The architect began by pulling down the fountain in Piazza dei Crociferi and moving the aqueduct's terminus to its present location, which had been improved ten years earlier by the rebuilding of Santi Vincenzo ed Anastasio with a Baroque façade. The pope's next move was an order to raze the Tomb of Cecilia Metella on the Via Appia and use the marble for the new fountain. In earlier centuries popes had destroyed pagan temples and tombs as they wished; but seventeenth-century Romans had learned to value their past, and there was such an outcry when Urban's intentions became known that he cancelled his plan.

Rome had no reason to expect delays in the building of a new fountain, but the difficulties were just starting. Sketches and plans were drawn and accepted and then rejected. There seemed no end in sight, no way to solve the problem. Acqua Vergine still ran, filling a large semicircular basin where people quenched their thirst, washed their clothes, and watered their horses and cattle. Finally a plan submitted by Nicholas Salvi, a poet and philosopher, was accepted, but the work was still delayed, then at last begun. Salvi died before its completion in May 1762, in the reign of Clement XIII—122 years and fourteen popes after Urban VIII had begun the work.

Mme. De Stael in *Corinne* and Hawthorne in *The Marble Faun* wrote about Trevi. Tourists and travelers, following a tradition whose origin is unknown, visited the tumbling waters by moonlight and tossed a coin into the fountain as a pledge of returning to Rome. It was a quiet, happy spot, an oasis; but a 1954 American motion picture, *Three Coins in the Fountain*, changed all that. Now even in foul spring weather or on dark, wet, early-winter days, you may find people crouched at the poolside, fascinated by Trevi's wild figures and the rushing water first brought to Rome in 13 BC.

CHAPTER 16

The Citadel of Rome . . . and Tosca

Bus 64, a double-decker that ran from the Stazione Termini to St. Peter's, was usually so overcrowded that passengers sometimes could not reach the conductor to pay their fares. We boarded 64 one day at Largo Argentina and stood next to three young American tourists, two men and a girl, who were talking about their trip: their stay at a New York hotel before flying to Europe (to Florence, in fact, where the girl had bought gloves priced as high as the same gloves in Via Condotti); their Rome lodgings (which they compared unfavorably with the New York hotel); and food. As the bus rolled onto Ponto Vittorio Emanuel, they spotted Castel Sant'Angelo.

"What's that?" the girl asked.

"Some kind of a prison, I think," one of the men replied. Nothing more was said.

Actually, Castel Sant'Angelo had been opened as a national museum in 1921. I think that our first visit to the old fortress satisfied forever our curiosity about the place. We looked over the papal apartments, the barracks, the big kitchens, the vats that had been used for olive oil.

189

We wandered through poorly lighted passages. We spent a long time in the armory, and then we went to the roof, our goal on all subsequent visits.

Piranesi's depiction of Castel Sant'Angelo is a monstrous round tower divested of humanity—hostile, chilling the soul with fear of unknowable evil and terror. What is going on behind these impregnable walls? Very little, in fact, was happening there in Piranesi's day, but almost everything unspeakable in Roman behavior had been enacted there during the sixteen centuries of its existence. Whatever Piranesi's design—whether he was simply impressed by the size of the structure or its sinister, bloody history—his mighty fortress, topped by the bronze statue of the Archangel Michael sheathing his sword and the stark outlines of the Mercy Bell that toiled after every execution, inspires dread.

No one knew or would ever know how many murders had been committed here—murders by poison and stabbing, starvation and strangulation, gunshot and decapitation, bludgeoning, hanging, and torture. No purification rites could ever cleanse this immense piece of masonry with its armory and kitchens, its sumptuous papal apartments and stinking dungeons, secret passages, tunnels that dizzily sloped, sealed chambers—nothing could erase the memory of the building's criminal past. Violence and death, horror and depravity, intrigue and conspiracy—everything that darkened the pages of Roman history was here in nightmarish examples. How much of this does Piranesi know as he sits there facing these formidable walls, younger than the Colosseum by only sixty years?

A Greek named Ignius was pope of the primitive Christian church when the Emperor Hadrian, who had gone to Naples to die of dropsy in a villa overlooking the unspoiled bay, ordered a new imperial tomb to be built on the right bank of the Tiber below the Vatican Hill and Nero's old chariot race track. (The hill was leveled in later years when the site was chosen for building the old St. Peter's.) Work on the tomb began in 135 AD. Hadrian died in 138, and the mausoleum was completed the following year by his adoptive son and successor, Antoninus Pius. The walls of brick, tufa, and concrete were overlaid with Parian marble. Statues adorned it. There was nothing more splendid in Rome, but its use as a sepulcher was brief—about eighty years. Marcus Aurelius, his son Commodus, Septimus Severus, and Caracalla were among the last emperors whose ashes were carried there in costly urns of ivory and gold.

For over two hundred years, the tomb was secure. In 410 Alaric the Goth invaded Rome, sacked the tomb, and seized the precious urns. There were other attacks during that century and the following one. In 537, when Vitiges tried to take the mausoleum, which by this time had become the citadel of Rome—a fortress and a prison—the defending garrison smashed the handsome statues and hurled chunks of marble at the men scaling the ladders. The beautiful white marble facing escaped serious damage and remained intact for another six centuries, after which it was removed and used as paving.

The worst century in the *castello's* history was the tenth, when the infamous Marozia, an incestuous, power-mad woman, a leader in the struggle between popes and anti-popes, took over the place. Her company of supporters included her three husbands—Alberic, Count of Tusculum; Guido, Marquis of Tuscany; and Hugo, King of Italy. The Romans, in time, rid themselves of Marozia; but there was further degradation in store when Censio (Crescenzio Nomentano), the consul who raised up the Anti-Pope Boniface VII, seized the *castello* in 974. Intending to destroy the temporal power of the papacy, he had two popes murdered—Benedict VI and John XIV. In 996 Pope Gregory V called on the Holy Roman Emperor Otho for help. The *castello* was taken and Censio beheaded.

Great changes transformed the structure. A moat was dug and four bastions were constructed. More and more names, those of heroic as well as shady characters, were written into the history, and the history itself became confusing and not always accurate, studded with mendacities, superstitious tales, rumors, and outright inventions. Benvenuto Cellini, one of the most exquisite artists of the Renaissance, turned artilleryman to defend the castello when Pope Clement VII took refuge there during the Sack of Rome in 1527. Two centuries earlier Cola di Rienzo, the Roman Tribune, hid there while the populace screamed for his blood.

During our visits, there was a guard in the weapons room who, as far as I could determine, spent most of the day reading. He sat on a chair raised above the level of the stone floor, and his area of surveillance was small. In the morning he read *Il Tempo* and then *Il Messaggero*, and when that gave out he turned to a weekly puzzle and humor magazine called *La settimana enigiaistica.* He wore his glasses on the tip of his nose, and from time to time he leaned forward, looked over the rims, and called out: "Non toccare! Non toccare!" (Don't touch!) The harsh warning, breaking the stillness of the gloomy museum, sometimes made people jump and look around, and it was usually a few seconds before they associated the voice with the man who regarded them so benignly from his perch. Most of his auditors, having no understanding of Italian, stared in mild bewilderment before returning to their inspection of daggers, swords, pistols, muskets, and helmets.

Sometimes when the room was empty he called "Non toccare!" without looking up. Now and then we stopped to chat with him on our way to the roof, where we sat and looked at Rome: at St. Peter's—so near we felt we could reach out and touch the dome; at the the pines of Janiculum, the Tiber below us, and all the city from Trinità dei Monti to Santa Maria Maggiore, from the campanile of Borromini's Palazzo della Sapienza to Santi Domenico e Sisto; to the north, the Palazzo di

Giustizia, condemned after less than a century of use; then, beyond the palace, Prati, the residential quarter built after 1870, and Monte Mario.

Few tourists came to the roof, but on school holidays in the spring and autumn the terrace sometimes unexpectedly filled up with noisy, excited teenagers who took pictures and played their wild, laughing games, and then as unexpectedly departed, still pushing, shoving, and yelling as they scrambled down the steps and through the low doorway.

We had our own little game up there under the high blue sky facing the city, and part of it was the question of how Cesare Angelotti, having escaped from Castel Sant'Angelo by means unknown to us, had managed to cross Ponte Sant'Angelo and make his tortuous way to the Bernini Church of Sant'Andrea al Quirinale opposite the Quirinale Palace. That was where Vivien Sardou, the French playwright and author of *La Tosca*, had directed him. In 1800, the time of the play's action, Pius VII was pope and the Quirinale was still a papal possession highly regarded as a summer residence. Where were the Swiss Guards? Sant'Andrea al Quirinale is a small church, as Roman churches go, and when Giacomo Puccini turned the play into the opera *Tosca*, his librettists, Giuseppe Giacosa and Luigi Illica, knowing that it would not do for the large chorus of Act I, changed the scene to the Church of Sant'Andrea della Valle, not far from Piazza Navona. From the roof of Castel Sant'Angelo, neither of Angelotti's routes—the one in the play nor the operatic one—could be seen; but we could visualize the way, the streets, the risks. How he went could not have interested Sardou, who knew so little of Rome that he thought the Tiber ran between St. Peter's and Castel Sant'Angelo.

To us, the Puccini characters—the radiant Floria Tosca; her lover, the painter Mario Cavaradossi; and the villainous Baron Scarpia—were real. Puccini knew they were fictional, but that didn't matter; they were believable. Like every other operagoer who went to Sant'Andrea della Valle—and we went there many times, especially in hot weather, when it was a cool place to rest—we always looked for the family chapel where Angelotti's sister, the Marchesa Attavanti, had hidden woman's clothing he could use to make his getaway from Rome. We looked in vain, but we never ceased to look.

At the Palazzo Farnese, now the French Embassy, where two rooms were opened to the public for a couple of hours on Sunday, *Tosca* lovers invariably asked the guard on duty whether this was where Scarpia met his end. If people believe, the truth may very well be what they believe. When A. Conan Doyle allowed Sherlock Holmes to die at the Reichenbach Falls, he was so bitterly criticized that he admitted his error, acknowledging that Holmes had been alive all the time his admirers were mourning his passing. When Thackeray was about to let Mrs. Pendennis die, his alarmed readers brought him back to his senses, and the lady recovered her health.

The mere statement that Sardou had concocted the story of the beautiful singer Tosca, and Puccini had furthered this deception, simply proved that skepticism and cynicism abound today. Who would deny Floria and Mario their last rapturous union on the roof where we sat—before Mario's execution by a firing squad and Tosca's suicidal leap from the parapet? Who would deny Uncle Tom, Eva, and Topsy, or Madame Bovary, Mr. Pickwick, and the Scarlet Pimpernel? And so *Tosca* had happened here where we sometimes sat so calmly looking out over the city.

Once, in the river below, a lone sculler came downstream on the yellow tide and stopped short of the bridge. We watched him turn and start back up stream with broad sweeps of his gleaming oars. Then we went below.

When we emerged from the *castello* that day we turned north to go past the closed Palazzo di Giustizia. The shadows were lengthening; the sculler was far upriver, heading for the boathouse moored above Ponte Matteotti or beyond. Almost any day now the weather would change.

CHAPTER 17

Sixtus V, Tireless Builder

Sixtus V, Felice Peretti, was born December 18, 1521 at Grottomare, a small town on the Adriatic. He was the son of a poor gardener who had migrated from Albania, and a domestic servant, a devout woman and a stern disciplinarian, who instilled in the boy her own ideas of work and duty.

The father was an easygoing talkative dreamer who assured everybody that the baby he held in his arms would one day be pope. He seems to have expected divine intervention, however, for he did nothing to train his son for a life better than his own. Instead of going to school, little Felice had to work scaring birds out of the fruit trees and tending pigs. He learned the alphabet and a little reading from the hornbooks of other boys, until a relative, noting how quick of mind he was, paid for his education and then saw him admitted to the Franciscan order at an early age.

Felice became a good preacher, celebrated before he was twenty for his flow of words. In his thirties he became acquainted with two future popes, Pius IV and Pius V, and with Ignatius Loyola. He served as

Grand Inquisitor of Venice and General of the Franciscans, and became a cardinal—Cardinal Montalto. As the name Peretti means "little pears," he used on his coat of arms a lion rampant under a pear tree. He was by no means popular; his sharp tongue and brusque domineering ways held people off. But his relatives who benefited from his access to riches loved him.

His path to the papacy was blocked in 1572 when Gregory XIII, Ugo Boncompagni—the calendar reformer—won the prize. Cardinal Montalto, disappointed, turned his energies into the building of an estate, Villa Montalto, later Villa Negroni, on land bordering the ruins of the Baths of Diocletian, where marble and brick were free for the taking. We can see the cardinal in all his bulldog tenaciousness, walking, talking, dreaming, knowing what must be done about Rome and the church to restore them to full glory, and waiting patiently for his time to come. Rome had been sacked fifty years earlier, but the blow had not been fatal; and with Montalto's election, astonishing changes would be made in the city where strength and imagination had always moved men to extraordinary deeds.

While he waited for Gregory to die, the cardinal edited the writings of St. Ambrose, the fourth-century church father and Bishop of Milan. Some of the Peretti family came to Rome to live in the new villa; these relatives included Francesco, Montalto's nephew and designated heir. In 1573 Francesco married Vittoria Accoramboni of Rome and Gubbio, a town north of Perugia in Umbria. One of eleven children of a respected notary, she was only sixteen, beautiful and clever—possibly too pretty and too clever for good. The cardinal had misgivings about her. As it turned out, his instinct was accurate; and subsequent events surrounding Vittoria well illustrate the alarming nature of the Roman world at that time and no doubt account in good measure for Montalto's stern, unyielding attitude as pope toward crime and criminals.

She had been married seven years when she met Paolo Giordano Orsini, Duke of Bracciano, head of a family that had vast land holdings and castles and for centuries had maintained its own private army. Orsini, an obese voluptuary, desired Vittoria at once, but there were obstacles not to be easily surmounted. He was married to Isabelle de Medici, who spent most of her time with their three children at the court of her father, Cosimo de Medici, in Florence, while Orsini preferred Rome. He was used to getting his own way and saw no reason why he should not possess Vittoria. She was twenty years younger than he, childless, and probably bored; but she was unwilling to accept anything short of marriage.

Orsini settled the matter in the brutal manner of the age. He went to Florence and took his wife to one of his castles, where she died. The story was that he strangled her after accusing her of infidelity with his cousin Troilo. Returning to Rome, the duke persuaded Vittoria's brother, Marcello, to carry out the second part of his scheme. Marcello sent a messenger to the Villa Montalto on the night of April 16, 1581, to tell Francesco he was urgently needed by a friend who would meet him at a point near the Quirinale Palace, then under construction. Francesco hesitated—no man liked to go abroad after dark without a strong body guard—but Vittoria taunted him about his manliness, and he left with the messenger, who carried a torch. They walked north over the rough ground, skirting the ruins, to what is now Via Venti Settembre and turned west near the spot where San Bernardo stands. Suddenly, as they neared the Quirinale, the killers appeared. They shot and stabbed Francesco and left him to die.

The cardinal grieved in silence and did nothing. Pope Gregory, familiar with the situation, suspected that the duke had arranged for the murder and forbade him to marry Vittoria, But the duke, not to be balked, brought Vittoria from her father's house to an Orsini palazzo near the Theater of Pompey and, in the presence of a woman servant, put a ring on her finger. He called the ceremony a marriage.

The pope, furious, sent the *barqello* and a small force of men to the palace and demanded the surrender of Francesco's murderers. Orsini's men-at-arms swarmed into the street, roared at the *barqello*'s men, killed one, and wounded several others. The *barqello* retreated. The pope issued a new order: Bracciano was not to see Vittoria. Vittoria left the palace and was arrested and sent to a convent. Late in December of that year, 1581, she was taken to Castel Sant'Angelo as a prisoner. The duke tried to have her released.

Six months passed. Then, after talking with the pope and Grand Duke Francesco de Medici, of Tuscany, brother of his wife, he agreed to give up Vittoria. He wrote to her, and she threatened to kill herself. In November she was released on condition that she return to Gubbio. She went to see the pope and Cardinal Montalto and departed for Gubbio. The duke was restless, but he did nothing until September, 1583, when he set out for the shrine at Loreto and an inspection of the fortifications at Ancona. This may have been a subterfuge to justify his presence near Gubbio. In any case his resolution not to see Vittoria weakened, and when he turned westward he passed through Gubbio, and Vittoria joined him. They went to the Bracciano castle, thirty miles north of Rome, and here they lived quietly, worried only by the duke's health—his legs were ulcerous. One version of the story is that they had a religious marriage at Bracciano. Another, more in keeping with the duke's tempestuous nature, is that they stayed at the castle briefly before going on to Rome, where they were living when Gregory died on April 10, 1585.

During the vacancy of the Holy See, all interdictions of a pope who had just died were suspended. The duke and Vittoria rejoiced at the prospect of a splendid wedding. The Conclave could last a long time, and there was no need for haste. They were in their apartments when a messenger arrived with news that Cardinal Montalto's election as pope could happen at any hour. Agitated by the news, the duke decided they would be married at once. He ordered his chaplain to prepare for the ceremony in the small family church of Santa Maria di Grotta Pinta within the walls of the palace.

A retainer of the house had been murdered at the outside gate that night, and his body lay on a trestle bier at the altar. The duke and Vittoria would soon descend the winding staircase, and no time was to be lost. The chaplain and the messenger raised a marble slab on an unused vault and dumped the body inside. The chaplain performed the marriage and entered the account in the church register. The date was April 24, 1585, four years after Francesco's murder.

The duke and Vittoria foresaw nothing but a bleak future. The duke's health was getting worse; their enemy was on the papal throne. Sixtus V remembered everything; there was no chance of a reconciliation. The duke and Vittoria left Rome for the state of Venice. At Padova he underwent treatment, and from Padova they went to Salo on Lake Garda, where he died on November 13. His will divided his estate between Vittoria and his Medici son, Virginio, somewhat to Vittoria's advantage. The duke's kinsman, Ludovico, a Venetian general who hated Vittoria, objected to the will. After the funeral he overtook Vittoria as she made her way to her home in Padova. In the name of the Orsini and Medici families, he forced her to surrender the will and give up all claims to the duke's property. But Vittoria was not so easily thwarted: She produced an earlier will, which the Venetian authorities declared valid.

Ludovico, enraged, sent a company of his *bravos* to Padova with a few choice gentlemen. They found Vittoria on the night of December 22, a Sunday and the eve of her saint's day, at prayer before a large crucifix. In the next room her brother, Flamineo, was playing his lute as he sang a Miserere. The masked intruders shot Flamineo and cut him to pieces with their knives as he tried to crawl to his sister's defense. Two men held her while Tolomeo Visconti cursed her and drove a dagger into her heart.

Two days after the murders Ludovico's house was besieged by the authorities. He surrendered on Christmas Day and was strangled in his prison cell by the *barqello*. As many of the killers as could be found were tortured and put to death. Vittoria's brother Marcello, who had lured Francesco to his death, was arrested six months later and beheaded on the pope's order.

The cardinal's way had been right: He had acted with prudence and patience, and the wrongdoers had been punished. His conscience was clear; nothing had diverted him from his intentions.

He was sixty-four when he was elected pope. If we believe the story of how he succeeded—and it would be a pity to doubt it in its entirety, considering the Italian genius for deception and manipulation—the cardinal counted on the Conclave to choose a stopgap pontiff, a short-termer rather than a hale man who might go on ruling for years (as Gregory had reigned for thirteen years) while their own chances of elevation ran out.

Montalto had been out of favor with Gregory's court, and many cardinals did not know him except by hearsay. His vigorous preaching, his zeal as an inquisitor, his rough philosophical disputes were only vaguely recalled. To the majority of those at the Conclave, he was the retiring scholar who tended his vineyard and orchard on the slope above Santa Maria Maggiore. Bearded, stooped, leaning heavily on a stick, he feigned before the cardinals a weakness he did not feel. Believing him to be in his eighties, a cardinal asked: "What brings that death's-head here?"

The Conclave was divided into six rival factions that could have prolonged the debate and meditation; but within two weeks they had united behind the man who allowed them to think that, once elected, he would let them take over the papal responsibilities. He looked frail, he faked a cough, he trembled, and he spoke without passion.

But in the moment of his triumphant election he threw aside the stick and, with the agility of a youth, went to the altar and intoned a Te Deum in a thunderous voice. Through the next five years, the church was to live with one of the most masterful administrators in its history.

Peretti's inquisitorial methods years before had been so harsh that Venice had asked for his recall to Rome, and age had not softened him. After his coronation he rejected the tradition that a new pope pardoned prisoners by the score. Sixtus had no pity for the men who were making life unsafe in Rome and the Papal States. He ordered the extermination of banditry and the death of all thieves and killers. Cargoes of heads began rolling into Rome and were exhibited in ghastly displays on Ponte Sant'Angelo; and executions were held with greater frequency in the city. A nobleman in a mountainous area, pressed to speed up the work of making the roads safe, lacked the courage to confront the brigands but found an ingenious way: He loaded a train of wagons with fruits and vegetables and a few casks of poisoned wine. The highwaymen fell on the freighters and dispersed them, celebrating their haul by drinking the wine. All perished. Sixtus praised the nobleman.

Gregory's extravagances and good works had emptied the papal treasury. Sixtus refilled it by imposing heavy taxes and reorganizing the ownership of property through a reexamination of old title deeds. In church affairs he reorganized the Curia and made other reforms in the government. He tried, without lasting success, to limit membership in the College of Cardinals to seventy. He corrected the Vulgate, though his work had to be emended later. He stood for no opposition to his conviction that the Catholic faith was the only true faith and that papal authority could not be questioned. He excommunicated Queen Elizabeth of England for persecuting Catholics and for having executed Mary Stuart. He excommunicated Henry of Navarre, head of the Huguenots; Henry III for the assassination of Cardinal Guise; and Jaques Clement for the regicide of Henry III. He gave assistance to the Armada of Philip II of Spain. Obsessed with the idea of placing symbols of Christianity wherever they could be seen, he put a bronze statue of St. Peter on top of Trajan's Column, and one of St. Paul on the column of Marcus Aurelius in Piazza Colonna. The pagan obelisks he set up were surmounted by crosses. He was impatient to get the dome of St. Peter's completed in his lifetime. When the architects asked for ten years, he put men to work day and night and finished the job in twenty-two months. He built the Church of San Girolamo degli Schiavoni, which had been raised two centuries earlier for Serbian refugees. He contributed to the beautification of other churches.

Some of his critics have called him a ruthless destroyer. Certainly he had no more respect for pagan ruins than had most men of those years. So he demolished the Septizonium, built in 203 AD by Septimius Severus near the southeast corner of the Palatine to impress strangers entering Rome by the Via Appia. Sixtus wanted the marble and travertine for his new creations. There is no record that anyone protested.

Nor did anyone protest in 1590, the year of his death, when a marble staircase of forty-five steps leading down to the basilica was installed in Sant'Agnese fuori le Mura far out on Via Nomentana. The marble was ancient, and the underside of the steps bore bas-reliefs which nobody took the trouble to study or try to preserve. Sixtus tore down the old Lateran Palace, which had been the papal residence before Avignon, and built a new palace and three museums; and close to St. Peter's, he erected the plain Vatican Palace, from a window of which popes now bless at noon the Sunday and Holy Day crowds in St. Peter's Square.

Sixtus loved Santa Maria Maggiore as he loved no other church. It was there and not in the new St. Peter's that he wished his remains to lie. The Sistine Chapel, where the pope's body was entombed, is the most magnificent chapel in Rome. It was designed by Domenico Fontana, who is said to have spent his own money on the tomb when the pontiff's purse was short.

Maria Maggiore was a pivotal point in the Sistine planning. When Sixtus climbed to the roof, he could see all Rome at his feet. A mile to the north, at the end of a narrow roadway, stood Trinità dei Monti on the Pincio. To the south lay San Giovanni in Laterano and Santa Croce in Gerusalenune and, off in the southeast, San Lorenzo fuori le Mura, three of the seven pilgrimage churches he intended to connect by building broad streets like Via Merulana, which already had taken shape in his mind across the Esquiline Hill. San Sebastiano and San Paolo fuori le Mura, the other two, would also be made more accessible.

The landscape Sixtus contemplated closer at hand was all too familiar to him. He could see his own Villa Montalto, which had drawn from deep wells the water needed for the household and the fountains. There were a few small habitations and a few old churches, Santa Pudenziana and Santa Prassede and San Martino di Monti, and down the hill San Pietro in Vincoli. Mostly it was a desolate landscape, old, impoverished, neglected—scrubby vegetation, a bit of a vineyard, empty fields. Yet if one walked past the ugly Moses statue of the Acqua Felice Mostra, he would come to one of Rome's great new monuments—the shining white marble arch of Porta Pia built into the Aurelian Wall in 1561 by Michelangelo at the behest of Pius IV.

If Sixtus regretted having come to power so late in his life, he never acknowledged it. He went ahead with his work as fast as he could. Though his dream of a new Rome was big, he could hardly have foreseen how quickly the changes would come—the rise of the Barberini Palace built by Pope Urban VIII, Matteo Barberini of Florence; the busy piazza and the handsome Bernini Tritone Fountain; and that strange Church of the Cappucini, built by another Barberini, Cardinal Antonio, a Franciscan.

He was filled with fresh zeal when he thought of the new papal palace, the Quirinale. It would support his urging that people should build on the hills. Wasting no time, he put more men to work there, though he must have known its completion would not occur in his lifetime. (It was finished about 150 years later in the time of Clement XII.) It had not started out as a palace but as the Villa d'Este, a plain dwelling which Cardinal Ippolito d'Este, the son of Lucrezia Borgia and Alfonso, Duke of Ferrara, turned into a charming country house. Gregory bought the property, which commanded a fine view of Rome. Sixtus loved the new palace so much that he went there to live—and there he died.

For some time after he moved, he had had his eye on a group of marble statues of two men and two horses, which somehow had survived through the centuries since their erection at the Baths of Constantine on a lower slope of the Quirinal Hill. Sixtus moved them to the space in front of the new palace. They were nameless, but people called them the Horse Tamers, or Castor and Pollux; and when they were in place and a fountain was built, the piazza took the name of Monte Cavallo. The water was Acqua Felice. (An obelisk stands today between the two groups, but it was not placed there until the late eighteenth century by Pius VI, when it was discovered near the Tomb of Augustinus. Sixtus would have approved. In 1587 he had set up the twin of this obelisk below the apse of Santa Maria Maggiore.)

Sixtus, who consecrated Trinita de1 Monti, built the high double staircase and leveled the ground in front of the church, but he did not, as many people think, set up the obelisk. A Roman imitation of the Egyptian, it was found in the Gardens of Sallust and moved to the Trinita de1 Monti Piazza in 1788 by Pius VI. The mistake in associating the obelisk with Sixtus is a natural one, since he was the pope who made obelisks fashionable architectural adornments of fountains and squares. Yet he actually handled only four in his brief reign. They were the Vatican Obelisk, the Lateran Obelisk, the one he erected behind Santa Maria Maggiore, and the one he installed at the Piazza del Popolo Fountain.

The Lateran shaft, the oldest piece of man's handiwork to be found in Rome, was dug up in the Circus Maximus. The one that went to the Piazza del Popolo was discovered shortly afterward in the same place, the low flat depression between the Palatine and the Aventine where chariots had raced. Sixtus might have used this one at Trinità dei Monti; but the beautification of Rome was always on his mind, and the piazza under the Pincio was the entrance to the Eternal City from the ancient Via Flaminia and therefore a more desirable spot than at the head of the street that ran down the hill and came to be known as Via Felice and later, Via Sistina. It was on the long, sloping, wearying hills of this country road, still a tiring exercise for those who go on foot, that he had trudged as a Franciscan monk and a cardinal. Along this way as pope he dashed from one building project to another, dragging with him his footsore court—the cardinals who had always mounted horses or mules or ridden in fine carriages. How they must have hated his peasant strength!

His predecessor, Gregory the Bolognese, was no less vigorous, mounting a Spanish horse or a white mule without assistance at the age of eighty-two; but Gregory's followers were mounted. Sixtus preferred his own sturdy legs, and after he went to live in the Quirinale, his long Sunday walks became a custom. On weekdays he was everywhere, climbing over high mounds of earth, mounting ladders, inspecting the cut marble, the ornamental details. Where Via Pia and Via Sistina intersected, he built four wall fountains and changed the name of Via Sistina south from Palazzo Barberini to Via delle Quattro Fontane.

All building before the invention of steam hoisting machines is a story of manpower, the hard muscle used in the construction of the pyramids and the Chinese Wall, Greek and Roman temples, aqueducts, viaducts, arches, port fortifications, canals, the Aurelian Wall and the Colosseum, the Roman bridges of Spain, the arenas of France and Istria, the cathedrals, palaces and castles of Europe. These works took years to complete, and never do the laborers appear in such a concentration of energy as they do under the stern eye of Sixtus when he turned to the obelisks.

The shifting of the Vatican obelisk from one side of St. Peter's to the space in front employed nine hundred men and 140 horses. Five hundred men were engaged in digging up the Lateran obelisk, and we have an even more vivid picture of brawn in the great trireme of three hundred oarsmen that towed the million-pound red granite Lateran shaft across the Mediterranean from Alexandria to Ostia. We know a lot more about that obelisk than we do about the one at the Vatican, but the fate of the barge that carried it is not known. It must have been a craft of immense size, for the one that carried the smaller Vatican obelisk astonished all Rome and was so long that the Emperor Claudius, Nero's successor, filled it with concrete and sank it to form a breakwater for his new port.

The Vatican Obelisk, a single piece of granite eighty-three feet tall from its high base, weighs 330 tons; the Lateran shaft is 105 feet and weighs 460 tons. The former was brought to Rome by Caligula and set up in the Vatican area known afterward as the Circus of Nero, a race-course where the impetuous young tyrant learned to drive four-horse chariots. The obelisk stood there while Constantine leveled the hill and built old St. Peter's, and it was still standing there in the early fifteenth century, when Nicholas V considered moving it. Nothing was done, because nobody knew what to do.

When Sixtus appeared, 130 years after Nicholas, he appointed a committee of cardinals and bishops who solved the problem, as far as they were concerned, by announcing a contest. Five hundred architects, artists, inventors, and crackpots from all over Italy responded. Fontana, a practical man, won the contest by showing Sixtus a small model of a wooden scaffolding or "castle" built around a miniature obelisk of lead, which he lowered by turning a wheel and raised with another turn.

The date chosen for Fontana to prove himself was April 30, 1586, one year after Peretti's election. There is a story, probably apocryphal, that should his plan fail he was prepared to flee from Rome and for that purpose had a relay of post-horses harnessed and ready to gallop off. But the enterprise did not fail. The soil around the shaft, piled up in the centuries, was cleared away, revealing four enormous blocks at the base. The shaft was then wrapped in straw mats and encased in wooden planks. At dawn Fontana and his men attended Mass in the open. All Rome had come to St. Peter's. All Italy awaited the results.

Fontana, his brother Giovanni, and his thirty-year-old assistant, Carlo Maderno, inspected the high castle, the windlasses and ropes. During an interval, they and the workmen confessed and received Holy Communion; and at two o'clock in the afternoon, Fontana mounted a raised rostrum, signaled with his hand—and trumpets blared the order to begin. Men and horses started turning the windlasses. The silent throng heard only the creak of the rude machinery, the grunts of the men, the sound of the horses—then, a perceptible wrench. The crowds watched in breathless fascination as the obelisk was lifted off its base. By the twelfth time around the shaft was a foot off its base, and there was no restraining the people, who roared jubilantly. The guns on Castel Sant'Angelo fired a salute, and all over Rome church bells joyously rang out.

On May 17 the obelisk was lowered horizontally on rollers and moved to the front of St. Peter's; but summer was blazing and further work was put off until September 14, the Feast of the Exaltation of the Holy Cross. Again Fontana and his men attended Mass and received the Blessed Sacrament as the crowds assembled. The tension this time was greater. Sixtus imposed silence on pain of death; and to remind everyone how serious he was, he had a gallows built. There was no need for it. The story about the San Remo sailor who cried out to water the ropes when he saw one start to burn from friction seems to have no foundation in fact.

The windlasses went around fifty-two times, and the obelisk was set down on its new base. Rome celebrated with dancing and song, feasting and fireworks, and the pealing of church bells, while Fontana presided over a banquet for his workmen. They feasted on bread, cheese, and ham, and every man had two bottles of wine for himself. Fontana received a papal title and seventy thousand scudi.

The Lateran shaft was discovered five months later, in February 1587. It lay, broken in three pieces, twenty-four feet deep in the spongy earth; and digging was impeded by the water that seeped in from an ancient stream. Three hundred men, working day and night, controlled the flood sufficiently to allow the obelisk and its smaller companion to be dragged to the surface. The big one had been cut for the Pharaoh Thothmes III in 1500 BC for the temple at Karnak. Constantine saw it in 330 AD and ordered it removed to his city of Constantinople; but it got only as far as Alexandria, where it lay for twenty-seven years until Constantine's successor, Constantius II, transported it to Rome. Nobody knows when or why it fell. Fontana put the three pieces together and sawed three feet off the bottom of the obelisk to flatten its burnt and broken base.

The Piazza del Popolo obelisk had been standing in Heliopolis, the City of the Sun, in Egypt, for thirteen centuries when Augustus saw it after the defeat of Antony and Cleopatra in 31 BC and shipped it to Rome. The shaft is seventy-nine feet tall, only four feet shorter than the Vatican Obelisk, and weighs 235 tons. Fontana raised it in 1589.

Sixtus died in the following year, on August 27, during a melodramatic thunderstorm that crashed over the heads of the crowds standing outside the Quirinale awaiting word of his end. Poor Sixtus! He had so loved the poor—even as he enriched his own family and Rome—but in the hour of his passing, the man who had risen to the most powerful position in the world was condemned. His taxes had been heavy, his passion for work sometimes oppressive. His brilliant accomplishments—the completion of St. Peter's dome, the Acqua Felice aqueduct, and the restoration of the hills; the new streets and obelisks; his work on the Vatican Library—all the things that Rome had hailed triumphantly—were forgotten in a moment as the mobs reverted to their natural treachery. Statues erected to the pope's honor were overturned and smashed as if he had been the people's enemy. Violence broke out, and pillaging started. An old rumor, invented by his foes, was re-circulated: old Cardinal Montalto had made a pact with the devil to seize the papal throne. Fontana, accused of falsifying basilica accounts, escaped to Naples and never returned to Rome.

CHAPTER 18

Lifestyle: Princes of the Renaissance Church

*I*n 1894 a scholar named Domenico Gnoli published an account of the census ordered by the Medici Pope Clement VII a few months before the Bourbon Sack of 1527. The census was not thought to have been accurate. Citizens lied or were evasive, or they were not at home when the census-taker called and so were never counted. Illiteracy abounded; the census-takers, sometimes semi-literate parish priests, misspelled names. Still, whatever its deficiencies, the census provided Signor Gnoli with much lively material, including a glimpse of the way the highly-privileged cardinals lived.

Their duties included supporting a given number of persons—courtiers and servants, as well as poor relatives, spongers, idlers, and possibly bastard sons. These dependents were not called persons but "mouths"—*bocche*, the plural of *bocca*, the Italian word for mouth. Alessandro, Cardinal Farnese, who was so rich that he could build the Palazzo Farnese and leave enough money to his grandson to build the sumptuous church the Gesu, fed 306. (The pope fed seven hundred). The others were as follows: Cesarini, 275; Orsini, 200; del Monte, 200| Cybo, 192; Pucci, 190; Ridolfi, 180; Piccolomini, 180; de Cupis, 150; Rangoni, 150; Campeggi, 130; della Valle, 130; Pisani,130; Armellini, 130; Scaramuccia Trivulzio, 103; Accolti, 100; Erkenfort, 100; Jacobacci, 80; Cesi, 80; Numalio, 60; de Vio, 45.

The Palazzo Farnese, loveliest of all Renaissance palaces in Rome, later became the French embassy. To operagoers it is also the setting for Act 2 of Puccini's *Tosca*. Michelangelo had a hand in its construction, as he had in everything in Rome in his lifetime, furnishing the handsome cornice. When we were there, two rooms were open to the public on Sundays between 11:00 AM and 1:00 PM, allowing one to get an idea of the building's splendid interior.

Cardinal Farnese, elected Pope Paul III, was a member of the minor but venerable country aristocracy of the Latium region. Since the Middle Ages, the family had owned land and a few castles near Lake Bolsena. For generations the Farnese men had distingiushed themselves as soldiers on the side of the papacy during the complicated rivalries between the Guelphs and Ghibellines. The popes had rewarded the Farneses with estates and privileges; and at the beginning of the fifteenth century, through the marriage of a Farnese heir to a Roman noblewoman, the family rose from the status of provincial nobility to that of urban aristocracy.

Alessandro was only twenty-five when he was named cardinal, largely because the Borgia pope, Alexander VI, was passionately fond of Alessandro's sister, the beautiful Giulia, la Bella of Roman gossip and innumerable stories, whom the sensual pontiff had lodged in the Vatican. For Alessandro, the red hat furthered his social position, and he allowed twenty-five years to pass before he took holy orders and celebrated his first Mass.

In the meantime he had four children, three boys and a girl, whom he legitimized. Their mother was never known to the public. He endowed them richly—how richly may be seen in a document which Lanciani describes. Lanciani confessed his puzzlement at the way in which Alessandro's grandson, at the age of twenty-four, could spend so much money. The grandson, who also was named Alessandro, lived in the Palazzo Farnese and was attended by three hundred servants, including an organist, a carpenter, a soprano, a gamekeeper, a barber, an upholsterer, an embroiderer, a saddler, a silk weaver, an apothecary, a weaver of silk stockings, a stable-master, a bookkeeper, a chief cook, an under-cook, a pastry cook, an amanuensis, a master of page-boys, a singer, a master of counterbass, a butler, a master mason, a gardener—and so forth.

There can be no doubt that, as a Farnese reared in luxury, he followed the example of his grandfather, who, to the joy and the general acclamation of the Roman populace, had ascended the papal throne in October 1534. Giovanna H. Solari, who wrote an excellent history of the Farnese family, has given us a vivid description of Paul III in the Vatican.

"The papal court was then a singular compromise of ecclesiastical pomp and secular style," she writes. "A man of great taste and pride, Paul lived surrounded by cardinals, prelates, dignitaries, and chamberlains in purple cassocks, and also by a colorful crowd of pages, courtiers, musicians, singers, and court jesters. Fifty footmen followed him everywhere he travelled. A head falconer with a flock of assistants was in charge of organizing the pope's hunts in the environs of Rome, took care of the hawks and the kennels, and imported new breeds of hounds from France. Two cooks prepared food exclusively for the pope, who, in deference to custom, ate alone at his own table but never by himself, for the banquet hall of the Vatican was always open to ambassadors, relatives, and friends. Yet, in the seeming confusion of the Vatican household, the innumerable mace-bearers, squires, halberdiers, attendants, Swiss Guards, and secretaries all had precise duties. And so had Luca Gaurico, the most famous astrologer of the time, who regularly consulted the stars on behalf of the pope; and every morning the pope arranged his day according to reports from the stars."

The only pope to build a Tiber bridge, Ponte Sisto, was Sixtus IV, Francesco della Rovere, a Franciscan from Albissola, near Savona, who was elected in 1471 at the age of fifty-seven and reigned for thirteen years. As Minister-General of the Franciscan Order, della Rovere was justly admired for his administrative skill and reforms; as pope, he was hailed as *Il Gran Fabbricatore*, the great builder. He built new roads and bridges. He built the Church of Santa Maria della Pace and rebuilt the ancient Santa Maria del Popolo. He reconstructed or repaired twenty other churches.

He reorganized the University of Rome and reformed sanitary conditions at Santo Spirito Hospital, the main ward of which was 365 feet long and accommodated a thousand patients. He repaired Castel Sant'Angelo and the Palazzo del Senatore on the Carnpidoglio. He established the Capitoline Museum by offering a gift of bronzes and marbles to the people of Rome. He reorganized the Vatican Library and built the Sistine Chapel, calling on the best painters of the Renaissance to decorate its walls—Botticelli, Perugino, Pinturicchio, and Ghirlandaio.

He had a weakness: he suffered from the papal disease of his time, nepotism. In Italian a *nepote* is a nephew, and Sixtus IV had a surfeit of nephews—nine or ten of them. Nothing good can be said of the lot, with one exception, Giuliano, an earnest young man who was to become Pope Julius II at the age of fifty, nineteen years after the death of his uncle. Giuliano was made a cardinal at the same time as another nephew, Raffaele Riario. Freed from the restraints of monastic confinement in a Franciscan convent, Raffaele indulged every appetite of his nature. He drank, gambled, whored, and wore rich garments.

One night Raffaele won sixty thousand scudi, which he decided at once to spend on the building of a palazzo befitting his rapacious exhibitionism. He did not live to see the palazzo completed, his debaucheries bringing him to his death-bed when he was only twenty-eight. Today he is remembered less as a worthless character in the gaudy Renaissance framework than as the builder of one of the noblest structures in Rome, the Cancellaria.

Sixtus IV raised two other nephews to the Sacred College and married off two more to the illegitimate daughters of the King of Naples. One married the daughter of the Duke of Milan and another, Girolamo, the daughter of the Duke of Urbino. Girolano plotted with the pope's bankers, the Pazzi, and the Archbishop of Florence to murder Lorenzo the Magnificent and his brother Giuliano while they were at Mass in the Duomo. Lorenzo escaped; Giuliano died where he fell. All the plotters were captured and executed.

Riario won his scudi from Franceschetto Cibo, whose uncle was to succeed Sixtus IV as Innocent VIII and reign for eight years. The Medici did not forget the della Rovere treachery, and when Leo X was elected as successor to Julius II, he confiscated the Riario property and kept it for the church.

There is a painting in the Vatican Galleries, a fresco by Melozzo da Forli, known throughout the world from its use in books, on postcards, and in film slides. Melozzo shows us Sixtus IV in the act of appointing Bartolomeo Sacchi—called Platina from his birthplace, Platina—as Vatican Librarian. On first seeing the painting, and for a time thereafter, we are inclined to accept it for what it no doubt was intended to be—the simple representation of a joyous little ceremony.

On studying it, however, we look in vain for joy. We see instead a strange disunity, each of the six men in the picture fettered in the isolation of his own thoughts. The painting is highly decorative—the architectural refinements of the chamber; the pope's chair with its fringed seat, tasseled back and arms, and heavily studded legs and stretchers; the rich ample folds of the garments, even the red-booted foot modestly showing itself under the pontiff's snowy white robe. The curious detachment of the characters is faintly disturbing. Platina, the great humanist, kneels before the pope but does not face him directly. The two men, so close in space and spirit, hardly seem aware of each other. The pope, a prelate plump and pleased, has made a satisfying appointment: The library will be in good hands. Platina has allowed his right index finger to point downward; his square handsome face and noble head have a saintly aspect. Between the scholar and the pope—partly blocking the former—is Cardinal Giuliano della Rovere, tall, impressive, gazing intently at his uncle, high priest of all Christendom, Vicar of Christ on earth, the fleshly Italian prince of princes, who has come here, though it took many years, from the chilly self-denial of a draughty friary.

The fourth figure in this small gallery of portraits is a cardinal-nephew seen in an interesting profile. He appears to be unaware that anything is happening. The fifth and sixth men stand behind Platina. Their full hair is curled and scented, and they are enveloped in velvet, satin, and brocade. They wear necklaces of gold, and their hands are hidden in the folds of their robes. They look spoiled in every sense of the word. And they were.

Giuliano della Rovere was eighteen years old, a tall, spare provincial youth, when Zio Francesco, his loving uncle, became pope. He was thirty-one, sound of frame, a good swordsman, a rich cardinal, when Sixtus died. The next pope, Innocent VIII—a Genovese named Cibo (which means "food" in Italian)—died after eight years in office, and by the time of his passing, Giuliano was nearly forty, vigorous, and clearly *papabile*.

But Giuliano's moral rectitude, his manly carriage and obvious superiority were no match against the intriguing Spaniard, Roderigo Lenzuoli-Borgia of Valencia, who won the election eight days after Columbus sailed on his first voyage of discovery and opened the way for all the new riches that would flow to the church. Cardinal della Rovere could do little but wait. While he waited he was distracted pleasantly, as he had been in his uncle's lifetime, by outings to the papal hunting lodge, La Magliana, a half-dozen miles from the city on the way to Ostia.

A project of greater interest also caught his fancy and provided an outlet for his energy: He built himself a small handsome castle of brick at Ostia—not Ostia Antica, the ancient port, but a town founded in 830 by Pope Gregory IV and named for him Gregoriopolis. Today it has around 2,400 inhabitants, a charming walled place of old houses, many of them restored.

The lovely castello looks as fresh today as it did the day the last masons departed. We liked to go there and listen to the castle guard speak of the past, and to go into the Church of Sant' Aurea, built by Baccio Pontelli, who also designed Giuliano's fortress. The church contains the body of Sant' Aurea, a martyr, and a fragment of gravestone believed to have marked the grave of St. Monica, mother of St. Augustine, who died at Ostia as she was waiting for a ship to take her home to North Africa. An air of antiquity sits easily on the town and the people, and we felt only peace there and were thankful that Giuliano had built as he did.

With the death of Alexander VI, Giuliano's hopes rose; but the Conclave turned to an older man, the sixty-four-year-old Todeschini-Piccolomini of Siena, who took the name Pius III. He died a month after his election, and this time Giuliano made it. The year was 1503, and he was fifty. As Julius II, bold, brilliant, and sometimes short-tempered, he would rule for nearly a decade, one of the greatest popes in history.

The one flaw in his character was his violent temper, which led to unpredictable outbursts of anger. His quarrels with Michelangelo over money he owed the sculptor at one point drove Michelangelo—who had a temper of his own—back to his native Florence. Julius, in a rage, sent soldiers in pursuit, but they failed to cow the great sculptor. It was only when the pope threatened to interdict Florence that Michelangelo returned to Rome.

The affair of the pope's magnificent tomb was another shameful example of papal temper and intransigence. Lesser artists completed the tomb, with its great central figure of Moses, and it never got to St. Peter's. It stands today in San Pietro in Vincoli.

Fifty years had passed since Nicholas V, concerned over the structural weaknesses of old St. Peter's, made it known publicly that he favored pulling down the basilica and replacing it with another. Six popes, including *Il Gran' Fabbricatore*, Sixtus IV, were aware of the building's deteriorating state, but they lacked either the nerve or the incentive to move them and did nothing. The Constantinian basilica was twelve hundred years old and tangible evidence that the survival and growth of the church were miraculous. Romans were superstitious about it.

Julius knew all the risks involved. He could expect a storm of abuse and derision and threats, but instead of deterring him, this fortified his resolution. He appealed for funds to all the rnonarchs of Europe, as well as the bishops and nobles, who responded with speed and generosity. The shaky, badly-patched old basilica was razed, and on April 18, 1506 Julius, wearing his miter and followed by a few attendants, descended into a hole dug twenty-five feet below the ancient pavement and there laid the first stone of the new St. Peter's. The occasion was one of splendor, formality, and tense excitement, and the pontiff, standing in the torch-lighted depths, heard the murmurous voice of the crowd above. Fearing its pressure might cause the walls to collapse, he took momentary fright and laid his stone crookedly. Then, handing the trowel to a workman, Julius scrambled up the ladder as fast as he could.

In another positive action of great significance, Julius did the unexpected. Interested in military exploits, he thought it shameful that the pope had to depend on unreliable mercenaries in times of emergency, when even the meanest baron had a strong band of fighters. Julius therefore raised an army of his own: six thousand Swiss soldiers recruited by arrangement with the Swiss Confederacy.

We have come to think of Switzerland as a nation of dull respectability, a neutral Alpine enclave filled with foreign tourists, secret numbered bank accounts, and milk chocolate and cheese factories. Winston Churchill's gibe is remembered: In many centuries of peace, all that the Swiss have done is to produce the cuckoo clock. But while there may have been stodgy Swiss in the sixteenth century, we get a far different appraisal of the people of that region—which the ancient Romans called Helvetia—when we read a book about the Sack of Rome by an English author, E. R. Chamberlin. To the "civilized nations" of Europe, he wrote, the hardy Swiss "appeared like so many disciplined savages. Intensely patriotic, fanatically courageous, capable of the very noblest self-sacrifice, they were also distinguished by an appalling ferocity, a cynical contempt and pitiless disregard for the rights of others and a deliberate and cold blooded cruelty. It was these Alpine herdsmen who broke the long ascendancy of the mountain man, the rich nobleman who could afford heavy armor and a strong horse to carry him. The Swiss reply to this glittering panoply of war was almost laughably simple, consisting as it did of a long shaft of wood tipped with a steel point, the whole measuring some nineteen feet from butt to tip: the pike. Its success depended upon one vital ingredient, the pikeman's utter faith in his neighbor. As long as one man held, all held, creating an actual hedge of glittering steel points that projected far beyond the vulnerable flesh that wielded it, a hedge that was unbreakable by the most determined cavalry charge."

It was men of this caliber and bloody tradition that Julius whipped into a papal army; and in August, 1506, he tasted victory when he marched up to Bologna at the head of his troops and expelled the usurping tyrant, Bentivoglio, restoring the province to the Papal States. This army existed until 1825, when Pope Leo XII converted it to a domestic bodyguard. Today it consists of one hundred men, including four officers, a chaplain, twenty-three non-commissioned officers, two drummers and seventy halberdiers. They stand guard at all the Vatican entrances wearing the costume they first wore nearly five hundred years ago—doublets and baggy pantaloons of violet and orange stripes, with berets drawn down over one eye. In this picturesque dress they stoically withstand the onslaught of thousands of amateur photographers from every corner of the world.

An earlier Pope Leo—Leo X, son of Lorenzo the Magnificent and successor to Julius II, Il Magnifico—found much of his pleasure in watching the hunt, dressed in simple riding attire. But Paride de Grassi, master of ceremonies at his court, liked the feel of silk and velvet. He looked with pleasure on the red hats of cardinals and Lenten purples and the golden threads of porphyryed copes, stoles, and chasubles. Pastoral staffs, jewelled croziers, and gemmed censers enchanted him. No incense was too exquisite for his taste.

De Grassi, therefore, was understandably distressed when the pope mounted a horse and rode heavily around the outskirts of the city or trotted with a large retinue down to La Magliana. His Holiness, De Grassi thought, looked ridiculous, a *buffone*, in the prescribed hunting gear of the day—a gray Flemish cloth jacket, a Spanish sombrero, and riding boots. How could good Christians pay homage to a figure like that and kiss the toe of a dirty riding boot?

Leo did look unworthy of the post he held. He was unwholesomely corpulent, and his flabby cheeks were pale. But his doctors had told him he needed exercise and that riding was good for him. He liked hunting, even though he could take part only as a spectator; and he naturally turned south to La Magliana, for no finer hunting lodge existed in Italy.

No better hunting, nor climate for the hunt, could be found anywhere on the peninsula. The forested hills and sunny glades and dark swamps teemed with game: majestic stags and lesser deer, ferocious bears, wolves, foxes, porcupines, hares, and vast numbers of birds. An entry in a sixteenth-century diary found in a Florentine palace described a day when two men armed with bow and spear bagged enough game near Anzio to overload a cart. In ancient times this region between Rome and Ostia and Porto had been a land of abundance, the broad fields and rich orchards yielding bounteous crops. But this was several centuries before the start of the Christian era. With Rome's decline, agriculture fell off, and the hills and flat country lapsed into their primitive state.

Here, at La Magliana, an old place with historic associations, Leo X found peace. It was the classic "Fundus Manlianus," a name corrupted by time into "Magliana." It was the family farm of Marcus Manlius Capitolinus, the Roman officer and former consul who had saved the Capitol in 390 BC from the night attack of the Gauls.

The story of that terrible night of bloody combat comes to us from Livy. The Gauls, having secretly studied the face of the Capitol

Hill, were confident they could scale it. They began their climb on a starlit night when the tired Citadel garrison slept and the sentries were dozing. So quiet were the Gauls that not even the dogs heard them. But the cackling of Juno's sacred geese and the loud flapping of their wings woke Marcus Manlius. He sprang up, seized his sword, and ran to the edge of the cliff just as the first Gaul reached the top.

Shouting the alarm, Marcus Manlius struck the invader with his shield and toppled him over the side. The falling man carried others with him. Many of the climbers lost their grip, dropped their weapons, and fell; and the roused Roman soldiers, running to the brink, hurled stones and javelins at those still trying to advance. The attack was halted, the Gauls who survived retreated, and quiet came to the Capitol.

The buildings of Fundus Manlius disappeared, but the site was not forgotten. In the Middle Ages a small church, San Giovanni di Magliana, stood there.

The late fifteenth-century popes enjoyed hunting as spectators. Pius II, who bore the impressive name of Aeneas Silvius Piccolomini, mentioned the sport in his commentaries; and Paul II—Pietro Barbo, a Venetian—arranged a hunt when Borso d'Este, followed by a pack of hounds and a string of falcons, came down to Rome to be crowned Duke of Ferrara. Many wild animals were slaughtered, and a gold medal was struck for the occasion.

Who began building the hunting lodge—actually it had all the conveniences and architectural and artistic virtues of a fine villa—is not known. Credit long went to Sixtus IV for laying the foundation; later the honor shifted to Innocent VIII. In any case accommodations existed at La Magliana as early as 1492, in which year an amusing incident occurred. The Borgia Pope Alexander VI was riding down to La Magliana in December, four months after his coronation, and no doubt thinking of his enemy, Giuliano della Rovere, when the keepers of the lodge, apprised of the pope's approach, fired off a rocket to welcome him. Suspecting that Giuliano, who was at his Ostia castello, had set an ambush for him, and fearful of his life, His Holiness turned and galloped back to Rome.

In spite of his flabbiness, Leo X did a lot of riding, sometimes to the discomfort of his courtiers, whom he led in long sorties through the woods as far as the sea. He did no hunting. He had no skill with bow or lance, but he loved to sit above the groundlings and watch the kill. It was a cruel, senseless, and wasteful sport, known to us in kind as it was carried on for centuries in Europe by kings, princes, and the aristocracy. The general practice, then as now, was to encircle a large tract of land where game was plentiful and, with a blowing of horns, beating of drums, and shouts, frighten the animals to a cleared space where they could be destroyed.

Hunting by itself would not have kept La Magliana going. Its real importance was as a fine suburban retreat. The air was purer than in Rome, and even when improvements were being made—new frescoes, the installation of statues, the construction of a staircase or a fountain—the noise was less nerve-wracking than it was at St. Peter's.

Papal interest in La Magliana gradually diminished, and Sixtus V, the occasionally fierce old Felice Peretti, was probably the last pope to spend many days there. Sixtus had been elected in April 1585 and reigned for five years and four months. Not long after his death the place was sold to the nuns of Santa Cecilia. The nuns continued living there until late in the nineteenth century, when they moved out and leased the property to the Civitavecchia Railway Company, which was constructing a line to Pisa. Engineers, surveyors, supply crews and laborers moved in. They drove pegs high in the painted walls for their coats; the smoke of their cooking blackened the delicately carved ceilings.

The countryside where the hunting lodge stood retains the name of Magliana, and there is a Ponte Magliana across the Tiber; but the old place, once the farm of the man who saved the Capitol and later the site of a gracious villa in the Renaissance, is gone. We used to drive down that way toward Fiumicino, but we never had the heart to look for what we knew we would not find.

CHAPTER 19

The Cenci and a Weeping Pope

*N*o crime in Renaissance Rome matched the brutish, senseless Cenci parricide. I suspect that if the setting had been in Naples, Venice, or Milan, the murder would hardly have interested us beyond our normal interest in an evil happening. But the Cenci principals were Roman, the active killers excepted. They were also of the noble class, the Eternal City's aristocracy. Rome had changed a great deal in the more than 350 years since the execution of the Cenci, but we could still reconstruct in our minds certain scenes.

The executions were carried out in Piazza del Ponte Sant'Angelo, across the river from Castel Sant'Angelo. Just north of the piazza there had stood the notorious Tor di Nona prison, where, in the fifteenth century, men were hanged, usually after midnight. Placards bearing their names and crimes were attached to the bodies so that early-morning passersby who saw them could carry the news abroad. Benvenuto Cellini was once detained in this prison. When Innocent X built the new prisons in Via Giulia, the old *carcere* was razed and the Teatro

Tordinona built on the foundations. The Tordinona was replaced by the Teatro Apollo, which stood until the river embankment was built.

Goldsmiths, bankers, and rich merchants lived in this corner of the Campo Marzio. In Via Bianchi, Cellini stabbed to death his old enemy, the Milanese goldsmith Pompeo. In front of San Celso, in this street, Lorenzo Colonna, the pronotary, was slain by the Orsini and Santacroce; and his mother, finding his head cut off, seized it by the hair and shrieked curses upon her son's enemies. Ignatius Loyola sent his Jesuit novices to preach hellfire and repentance to the roughs and mountebanks (*saltimgbanchi*) who gathered there.

Beatrice Cenci was twenty-two years and seven months old when she was executed on September 11, 1599, for complicity in her father's murder. Her older brother, Giacomo, thirty-one, and her stepmother, Lucrezia, were put to death at the same time. A younger brother, Bernardo, eighteen, was spared by Pope Clement VIII but forced to sit on the scaffold throughout the ghastly proceedings. Afterwards he was sent to the stinking, verminous papal galleys at Civitavecchia, forty miles up the Tyrrhenian coast, and held in bondage for seven years.

Executions were common enough in Rome—a few months after the Cenci died, Giordano Bruno of Nola was burned as a heretic in the Campo de' Fiori—but never in the city's bloody history did one rouse the people to such a frenzy as did that of the Cenci. There was no sympathy for the slain man. Count Francesco Cenci was monstrously evil, bestial in his habits, cruel, lustful and dishonest. He was forty-nine, in deteriorating health, but as savagely vicious as ever when he was killed by two assassins on September 9, 1598, in a castle at Petrella del Salto in the desolate mountains of the Kingdom of Naples, between Rieti and Avezzano, about sixty miles from Rome. His murder, unbelievably crude, was as foul as his life had been.

It was Beatrice, fair of face, serene, and of such fortitude that people likened her to a saint, who moved the populace to a great outpouring of grief. The legend of her excellence and virtue had begun to form even while she lived out her last long hot summer in prison. It flourished through the years immediately after her death and persists today, in spite of dispassionate studies such as the one made after the first World War by Corrado Ricci, which show that she was not a virgin; that Olimpio Calvetti, one of the killers, was her lover, by whom she bore a son; and that she was the prime instigator in the slaying. At a moment when the two murderers appeared to falter, Beatrice bade them get on with their work.

Rome was a small city in 1599. On the return of the popes from Avignon in 1377, the population was down to 17,200. Because of its lack of drinking water, it grew slowly and had risen to only thirty-five thousand in 1527 when Spaniards and German mercenaries sacked the city, burning, pillaging, raping nuns, and mercilessly murdering men, women, and children. The imperishable city recovered from its cruel visitation, the physical scars faded, and within fifty years Rome was entering upon one of its most brilliant periods of building.

There were no newspapers in the modern sense, but the public never lacked information. Through *avvisi* (newsletters, public announcements, gossip sheets—all these terms fit the word) everything was revealed. Some *avvisi* were privately printed and sold in the streets or privately posted. Through *avvisi*, as well as by word of mouth, people heard of the murder of Count Francesco Cenci, the search for his slayers, the arrest of Lucrezia and her stepchildren, and their trials: the protracted examinations and torture and the torture of witnesses. Whatever leaked out or was stated officially—a massive tangle of fact and rumor—was passed along daily, many times a day, in the papal court, in government circles, in foreign embassies, in churches, convents, shops, and streets. The endless repetition deformed much of the truth. Additions and subtractions were freely made, and, as the apotheosis of Beatrice advanced, the villainous nature of her father was blackened—justifiably, it must be said, although Shelley, two centuries later, was chided for having made Francesco so uncompromisingly wicked in his play, *The Cenci*.

The family, an old one, claimed descent from Crescentius Centius. Francesco's father was a Monsignor Cristoforo Cenci (the name means rags in Italian), treasurer general of the Apostolic Chamber, deputy collector of tithes of the Papal States, canon of St. Peter's, director of the parish of San Tommaso dei Cenci, and as sly a peculator as one could imagine in that age of venality. His thievery was so great that his estate later had to restore thousands of scudi to the papal treasury. Cristoforo was not an ordained priest but a clerk (*chierico*), not authorized to say Mass, and not bound to celibacy. He died in the summer of 1562 after a deathbed marriage to Beatrice Arias, who had abandoned her legal husband many years before and gone to live with the unscrupulous nobleman in the gloomy old Palazzo Cenci, an undistinguished hulk of dark buildings still standing near the former Jewish Ghetto.

Beatrice Arias was the mother of Francesco. The Monsignor had had him legitimized and had named him his heir, and the delayed union with Beatrice, who had been recently widowed, was part of the process of giving the boy the security of a rightful name. Beatrice received a generous income for life and died in 1575. In the thirteen years of her double widowhood, she revealed an astonishing cunning. She remarried—her third husband was a lawyer of base origin—and boldly and adroitly practiced a nepotism that Cristoforo himself would have admired.

The boy Francesco, some months short of his thirteenth birthday when his father died, inherited one of the largest fortunes in Rome. It included the Palazzo Cenci and two other palazzi in Rome, as well as large tracts of farmland and forest, vineyards, villas, and whole villages, some of them in the Kingdom of Naples. Francesco was born with a violent disposition: At eleven he was tried before a criminal court for having clubbed and bloodied one Quintilio de Vetralla; at fourteen he was in trouble over a child he had fathered. He was so precocious sexually that his mother and his guardian, Monsignor Francesco Santacroce, arranged a match for him with the guardian's niece, Ersilia Santacroce. Ersilia died twenty years later in April 1584, two days after the birth of her twelfth child, who lived but five days. Of the eleven other children only seven lived beyond childhood.

How many children Francesco fathered "by contraband," as the Italians have it, was not known. If his mother and his guardian had expected marriage would cure the boy's insatiable sensual appetite, they were wrong. Rough, willful, a stranger to pity and remorse, he took his pleasure where he found it. He did not stop with girls and mature women: Males attracted him, and he was tried for sodomy in the Roman courts. In that age sodomy was equated with heresy and punishable by death at the stake, which Cenci escaped by paying large fines.

His rancor toward everybody was incurable. He was imprisoned in his own house and, for a time, at Petrella del Salto, for attacking defenseless servants and peasants; he cudgeled his sons, who stole from him and ran away from him. He never bothered to hide his sexual excesses from his family. His animal outbursts of rage terrified all within hearing. Those who knew him well loathed him as a lying bully. Ersilia, his childhood bride, alone seems to have tolerated him. When she died he felt her loss mainly because she had accepted him and been submissive. His mistress, Maria Pelli of Spoleto—La Bella Spoletina—was less obedient: She even brought an action against him for extreme cruelty.

Why Lucrezia Petroni, a thirty-eight-year-old widow and mother of nine children, decided to marry Francesco, as she did late in 1593, is not hard to understand: He was rich. But it was a fatal step. He insulted and beat her and held her prisoner in Rome and in the mountains.

Rome had always been a place of violence. Hare, listing the busts of eighty-three ancient Romans and their ladies in one room of the Capitoline Museum, noted that forty-three of the eighty-three persons represented in marble had been murdered. The sixteenth-century Cenci made notable contributions to the city's records of bloodshed: At nineteen, Rocco Cenci, as bellicose as his father, was killed in a duel by an illegitimate Orsini; Cristoforo, twenty-six, his brother, was murdered by his rival in a sordid love affair. (Paolo died of a fever at sixteen.)

Beatrice, seven when her mother died and sixteen when her father remarried, and her sister Antonina, four years older, spent their early years in a convent. Antonina, a girl of amiable nature, was happily married at twenty-one to Luzio Savelli of the great Roman family and died a year later in childbirth. While the sons sued their father to get money from him, and he countersued and accused them of thievery, Beatrice languished in the Palazzo Cenci and later at Petrella. Her father's behavior became more shameful, though there is no evidence that he had incestuous impulses. The charge of incest was suggested by Prospero Farinaccio, the Cenci lawyer, only a few weeks before the executions, almost in desperation it was thought. If Francesco had thought of raping his daughter, there was no way to prove it. But as he continually abused her verbally and physically—he beat her with a bull's pizzle—she roused the sympathy and desire of Olimpio Calvetti, the *castellano* at Petrella.

Olimpio was middle-aged, tall, handsome, strong, vain, and a hothead in the classic Italian manner. He had killed two men in two separate fights, but the age's system of criminal justice—the uncodified laws, the trials by torture, the cruel and illogical administration that allowed murderers to go unpunished while blasphemers or anyone who might make an offhand scurrilous remark about a priest was sent to the galleys—all this had left Olimpio a free man under the powerful protection of the Colonnas. He became Beatrice's lover, and when, having secretly given birth to a son, she continued to complain of Francesco's brutalities, Olimpio was easily persuaded to kill him. He enlisted the assistance of Marzio Catalano, a native of the village, who had been the count's coachman and remained in his employ from time to time.

At daybreak on September 9, 1598, they went to Cenci's bedroom, and Olimpio hit Francesco's head with a stonecutter's hammer, striking him repeatedly, while Catalano beat the count's shins with a rolling pin to prevent him from rising. They then clumsily hauled the body to a balcony, broke part of the protective railing to make it appear as if the count had had an accident, and dumped the mutilated corpse into the trees and shrubbery below. The two women disposed of the bloody bedsheets. The Cenci returned to Rome and went into mourning, but the murder was obvious, and in December Lucrezia and Beatrice and the sons were arrested.

We don't know when Clement VIII learned of the Cenci crime and the detention of Beatrice and the others. The pope had left Rome on April 12, 1598 to go to Ferrara, following the army of his nephew, Cardinal Pietro Aldobrandini, who had seized the city on the pretext that Cesare d'Este, heir apparent of Duke Alfonso II, was illegitimate. The annexation of the rich and beautiful city, one of the loveliest in all Italy in the sixteenth century, had caused great rejoicing in Rome, and when Clement departed from Ferrara at the end of November, preparations for a joyous celebration began.

Romans were never happier than when they were building triumphal arches, decorating balconies, and rehearsing elaborate ceremonies, and the work went on feverishly; but the pope took his time, and bad weather and bad roads held his progress to a crawl. It was December 20 when he reached the environs of Rome and halted. The skies were gray, the Tiber sullen and higher than usual.

In the morning great crowds came out to watch a long procession of clergy, the confraternities and city magistrates carrying to St. Peter's the consecrated Host, which Clement had sent on in advance of his train. In the afternoon he entered the city on horseback, attended by Cardinal Aldobrandini and another nephew, Giovanni, lately promoted to general in the papal army. The second procession included several cardinals, the Governor of Rome, all the monastic orders, the clergy of the parochial and collegiate churches, the canons of St. Peter's and the Lateran, choristers, officials of the Cancellaria and of the people, the militia, the District Leaders, the Keepers of the Archives, the senators, ambassadors, and many knights, court officers, and other eminent citizens.

The splendidly-arrayed throng moved down the Corso to the Palazzo di San Marco, now called Palazzo di Venezia, and turned west, passing the Jesuit's grand new church, the Gesu, and some blocks on, Sant'Andrea della Valle, traversing the streets beyond. As the procession crossed the Ponte Sant'Angelo, mortars and culverins were discharged, and fifes, trumpets, kettledrums, and tambourines sounded in a spirited show of victory. The pope reached St. Peter's at four o'clock. The Cenci, listening to the music and cannon fire and the roar of the populace, must have hoped that Clement would take pity on them.

Rain had fallen intermittently for days. Now it fell heavily, and the river rose rapidly as melting snows in the hills of Umbria and downpours along the Tiber's 250-mile course also fed it. The city's gay mood darkened as the waters, rising higher and higher, flowed into Rome bearing the bodies of drowned farm animals—oxen, horses, sheep—and of men, women, and children. Suddenly the flood arrived, and people scrambled to save themselves, running to the security of the hills and to rooftops, where they waited to be rescued.

Old houses collapsed; people—scores, hundreds of them—fell into the waters and drowned. Christmas Eve was a night of terror—dark, cold, wet—and Christmas a day of silence: no Masses, no celebrations, no church bells. The city bacame a lake, the river a brown torrent. Two arches of the Ponte Palatino, the ancient Pons Aemilius, which had been restored by Gregory XIII, were swept away. (The bridge is known today as Ponte Rotto—Broken Bridge.)

The death toll, never officially established, ranged from fourteen hundred to four thousand, the best authorities agreeing it was fifteen hundred. The loss of property, including wine, oil and food stores, clothing and furniture, was immeasurable. The people were very hungry, if not close to starvation, before Clement heroically moved in vast supplies of food. The waters subsided, good humor returned to the city, and the work of rebuilding began.

Interest in the Cenci case revived. In May, 1599, Olimpio was murdered—stabbed to death and beheaded—in the mountains at Cantalice, near Petrella, by two men who had been hired to remove him as a potentially dangerous witness against Monsignor Mario Guerra, an admirer of Beatrice's and a suspect in the plotting of her father's slaying. Catalano was arrested a short time later and brought to Rome. He confronted the Cenci, and their doom was sealed. Catalano was not very bright: neglected in prison and too weak or timid to protest his treatment, he slowly starved to death.

The trial of the Cenci seemed to go on interminably, ending only a week before the executions. Their chances for mercy lessened when the pope allowed Marcantonio Massimo to be beheaded on June 15. They suffered a second setback, as we learn from a letter sent from Rome to the court of Urbino relating that Andrea Caproni had been seized in the household of Duke Cesarini "for having dealt certain wounds to a brother of his own" and cynically adding that "these young men are imitating the sons of Francesco Cenci." Finally, news came from Subiaco on September 6 that on the previous day, Paolo Santacroce had killed his mother after having vilely slandered her when she refused to name him her heir. So much bloodletting among the nobles, though hardly new, disturbed Clement. The aristocracy was setting a bad example; His Holiness was in no mood for leniency. In the forty years since little Francesco had attacked Quintilio de Vetralla, the Cenci had been a plague.

The people knew this but had tender thoughts of Beatrice. They also knew that a verdict of guilty would permit the pope to seize the Cenci wealth. (After the executions Clement did, indeed, confiscate the Cenci properties, which included part of what is now the Villa Borghese. Partial restitution was made later to Bernardo and other Cenci heirs.) Beatrice and Lucrezia had been removed early in the summer from Castel Sant'Angelo to the Corte Savella prison in Via Monserrato, opposite the Church of Santa Maria di Monserrato. Until the eve of their execution, they had no definite knowledge of what was going to happen to them; but they expected the worst and made their wills.

On the evening of September 10, when Beatrice and Lucrezia had finished supper, the pope's courier arrived with the document that set forth the death sentence. Francesco Cenci is referred to as a "most wretched father" and a "most unhappy husband." The punishment of the Cenci would be an example to others who might be tempted to commit similar dastardly crimes.

Toward midnight the Comforters arrive at the Corte Savella and at the Tor di Nona where the brothers lie—eight members of the San Giovanni Decollato (St. John the Beheaded), a confraternity founded by the Florentines in Rome to attend the condemned in their final agony and to bury, in the grounds of their own tiny cloister, those who died friendless but penitent. The impenitent got rude treatment: Their cadavers were thrown into a ditch at the Muro Torto, a part of the Aurelian Wall near the Pincian Gate, where common prostitutes were buried. The brothers of the confraternity were highly respected men of austere principles. Michelangelo had been a Comforter. In their death duties, they wore black gowns girdled at the waist with rope, and tall black hoods pierced by two slits for the eyes; they carried lanterns at night and tablets on which were painted scenes of the Crucifixion. A handle on the tablet allowed it to be held before the face of the condemned, as he was exhorted to be resolute in his behavior and strong in his faith.

These Comforters were brave men of simple good will, but their mere presence induced terror, and no hapless Roman or stranger who chanced to meet them by moonlight or in the darkness of some echoing alley on their way to pray with a poor soul who was to die within the hour was likely ever to forget the encounter. One can imagine the brothers on that sultry September night in 1599 leaving their little church not far from the Teatro Marcello and walking along the riverbank to Ponte Sisto, where they veer away to follow the straight line of Via Giulia that will bring them to the prisons. They have not seen the terms of the court's sentence and assume that Bernardo is to die; but his age has saved him—he was only seventeen when the murder was committed.

One group of Comforters is admitted to the cell of the Cenci brothers. Bernardo has already heard that he will live. He joins Giacomo in prayers through the long sleepless night. They make their confessions, and at four thirty they hear Mass and receive Communion. The prayers go on, litanies without end, Pater Nosters and Aves, and special prayers, the story of the Passion and Death. Giacomo is grim. Bernardo weeps. Bernardo never stops weeping.

At the Corte Savella prison, the other Comforters attend Lucrezia and Beatrice. Prayers and exhortations: God is good, God is merciful. He is a forgiving God. He allowed his only begotten son to be tortured and killed for man's salvation. Coraggio! Soon you will be with Him in Paradiso. The women hear Mass at five thirty and make their confessions. They receive Communion and mumble prayers that seem drained of meaning.

At nine thirty, Giacomo and Bernardo are taken out of the Tor di Nona and placed in separate carts to be drawn through the streets. Giacomo has been stripped to the waist and heavily shackled. The sentence of the court has ordered public torture for him. The Comforters ride with him, praying and holding before his eyes a tablet bearing the Crucifixion scene. In a corner of the cart the executioner has set up a charcoal fire to heat his pincers. Bernardo rides alone, abandoned to his grief. Since dawn all Rome has been moving into this part of the city that lies in the bend of the river across from the ancient rust-colored Castel Sant'Angelo.

The carts inch forward, and the executioner withdraws from the coals the pincers and grips Giacomo's flesh, tearing at the muscles and tendons. Giacomo screams. Women moan and sob or turn away. Giacomo screams again, and Bernardo faints. Men close to the carts make threatening noises and seem as if they would shoulder their way past the soldiers and rescue the brothers. Fear and their own morbid curiosity hold them back; such a melancholy proceeding as this must go on. There is anger in the hearts of the people and a profound hatred for Clement VIII, who is permitting such shameful punishment.

Word passes that he has left the Quirinale and gone to San Giovanni in Laterano to say a Low Mass for the Cenci in private. The people mutter curses against him, even as they pray for the Cenci. "Poor souls," they murmur. "Poor, wretched folk." But this is Rome, where a man's spiritual salvation is the first consideration: Innocent or guilty, the Cenci will have happy deaths within the shelter of the church.

The carts roll through the narrow streets, past elegant palazzi and humble dwellings, past silent convents and churches and heavily-shuttered burrow-like shops. People stand at windows and on balconies and roofs to watch the grisly exhibition. At the head march the Brothers of the Stigmata, "unshod, with Apostolic sandals," as a contemporary writer describes them, "clad in cassocks of ordinary serge of ash color, with a heavy rope for girdle and attached to the girdle a crown of thorns of wood." Behind the monks presses a great and varied swarm—pious companies and confraternities, sad voices raised in prayer as they trudge solemnly along, and then more detachments of soldiers and men and women, girls and boys, a formless rabble united by unspeakable sorrow. Their feet stir up clouds of yellow dust that hangs in the windless air.

The doleful procession moves through Via dell'Orso, Via del Giglio, crosses Piazza dell'Apollinaire, passes Tor Sanguigna and Piazza Navona and the ancient mutilated sculpture called Pasquino, and goes on past the Palazzo della Cancellaria, which contains the Church of San Lorenzo in Damaso, where Bernardo had been baptized. It flows sluggishly to the Piazza Farnese and into Via di Santa Maria di Monserrato to the Corte Savella prison and halts. Sweat rolls down the faces of the marchers. Their clothes are drenched. Lucrezia and Beatrice are brought out and join the procession on foot, the frightened women attended by four Comforters and propelled almost involuntarily forward, as the shuffling throng moves toward the piazza in a cloud of saffron dust.

Many of the occupants of the palazzi and houses abandon the security and comfort of their posts and join the people in the street.

Another stop is made at a chapel where it is the custom to allow condemned persons to attend their own Requiem Mass. Giacomo, bloody and torn and unable to stand, is carried inside and sees his sister and his stepmother for the last time. Bernardo is weeping. Outside the people wait patiently, listening to the chanting, the Dies irae, the prayers for the dead.

The weather is stifling, a relentlessly hot Roman summer day. Women recite their rosaries or talk about Beatrice. They have heard much about her, but few have ever seen her. They talk about her youth—some think she is only sixteen or seventeen—and her beauty, grace, and courageous bearing. Letters written to various courts of Italy—to Modena, Urbino, Ferrara—after the execution all praise the girl's virtue and public behavior. The records of the trial reveal her arrogance and insolence, but the spectators don't know this; and if they had heard anything unfavorable to her, they would be inclined to disbelief.

A scaffold stands in the center of the piazza ringed by solid ranks of soldiers. The bridge has been closed, but a horde of men and women, approaching from Trastevere and the Borgo, have destroyed the barriers by the weight of their numbers, dispersing the guards and pressing forward. In search of good points from which to watch the executions, some climb the parapets and either lose their footing or are pushed off the bridge into the water. Seven or eight drown.

The rooftops and balconies overlooking the piazza are packed, and the crowd is backed up into all the surrounding streets. Castel Sant'Angelo bristles with the heads of the living: Bastions, towers, outworks are fringed with them. Figures cluster at the highest points. The babble of voices swells, the low hubbub becomes a low rumble, a restrained roar. The people grow impatient. The pressure of those in the far reaches of the crowd who cannot see mounts steadily. The heat, the stink of dirty clothes and unwashed bodies, the suppressed emotions crying for release—anger and sorrow and anxiety and frustration, the pitiless sun, hunger and thirst—are too much. Hundreds of men and women collapse. Women scream, men shout. The din rising along the old river is the voice of love and hatred and despair—the voice of a people who could unfeelingly count the lashes an offender publicly received stretched on the *cavaletto* and in a moment applaud a passing cardinal, who could stop the punishment with a wave of his hand.

At last there is a movement in the piazza, and silence falls on the spectators and on all Rome. Bernardo is being taken from the chapel to the scaffold. He is weeping as he is led to a seat from which he will watch his brother, sister, and stepmother die. A wail of sympathy comes from the people, falls away, and rises again as the crowd catches sight of Lucrezia. She totters. The Comforters keep her on her feet, as she slowly mounts the steps of the scaffold. *Povera donna*! There is no color in her face, her body goes limp. She is stretched out on the bench, her head on the block, and the axe falls. Her head drops into a heavy wicker basket. Then the body and head are carried to the ground at the foot of the scaffold.

Bernardo has swooned. He faints again as he watches his lovely golden-haired sister draw near. She is wearing a long-sleeved turquoise dress, a purple underskirt, a turquoise veil on her head and white velvet slippers with red cords. She crosses the piazza in silence, unmoved by the tears and sobs and prayers of the people. To some she appears already to have departed life. She looks out over the immense blur of faces, and a cry starts up, low at first, then mounting in anguish in the burning air. Quietly she extends her body and the axe falls.

Now comes the most horrifying moment in the long, hideous business. Giacomo, weakened by torture, a mutilated, pitiful creature, is brought forward on his cart. He passes the headless bodies of his sister and Lucrezia. The indefatigable Comforters support his ravaged body. From the scaffold he speaks, summoning the last of his sobbing strengths: Bernardo, he says, is innocent. As if the effort to utter these last words is too much for him, he crumples to his knees and extends his body, his head on the block.

But this is to be no simple death. Cruelty has no bounds; the people must be taught a stern lesson. The hooded, brawny, bloodstained executioner raises a sledge and brings it down with all his strength on Giacomo's skull, crushing it into a pulp. Then he and his assistants are on the body, hacking and cutting, slitting the throat, removing the shapeless head, and quartering the trunk. They hang the revolting mess on hooks protruding from the upper framework of the scaffold.

The Confraternities form a line and begin reciting a litany. The Court, the ministers of justice, the soldiers slowly depart, and Bernardo is conducted back to the Tor di Nona prison. He will go to the galleys at Civitavecchia, but these are galleys that do not go to sea. The pope has no navy. His galleys are prison hulks.

The piazza is still jammed, and people come closer, weep anew, and pray, as girls lay fresh flowers at the women's heads. When leave is granted for the removal of the remains, Giacomo's parts are lowered and laid out *in figura* on a stretcher and carried to San Giovanni Decollato, a mile away. In the evening the broken body is delivered to his relatives and, in accordance with his wish, interred in San Tommaso dei Cenci, where his murdered father is buried. Relatives of Lucrezia claim her corpse, and the Companions of the Stigmata carry her to San Gregorio della Divina Pieta, not far from the Palazzo Cenci.

The body of Beatrice still lies on its bier at the scaffold's foot. All through the afternoon the curious and the morbid wander through the piazza, fascinated by what has happened and reluctant to go away and once more pick up their lives. As the afternoon wanes and Castel San'Angelo is suffused with the light of the setting sun, the piazza begins filling with people. Swifts dart in the cooling air. Members of the Confraternities, bands of tonsured, sandalled monks, notables in carriages, peasants and foreigners, pay a last visit to the spot where Beatrice lies.

At last it is time for the funeral. The shrines to the Madonna, the only street illumination in the city, have been lighted. In the darkness of the piazza, candles flicker and torches flare, and as the Brothers of the Stigmata shoulder the bier, a high tenor voice breaks the quiet with the *Dies irae*. Others take up the sad music, as the assemblage sets in motion.

The brothers walk to Via Giulia and plod south with tears and lamentations, followed by chanting monks and priests, men and women telling their rosaries, childhood friends of Beatrice grieving for the lost young life. They pass the dark, silent palazzi and churches, the tall garden wall of Palazzo Farnese, and come to the Tiber. Still singing and praying, they cross Ponte Sisto to Trastevere and start the tortuous climb up the steep tree-lined Via del Janiculum to San Pietro in Montorio, where Beatrice had asked to be buried.

The bier is set down in the center of the little church, but the people do not disperse. There are still tears to shed, prayers to be said, and flowers to be placed in the church amid the freshly-lighted candles. The middle of the night passes, another litany is recited, and another, and now the air is tranquil.

Peace lies over the church and the ancient hill, and in the stillness the mourners start down the slope. When all but a few have departed, the body is lowered into a grave in the apse. By its side the head is placed on a silver platter.

CHAPTER 20

Bomarzo: a Garden of Stone Monsters

*A*t one of the highest points on the winding road between Poggibonsi and Volterra—a curve where all but the most maniacal of Italian drivers must slow their pace—there is a sign so charming in its simplicity that one smiles. *Admire the beautiful towers of San Gimignano*, it says; and there, far away beyond the vineyards, the patches of pine forest, the red tile roofs of farmhouses, and the shimmering olive groves, rise the medieval towers of the old town—thirteen now, where once there were seventy-six.

Memories of the Tuscan landscape are always sunlit, the skies blue even when one remembers rain and dampness and winter's chill. The mind accepts days of scuffling winds and dead fogs and frost as it accepts the region's turbulent history, comprehending it all as part of Tuscany—of Florence and Siena, Lucca and Pisa, the hill towns and fruitful valleys. Tuscany is orderly. It is neatly catalogued, explained in books. Its past has been examined; it has no secrets. Like the *belli torri* of San Gimignano, it is there to be admired and enjoyed.

Tuscany was on my mind one October day when we drove out of Rome and headed north on the Autostrada to go to the Gardens of Bomarzo. We had read about the gardens and their fantastic sculptures, and we kept telling ourselves that if the gardens had been in Tuscany they would hardly have been abandoned and almost forgotten for several centuries. Resident Englishmen or Americans would have found them out.

But Bomarzo is a good many miles south of Tuscany in a relatively obscure corner of Latium. It is fifty miles north of Rome and a dozen miles northeast of Viterbo, a papal stronghold in the Middle Ages. Although Viterbo thrived, especially in the nineteenth century, and the extensive Etruscan remains in the area—and the Renaissance villas of the Monte Cimini—all attracted visitors, Bomarzo declined. (Sacheverell Sitwell, an authority on the Baroque, had called the gardens of the Villa Lante, a few miles west of Bomarzo at Bagnaio, the most enchanting spot in Italy, if not in the world).

The few travelers who passed that way seem to have ignored the narrow, steep, and stony town of Bomarzo; and, having no reason to go there, they missed the Orsini villa and the Parco dei Mostri, or Park of the Monsters, as it is now known. In a way this was all to the good, for the years of neglect and the absence of the precise sort of information we have come to expect in Italy deepened the mystery of Bomarzo and imparted to the gardens a sinister aspect that good care and a constant flow of visitors would long ago have softened if not altogether dispelled.

The park dates only from the late Renaissance—sometime after 1561, it is thought. It is the Renaissance of gibbous dwarfs and drunken buffoons, crooked minds and grossly humorous distortions, and Bomarzo has been called a gigantic jest. If it is, it is an unsettling jest that cannot be accurately defined or catalogued. It calls for an explanation, but the explanations that have been advanced are shaky, having the air of improvised footnotes.

I don't think it is the statues themselves, bizarre as they are, that trouble the mind of the beholder who walks among them or in the tangle of woodland below the villa. They are no more repellent than many monumental pieces to be seen in the Orient and in Mexico, Yucatan, and South America, and they reveal far less inventiveness than Gothic grotesques. The difference is that, whereas we have a reasonably good idea about the others, Bomarzo's works continue to puzzle us.

We can believe in the reality of a Gothic devil, because the whole array of Gothic figures in sculptured art has a gaily mocking quality. There is no evil in a grinning gargoyle; but Bomarzo suggests an evil presence, an invisible wickedness emanating from an inexplicable past. There is a hint of depravity. Else why on earth were these figures carved out of the massive volcanic boulders strewn up and down the harsh landscape!

An Argentine writer, Manuel Mujica Lainez, found his own answer, first in a novel titled *Bomarzo* that became a best-seller, and later in a six-part text in prose and verse that Alberto Ginastera, his fellow-countryman, used for a cantata and the libretto of his opera. Lainez, who had read about Bomarzo, visited the gardens and came away seeing the place as a Freudian autobiography of the gardens' creator, whom he pictured as a weak and savage hunchback, tormented in body and spirit, living a life of violence and sexual aberration, finding an outlet of sorts in a park of monsters. This highly-imaginative fictive approach may libel an innocent man, whose motives in constructing the gardens could very likely have been merely a desire to be ingenious and amusing at a time when he and some of his contemporaries had tired of the splendid formalities of the handsome garden layouts of Giacoma da Vignola, with their cascades and fountains, nymphs and grottoes.

Anyway, all that we actually know is that Bomarzo sprang from the brain of Pier Francesco Orsini, Duke of Bomarzo, called by some authorities Prince Vicino Orsini. He was the husband of Giulia Farnese, the niece of another Giulia Farnese who was also married to an Orsini and was the mistress of the Borgia Pope, Alexander VI. The Bomarzo Giulia, or Julia, has been described as a virtuous and generous woman, greatly beloved by her husband, who had his own and her initials, intertwined in pleasing designs, placed throughout the villa. He also built in the gardens a small lovely classical termple, which was to have been her mausoleum but never was used.

Who carved the figures? One story is that the work was done by Turkish prisoners of war taken by the Venetian-Spanish-Papal forces that defeated the Turks at the great naval battle of Lepanto on October 7, 1571. This account is embedded in Orsini family history, but there is no evidence that it is true.

The gardens are owned by the commune of Bomarzo, which charges a small admission. We had made inquiries in the town, and on our arrival at the estate we found a dirt road that led off the main road from the Orsini villa to an open space used as a parking lot. The entrance to the park, a few rods away, was reached by another road, a mere trace of ancient wagon ruts in the weeds. The whole place, including the guard's shelter, had an air of poverty and neglect, and matters had not improved since weekend visitors—mainly from Rome, one suspects—had started coming there. Italians are ardent picnickers who invariably leave evidence of their hearty eating, and there was considerable litter.

The statues have been exposed to the weather so long that they have an eroded look, and those in the shade have an accumulation of thick moss at their bases. Some of the statues are unmistakably Oriental, particularly one of a lioness fighting a dragon for possession of her cubs. The dragon's fierce expression—its mouth is open, its eyes bulge, and its face is a mass of wrinkles—is like that of a Chinese or Japanese theatrical mask. I'm not sure that this proves anything. The Italians had a heritage of carved monsters: the griffin, half-lion and half-eagle out of Greek mythology (griffins may be seen, couchant, outside the duomo at Ferrara); and the chimera, an even more extravagant product of the Greeks, a she-monster with the head of a lion, a goat's body, and a dragon's or serpent's tail.

There are full-breasted, round-bellied mermaids at Bomarzo, one wearing the headdress of a Javanese dancer, another with massive scaled legs spread in an enormous split at right angles to her upright body. There is a huge elephant, and a colossal naked man who is tearing apart a screaming girl. The elephant, bearing on its back a howdah that resembles a medieval fortress, looks as harmless as a circus beast until one walks in front of it and sees that it is strangling a Roman warrior in its trunk.

The homicidal giant is shocking, mainly because there is nothing to prepare us for his horrifying display of strength. We glimpse him first in profile, his head and shoulders rising above a protective railing that runs along the top of a wooded hollow. His gaze, turned from us, appears fixed on a noisy brook below, where the sun, falling through the foliage, showers spangles of gold. From this elevation there is a serenity in his great head; but when we descend a path to his feet, look upwards, and see his muscular nakedness and the helpless girl, the full power of his ferocity is shattering. Her head rests on the ground, and her legs reach up to the burly shoulders. It is the idiot blankness of the man's face that is numbing. He feels nothing as, with no apparent effort or any savage intent or anger, he blindly obeys an instinct to kill.

Elsewhere in the gardens there are a three-headed dog, mammoth pine cones, fluted vases, luxuriant bursts of stony vegetation, and the

John Ferris

heads of ogres and animals with gaping mouths that one can enter. There is also a massive stone pool in the midst of a formal court, overgrown with weeds and partly hidden by thickets at the time of our visit. Finally, there are small pornographic carvings here and there that may have stimulated the duke's guests or simply amused them.

Strolling among the statues, trying vainly to pierce the mystery, one imagines that first night, four hundred years ago, when the owner of Bomarzo led the members of his rural court and his guests from the villa to show off the monsters. Fiery torches illuminate the weird scene as the elegantly-clad men and their ladies—the virtuous dames, the sweet flirts, the courtesans—troop down the hill. How astonished they must have been! What squealings and cries of horror or delight filled the night as the bright procession moved among the hideous shadows!

What happened in the years before the gardens fell into disuse—they were rediscovered early in the twentieth century—is conjecture of a very unsatisfactory kind. Our knowledge of the duke is fragmentary: The little that has been turned up shows him to have been a man troubled by the mysteries of life and death. We need not care too much; he could well have been tortured by nightmares of violence, sex, and anxiety. In any case, it is not illogical to assume that the creator of a garden of monsters was a monster himself.

All the way back to Rome, by way of Viterbo and the old *stradale normale* that runs down from Siena, we talked of the gardens. The mystery nagged us. Then for no reason at all, except that it was on the dark side of life, I thought of the church of the Cappuccini in Via Veneto and the old monk inviting us to make ourselves at home.

So, among his own horrors, the duke may have greeted his guests.

CHAPTER 21

Catacombs . . . The Seven Sleepers . . . Columbaria

We drove late one September morning to Lake Albano and from the highest point of the old crater looked across the water to Castel Gandolfo. Afterward we went to Lake Nemi and talked indifferently of the cruel story of the goddess Diana and her worship, and of her priest, killer and killed: that strange, lonely murderer, stalking to slay a man who had stalked and slain his predecessor. Killer became priest became victim in gory timeless succession. Moved by the impressive legend, Sir James Frazer wrote *The Golden Bough*.

It was autumn, but the midday sun was hot when we left Nemi and went to Velletri, where we sat at a cafe table in a pleasant bower of ripening figs and talked about how it was at this time of year at home, and of long weekends in the house in Litchfield County, Connecticut. We had an old chunk stove there that took fire briskly, and when the first signs of pink showed on its little round belly we always turned the damper to hold the flames down. Dusk came early to the Connecticut valley, while the hilltops still were orange and scarlet and yellow and the copper beeches turned their leaves in the waning light.

Mourning warblers fluttered across the empty stubble field. The gate to the rose garden was closed, and all the elms stood naked, plundered by winds that came in the night. Summer was going quickly, leaving only the signatures of long hot days: withered purple loosestrife in the doorsill jar, a stain of strawberries on the white duck pants. On the mantelpiece the broken clock, the stubs of straw-hat theater tickets.

Autumn and its scowling days, blue-and-rust days, and days when the shadows under the larches were invested with golden tints, the white ash trembled, and the fox walked alone upon the hill. Days of raw wet winds thrashing the soft compliant limbs of willow and fir. Autumn in New York: the bright expectancy, and in a few weeks, frosty stars.

But we shook off the temptation to go home and stayed on in Rome; and one day, All Souls' Day, November 2, we drove down to the southern catacombs, through Porta Sebastiano and past the Church of Domine, Quo Vadis to the entrance to San Calixtus. Many people stood around, and two touring buses were parked at the roadside. We had come this far several times before, but we never went below ground, and now we turned away.

Our interest in the catacombs was slight, a vestige of youthful instruction. They had been places of wonder blessed by heroic men who resembled Peter and Paul and prayed in divers tongues, principally Latin and Greek. The rituals of these primitive Christians were not wholly strange to us, for in them we could see the soft outlines of our own Mass and other forms of worship that we knew.

What impressed us was the fact that these solemn activities went on underground: that these poor hunted men and women who spurned the pagan gods had hollowed out of the solid earth galleries where they met secretly. We were fascinated by their burrowings—sweaty, patient, tireless creatures working away in the gloom, believers in the resurrection of the body, laying their dead in narrow tombs chiseled and scraped out of the volcanic rock. They buried small personal properties with the dead, whom they knew would wish to look well on Judgment Day; and they decorated the tombs with pious inscriptions and symbols, marked them with the names of the occupants, and painted frescoes in enduring colors. The catacombs were a part of Roman history we had studied attentively, but it did not follow that when the opportunity came to see them we should feel a duty to do so.

A companion piece to the story of the catacombs was one taken from the *Liber Miraculorum* (Book of Miracles) of St. Gregory of Tours. It was called *The Seven Sleepers of Ephesus* and recounted the fate of seven brothers who were converted to Christianity during the persecution of Decius in 250 AD. Fleeing from a band of the emperor's soldiers, they took refuge in a cave. The soldiers blocked the cave entrance with big stones, but the brothers, fortified by their belief in the resurrection, went to sleep. It was a long sleep, lasting nearly two hundred years. In the year 447, vhen Theodosius II was emperor, the brothers awoke and came forth into the light of a fresh new world that now was Christian.

If the purpose in giving us the story was to strengthen our faith, it failed. It was the cave, the underground, we found memorable.

The catacombs were ransacked by the Goths under Vitiges in 537, and again by the Lombards in 755. Pope Paul I in 757 began to remove the bodies to various churches within the city, and Pascal I followed his example on a larger scale in 817.

This practice went on under Sergius II (844) and Leo IV (847). All bodies found in the catacombs were now regarded as those of martyrs, and relic hunters did much devastation, carrying away whatever they could lay hands on. After the ninth century the catacombs, entirely neglected, were forgotten and their position lost with one exception: the *sotteranea* of San Sebastiano ad Catacumbas.

Seven hundred years passed before the catacombs came once more to the public mind. On May 31, 1578, some workmen digging in a vineyard off Via Salaria, two miles beyond the walls, uncovered a Christian catacomb. Rome was excited, but no official action was taken. The workmen were allowed to despoil the crypts, and eventually all traces of the catacombs disappeared.

The interest wakened by the Via Salaria excavation rekindled the people's curiosity, and scholars, pursuing the subject through ancient writings, showed the way to new discoveries. Openings to subterranean cemeteries, hidden for centuries by displaced earth and wild undergrowth, were entered and explored. In London, in 1599, Antony Munday published a book about the catacombs that was likely to deter many of those eager to see them: There was a risk of getting lost, Munday wrote, and never being found alive. To prevent such accidents, Munday continued, people tied themselves to a line.

The terror of being lost underground was described by Padre Antonio Bosio, the pioneer of catacomb explorations. Padre Bosio made his first visit to a catacomb on December 10, 1593, in the company of friends. They went too far, lost their way, and their lights burned out.

"I began to fear," Padre Bosio said after his rescue, "that I should defile by my vile corpse the sepulchre of the martyrs."

Undaunted, though, by the dreadful experience, Bosio went on for thirty years exploring the catacombs, earning for himself the happy title of "Columbus of the underground new world."

One result of the scholarly research was to explain the etymology of the word "catacomb." It came from two Greek words meaning "down" and "hollow" that were first applied to the conformation of the ground of the cemetery at San Sebastiano. The full title of the place was Cemiterium ad Catacumbus, or Cemetery in the Hollow. "Catacombs" was easily substituted for "cemetery," thus becoming the place and not merely a descriptive tag. So the word catacomb, first applied to an obscure Roman burial place, was given to burial places everywhere, even in lands ruled by the infidels.

Normally tolerant and understanding, Lanciani and his master, De Rossi, were distressed and sometimes outraged by the way the catacombs had been desecrated and robbed. Nothing of any great intrinsic value had been taken: no large pieces of precious jewelry, nothing but homely trinkets, since the dead, with few exceptions, were poor. But to an archeologist there are no trifles, everything has meaning: the object itself, where it is found, its position in relation to other things put there many centuries ago. The Goths and Lombards had taken much, but much had remained, and more had been removed by visiting strangers and the Romans themselves in the early Middle Ages. Even in the early nineteenth century the men authorized to explore the catacombs were insufficiently-trained archeologists. It was not until late in the century that De Rossi published his *Roma Sotteranea* and laid down the rules for scientific examination of the underground burial grounds.

Lanciani listed the things most commonly stolen out of greed, or the innocent wish to own a relic, something of spiritual value because of its association with the dead: cameos and rings; glass bowls or phials which had contained blood or wine; coins, medal lions, bronze statuettes, amphoras and lamps. Pieces of the wall were cut away, frescoes rudely torn and carried off to be framed in glass in a distant French or Bavarian church or monastery.

Still, there was a great deal to be explored. The catacombs had been carefully planned and built by Romans. The supervisors of the work were skilled to some degree in engineering, and the *fossores* or diggers were patient, honest workers. The catacombs were achieved through cooperation. The Christians owned the land, which had come to them either from a rich landowner as a gift or in an exchange of money, and the partakers of the deal were usually members of a burial society. The dues or outright contributions made by members were small.

The places might be hazardous labyrinths to latter-day explorers, but the builders of the catacombs followed a design that was flawless, so far as they were concerned. Measurements were exact; no waste of space could be tolerated. The ceilings were eight feet high, the passageways from three to five feet wide. The *fossores* meticulously avoided trespassing on adjacent properties and so, having completed their digging, were forced to construct a new catacomb below the first when the graves of the first were filled. One catacomb, explored in Lanciani's day, was six levels deep.

Upward of fifty separate catacombs, most of them of limited extent, have been discovered. There is one, for example, under Sant'Agnese fuori le Mura, far out on Via Nomentana. Closer to Porta Pia, in a back street off Via Nomentana, is another very small one with an entrance through a house. We lived near that one once for several months, but it did not occur to us to have a look at it. The catacombs were never dug at random: The builders chose places where no underground springs, plentiful in Rome, would flood the galleries, and on ground high enough to remain dry in wet weather.

The total length of the galleries explored by the end of the nineteenth century was over six hundred miles, and the number of the dead exceeded six million. The patrons of the catacombs had no reason to doubt the security of their resting places; their graves would be inviolate. They had no idea that, as Christians persecuted by the pagan emperors, they were working toward sainthood; and they had no inkling that the status of martyr and saint conferred upon them by the early popes would lead to the rude invasion of their peaceful cemeteries—that they would be taken from their snug earthy beds and carried off to a Roman church or one more distant in France, the Netherlands, or Germany. Yet that is what happened.

By the end of the sixth century, Rome had ceased to be the legal and political center of the world, but Christianity had survived. The church was triumphant, and those pilgrimages began that have never stopped. In numbers ever larger, pilgrims flowed down to Rome from the north or came by ship from the east. It was not the glories of empire that attracted them, but the holy places associated with Peter, Paul, and the other martyrs. The universal heritage of Roman law, art, and thought was of less account than the story of the simple fisherman of Galilee and the Roman Jew, Saul of Tarsus, who became Paul, the mighty propagandist and interpreter of the new faith; and the lives of Cecilia and Agnes, Lawrence and Sebastian, and many others, not very well known then and now virtually unknown outside church writing and church frescoes.

There is a story that Nero was furious when he learned that Peter had been crucified upside down. The emperor's arch enemy had escaped his hands; Nero had envisioned the man's death only after the most frightful tortures he could devise. Today when we think of Christians condemned to death, we commonly limit the type of execution to a few forms: beheading, crucifixion, burning at the stake, and mangling by wild beasts. But the sight of Christians, wrapped in animal skins and furs, being torn apart by famished lions could cease to satisfy a vicious nature; decapitation took but a swish of the sword; and turning an oil-soaked man into a flaming torch was effective only after dark.

To see how far cruelty could go, one ought to visit San Stefano Rotondo and study the frescoes. Unfortunately the church has been *in restauro* for some years, and because of the danger of collapse it is closed to the public. But permission to enter may be granted if one knows the right person to ask. Augustus Hare calls the interior "exceedingly curious architecturally." It is 133 feet in diameter, with a double circle of granite columns, thirty-six in the outer and twenty in the inner series, enclosing two tall Corinthian columns, with two pilasters supporting a cross wall. In the center is a kind of temple with relics of Stephen, whose body lies elsewhere.

The frescoes fix themselves indelibly on the memory of the beholder, starting with the Crucifixion, with two of the Holy Innocents who suffered death in Herod's massacre lying at the foot of the cross, one on each side. Touching, yes, but what follows is, in Hare's word, revolting—the torture and death of hundreds of men and women condemned by seventeen emperors, from Nero to Julian the Apostate. These are not scenes of savage behavior drawn from feverish imaginations; they are, insofar as we can judge, meant to be literal representations of the deaths of real men and women, based on accounts of those who witnessed them, or on the word of others who learned of them from those who did. The victims are identified, and all are called saint.

Here is Peter, crucified; Paul, beheaded; Vitale, burned alive; Thecla, tossed by a bull; Gervase, beaten to death; and John, boiled in oil. Here is Domitilla, roasted alive; Lucia, thrown into a well of serpents; Catherine of Alexandria, broken on the wheel; Agatha, her breasts cut off. The horrors seem endless: Peter, Bishop of Alexandria, and forty soldiers left to die, up to their waists in a frozen lake; death by roasting on a grid or in a red hot chair or by a brazen bull; death by crushing between two stones; Erasmus, laid in a coffin into which boiling lead was poured. Men are torn apart by wild horses or dragged through the streets by wild horses. There are burnings, stabbings, beheadings, drownings, and more.

It was no wonder that pilgrims, already familiar with stories of martyrdom, prayed to those brave souls to intercede for them before the throne of God. They looked for relics, however small, to take home with them. Rome provided them with relics, genuine and fake. Rome offered them guidebooks to churches and catacombs, and some of the pilgrims, reluctant to leave, stayed on and even started small colonies—the English, for example, settling near St. Peter's, in what was to be called the Borgo.

But such a simple relic as a saint's finger or a lock of hair could not satisfy bishops and abbots, whose new and flourishing communities demanded nothing less than a whole cadaver or, at the least, a saint's head. Only the best would do. Thus in all innocence and piety began that extraordinary period of trafficking in the bodies of martyrs. Records of transactions that took place often reveal an incredible spirit of venality. Men, obsessed with the desire to procure a body, entangled themselves, or became entangled, in a net of lying, cheating treachery by the unscrupulous agents, monks, or courtiers they employed. Bodies were switched in transit, identifications falsified. Not every man was dishonest, but there were enough who believed the end justified any means to give the business a bad name.

So the cajoling, the threats, the bribery and swindling went on and eventually ran their course. Pope Gregory the Great told the story of two Greek monks who came to Rome and lived for a while with other Greek monks on the Palatine. One night the two newcomers went to a field near San Paolo fuori le Mura and dug out the skeletons of four men who had been buried there. The monks put the bones in four bags and carried them back to Rome. After some time had passed, these two monks prepared to return to Greece to sell the bones; but they were halted at one of the gates and arrested, and the bones were restored to the field where they belonged.

The popes were under pressure to release bodies. Gregory had to write a letter in the most delicate diplomatic language to the Empress Constantia refusing her request for the head of St. Paul. Dreadful, unspeakable punishments from Heaven befell those who wrongly disturbed the holy dead, the pope wrote. He promised to send her a piece of cloth that had been placed near the saint's body long enough to be imbued with influence.

Until the third century BC, the Romans buried their dead. Cremation then became the custom and lasted until the second century AD, when interment of the body again became the fashion. The ashes of the cremated were placed in urns and the urns deposited in private vaults, in graves, or in columbaria. A columbarium was a building, the inner walls of which were lined with niches for urns. Columbaria were often built on speculation, and space was sold just as space was sold to individuals or to burial societies in the vast cemeteries that lay beyond the old Servian Wall. Some columbaria held several thousand urns. The graves were deep—one where the coffin of Cicero's daughter was found was twenty-four feet deep. As burial was forbidden in the city, the area outside became an incredible necropolis, a city of the dead covering hundreds of acres, a ghostly land filled with no fewer than three hundred thousand shelters for the ashes and skeletal remains of millions of people.

It was once generally thought that the spaced tombs along Via Appia were typical of Roman planning, but Lanciani said that these tombs were only the front line of a massive jumble of marble and granite, where the end never seemed in sight to the bewildered wanderer. Christians believed in the resurrection of the body, when it would be reunited with the soul. The pagans believed that death was the release of the immortal spirit; the body was gone for all time. They sometimes expressed their feelings—anger, regret, sorrow at partings, and so on—on their grave stones. Some stones carried concise but remarkably full biographies of the deceased, in a manner that would have pleased Mr. Leopold Bloom as he walked in Glasnevin Cemetery at the funeral of Paddy Jignam. Good idea if they were identified, thought Bloom . . . commercial traveler, a woman who made good Irish stews. Saucepan on her head.

Before these huge cemeteries disappeared, the Roman authorities put men to work copying thousands of the names on tombstones, the biographies and the sentiments of outrage or resignation. Who were these people who had once filled the land? Tradesmen and soldiers, charioteers, gladiators, statesmen, prostitutes, philosophers and priests, lawyers, tailors, freedmen, slaves and poets, cattle drovers, farmers, sculptors, artists and artisans, teachers and consuls, engineers, singers, bath attendants, road builders, painters, grain dealers and sailors, river boatmen, low comedians, and the great Caesar himself, a shade, one with Cassius and Cato—knaves and heroes, gentle Augustus and unspeakable Messalina.

Some, of course, more than most make the extra effort not to be forgotten. Gaius Cestius, a rich praetor, tribune of the plebs, and member of the college of Septemviri Epulones, who had charge of solemn banquets, built himself a magnificent tomb of marble, in which his ashes were placed when he died in 43 BC. Pyramidal in form, 121 feet high and one hundred feet square at the base, it rose in a thinly-forested spot on the road to Ostia, just beyond the Aventine, where it could be seen and admired, as it has been for more than two thousand years, though its shiny white marble had been darkened by the grime of centuries before engraver Piranesi first saw it in the eighteenth century, sprouts of vegetation clinging to its sides.

Although Cestius was a man of quality, he was no fashion setter in tombs. The pyramidal form of sepulchre never caught on among the

Romans. Few people, of course, could afford tombs, and, as we have seen, most were quite happy to look forward to a small funerary urn in a niche of a columbarium where, possibly, their ashes would be secure in the company of friends—the incarcerated remains of childhood playmates, old lovers, and friends.

These simple arrangements would hardly do for emperors and the very wealthy, compelled by custom to put on a better show. So it was in the reign of Augustus that Quintus Metellus Creticus raised to his beloved daughter Cecilia a massive circular tomb sixty-six feet in diameter, on the Via Appia. In the thirteenth century the Caetani, one of the warring families of the Middle Ages, desecrated the tomb, turning it into a keep for the castle they had built nearby. In spite of this savage treatment, the tomb survives in all its marmoreal beauty.

Two miles farther down the road stands another round tomb, the largest on the Via Appia. It dates from the Republic and is known as the Casal Rotondo. It is said to have been erected to the memory of the poet Messala Corvinus by his son, Valerius Maximus Cotta. The diameter of its base is 120 feet. It is more than an ancient tomb: Somebody lives on its lofty summit in a small house with an olive garden. There is also a washline, that tell-tale Italian sign of habitation: wet clothes drying in the sun.

Homely and odd as the state of the Casal Rotondo may be—it was long ago stripped of its marble sheath—it doesn't bear comparison to the striking changes that overtook the Mausoleum of Augustus, built in 28 BC. Its diameter is 292 feet. In the Middle Ages, another of those bellicose Roman families, the Colonna, seized the tomb and turned it into a fortress. Later it was despoiled of its travertine, and in 1780 its interior was transformed into an amphitheater for entertainments. Still later it became a concert hall and was used as such until 1936.

In Lanciani's *Pagan and Christian Rome*, we read one of the saddest stories in the annals of Roman archeology. It began, for Lanciani, in the early morning of May 12, 1889, when he was called to witness the opening of a marble coffin that had been discovered two days before by men working on the foundations of the new Palazzo di Giustizia that was to rise just a little to the north of Castel Sant'Angelo.

"As a rule," Lanciani wrote, "the ceremony of cutting the brass clamps which fasten the lids of urns and sarcophagi is performed in one of our archeological repositories, where the contents can be quietly and carefully examined away from the excited and dangerous crowd. In this present case the plan was found impracticable because the coffin was ascertained to be filled with water that had in the course of centuries filtered in, drop by drop, through the interstices of the lid."

The idea of hauling the coffin to the Capitol was abandoned because of its excessive weight and the reasonable fear that too much moving and possible jarring would disturb the arrangement of the contents. The coffin was inscribed simply with the name CREPEREIA TRYPHAENA and decorated with bas-reliefs representing the scene of her death.

A fairly large crowd of workmen and outsiders had collected and now pressed forward for a look, as Lanciani's assistants broke the coffin seals and put the lid aside. They stared down at a horrifying sight. Through the veil of clear water, they saw that the skull was covered, as it were, with long masses of brown hair. Shocked and frightened, those close to the coffin fled, floating in the liquid crystal. Word of the strange growth on the skull spread and, fed by exaggerated additions, was repeated for many years in that part of Rome.

Lanciani was puzzled only for a few moments before he shrewdly guessed that the floating tresses were not hair, but long glossy threadlike

263

tendrils of aquatic plants. The water that had seeped into the coffin had carried tiny seeds that had settled on the concave surface of the skull.

Now we see Lanciani, the scholarly archeologist at work, painstakingly observing every detail, calling on the knowledge he has amassed since boyhood.

"The skull," he wrote, "was inclined slightly toward the left shoulder and toward an exquisite little doll, carved of wood, which was lying on the scapula, or shoulder-blade. On each side of the head were gold earrings with pearl drops. Mingled with the vertebrae of the neck and back were a gold necklace, woven as a chain, with thirty-seven pendants of green jasper, and a brooch with an amethyst intaglio of Greek workmanship, representing the fight of a griffin and a deer. Where the left hand had been lying, we found four rings of solid gold. One is an engagement ring, with an engraving in red jasper representing two hands clasped together., The second has the name PHILETUS engraved on the stone; the third and fourth are plain gold bands. Proceeding further with our exploration, we discovered, close to the right hip, a box containing toilet articles. The box was made of thin pieces of thin pieces of hard wood, inlaid *alla Certosina*, with lines, squares, circles, triangles, and diamonds of bone, ivory, and wood of various kinds and colors. The box, however, had been completely disjointed by the action of the water. Inside there were two fine combs in excellent preservation, with the teeth larger on one side than on the other; a small mirror of polished steel, a silver box for cosmetics, an amber hairpin, an oblong piece of soft leather, and a few fragments of a sponge. The most impressive discovery was made after the removal of the water, and the drying of the coffin. The woman had been buried in a shroud of fine white linen, pieces of which were still encrusted and cemented against the bottom and sides of the case, and she had been laid with a wreath of myrtle fastened with a silver clasp about the forehead. The preservation of the leaves is truly remarkable."

Gazing at the bejeweled skeleton, Lanciani asked himself questions that still recall the excitement felt by all Rome. Who was this woman who suddenly sprang from the darkness of seventeen centuries—from a marble coffin embedded in the blue clay of the Tiber bank? At what age did she die? What caused her death? What was her condition in life? Was she beautiful? Why was she buried with her doll? Lanciani eventually answered his own questions.

She had lived at the beginning of the third century after Christ, during the reigns of Septimius Severus and Caracalla. Lanciani came to this conclusion after studying the form of the letters and the style of the bas-reliefs engraved on the sarcophagus. She was not noble by birth; her surname was Greek and showed that she belonged to a family of freedmen, former servants of the noble family of the Creperei. Nothing could be known of her features, except that she had a strong and fine set of teeth.

"Her figure, however, seems to have been rather defective, on account of a deformity in the ribs, probably caused by scrofula," Lanciani wrote. "Scrofula, in fact, seems to have been the cause of her death. In spite of this deformity, however, there is no doubt that she was betrothed to the young man Philetus, whose name is engraved on the stone of the second ring, and that the two happy lovers had exchanged the oath of fidelity and mutual devotion of life, which is expressed by the symbol of the clasped hands. The story of her sad death, of the sudden grief which overtook her family on the eve of a joyful wedding, is plainly told by the presence in the coffin of the doll and the myrtle wreath, which is a corona nuptialis. I believe, in fact, that the girl was buried in her full bridal costume and then covered with the linen shroud, because there are fragments of clothes of various textures and qualities mixed with those of white linen."

Lanciani was astonished and delighted by the doll. This exquisite *pupa*, as he called it, was a work of art in itself. It was made of oak to which time and water had given the hardness of metal.

"It was modelled in perfect imitation of a woman's form, and ranks amongst the finest of its kind yet found in Roman excavations. The hands and feet are carved with the utmost skill. The arrangement of the hair is characteristic of the age of the Antonines, and differs but little from the coiffure of Faustina the elder. The doll was probably dressed, because in the thumb of her right hand are inserted two gold keyrings like those carried by housewives. This charming little figure, the joints of which at the hips, knees, shoulders, and elbows are still in good order, is nearly a foot high. Dolls and playthings are not peculiar to children's tombs. It was customary for young ladies to offer their dolls to Venus or Diana on their wedding day. But this was not the end reserved for Crepereia's doll. She was doomed to share the fate of her young mistress, and to be placed with her corpse, before the marriage ceremony could be performed."

We stopped once, coming home at a late hour from Tivoli, and listened. Those mutinous night winds rising and falling across the dark moonless Campagna, were they the spirits of all who had died, Romans and strangers in numbers never to be known? All gone now, up there in the blackness, a long sigh, a soft moaning.

CHAPTER 22

Rome Inherits Buried Treasure

*I*n 1870 nobody had any idea how much lay buried in the city Hawthorne and Crawford had thought a vast cemetery, a city built up in layers through two millennia—a city that had, in the fourth century, 46,602 tenements, 1,790 palaces, and one thousand public buildings, such as baths, temples, basilicas, theatres, amphitheatres, circuses and porticoes. Some of the marble and metal of these structures and their contents had been salvaged, but generally little had been done in ancient Rome about carting off the debris of a house that had collapsed. New houses were built on the ruins of old ones: The Church of San Clemente, to take a notable example, was built in 1099 by Pope Pascal II above the ruins of a basilica built seven-and-a-half centuries earlier upon the foundations of a second-century patrician house under which lay the ruins of the Republican era containing a Mithraic shrine.

Archeologist Lanciani and his colleagues were concerned with more than mere discoveries. One of their goals was the reconstruction of the ancient city beyond what they could be fairly sure of doing on the Palatine and in the imperial fora. One difficulty was the virtual impossibility of ever knowing with any accuracy the topography of Republican Rome—or the earlier kingly city—or even to agree on the number of the original hills.

One of Lanciani's maps of ancient Rome is a hydrographic and chorographic (correct) chart on which he drew the waterways—the ponds, creeks and rivulets—in light blue and set down in bold double red lines a few of the city's modern thoroughfares as guidelines, among them the Corso, Via Venti Settembre, Via Nazionale, Via Giulia, and Via Merulana, the wide avenue that runs from Santa Maria Maggiore to San Giovanni in Laterano. The Aurelian Wall, which was not built until the third century of the Christian era, or around a thousand years after the founding of the city, is delicately traced in black through its twenty-one miles (it had sixteen gates and 383 towers); and the hills, outlined in a fuzzy buff, appear as they were originally—the Aventine, Palatine, and Caelian isolated; the Quirinal, Viminal, and Esquiline as projections of the wide undulating plain above; and the Capitoline joined to the Quirinal by the high ridge that Trajan cut away when he made his own forum. These were the seven traditional hills, and Lanciani added the Vatican Hill (which had been leveled before old St. Peter's was built), the Janiculum, and the Pincio. He also identified two more hills that are usually regarded as part of the Esquiline: the Cespius, where Santa Maria Maggiore stands, and the Oppius, site of San Pietro in Vincoli.

The old hills of the kings had been nibbled, eroded, pared, cut down in some places, and built up in others in one of the strangest shiftings of contours imaginable—strange because Rome somehow held onto what soil it had and wasted little. Lanciani, fascinated by these movements of soil, noted that Alessandro, Cardinal Farnese, afterward Pope Paul III, had dug an enormous hole when he built the Palazzo Farnese. The dirt was wheeled up to the top of the Palatine, where it remained for three centuries before it was hauled away and used as a landfill between the Aventine and Santa Balbina, a fifth-century church near the Baths of Caracalla.

The rise of the Roman soil had begun in the age of the Tarquins, when the Velabra was drained and filled. (Lanciani, studying coastal changes at Ostia and Fiumicino, estimated that the Tiber washed down eight-and-one-half million tons of sand to the sea every year. The Torre San Michele, built by Michelangelo in 1567 at Ostia, was a mile and a quarter inland three hundred years later; and another tower, built on the sea by Pope Clement XII in the 1730s at Fiumicino, was cut off from the water's edge by a line of sand dunes, nearly a thousand yards wide, by the late nineteenth century.)

Unhappily, changes occurred when the barbarians cut the aqueducts and Romans abandoned the fruitful hills and the Campagna, which had grown to be like a great park studded with pleasant villages, farms, princely residences, temples, fountains, and tombs. Back to the cover of the walls had come a dispirited people. Waterless, they moved down to the Tiber. It would be a long time—a thousand years—before their descendants and newcomers to Rome could be persuaded by Pope Sixtus to build villas on the Quirinal, the Viminal, and the Esquiline.

Lanciani, who loved his work, at times could scarcely contain his enthusiasm. But how could he or any other archeologist—or any laborer, if it came to that—have felt differently in this age of discovery? They were pursuing a science and an adventure, looking for buried treasure far more precious than diamonds, gold, or emeralds. Unlike millionaire art collectors or the museum directors working in a competitive market, they were engaged in recovering what they could of the artistic and utilitarian past. Pride, as we understand it when applied to one who has just made a rich acquisition, was not one of their sins. They expected everybody to rejoice when a bronze statue of Bacchus was fished out of the Tiber, and when precious marble inscriptions were uncovered during the demolition of a floor in Santa Maria in Trastevere.

The tantalizing thought was: How much had been lost? In a manuscript volume in the Vatican Library's Syriac collection, a short description of Rome had been found, written in 546 AD by Zacharias, a Byzantine historian and Bishop of Mytilene in the Island of Lesbos. This account indicated that when Zacharias wrote, there were in Rome eighty gilt bronze statues of gods; 3,785 bronze statues of gods, emperors, generals and other subjects; and twenty-five statues of bronze that, tradition said, had been brought from Jerusalem by Vespasian. The statue of Marcus Aurelius, which then stood on the Campidoglio—the only large bronze equestrian statue to have survived in Rome—owed its life, we are told, to the popular belief that it was a statue of Constantine. (It had stood for years at San Giovanni in Laterano until Paul III removed it to the new piazzetta.)

Works of art in bronze and, in fact, in all metal were expendable among people more concerned about money than art. Marble could not be easily hauled away and thus was comparatively safe for many years, except from the limeburners; but bronze could be melted and sold. It was so scarce in the seventeenth century that Bernini stripped the Pantheon of its roof to get material to finish his baldacchino in St. Peter's.

Describing the Claudian port of Ostia, through which passed thousands of tons of marble, Lanciani says that halfway through the nineteenth century, "a gentleman possessed of great perseverance, Sig. Faustino Corsi, counted in Rome 7,012 ancient columns or important pieces of ancient columns which had escaped destruction." The number had increased to nearly nine thousand after excavations began under the new government. "Considering what an amount of destruction, of breaking up, or burning into lime, has been accomplished in Rome since the fall of the empire, there is no danger of exaggerating if we place the total number of columns landed at Ostia at fifty thousand at least; and columns represent but a small item in the marble trade of ancient Rome." Marble clothed the towering Baths of Diocletian, the Baths of Caracalla, the Temple of Minerva Medica, the Basilica of Maxentius, and Castel Sant'Angelo.

Lanciani's books are full of details of extraordinary discoveries, most of them, it would seem, happy accidents. One was the finding of fragments of the *acta fratrum Arvalium* (Annals of the Fratres Arvales), a brotherhood that closely resembled in organization and religious character the sisterhood of the Vestals. The first pieces turned up in the Middle Ages, and it was determined from them that the Arvales held their meetings in a wood five miles from Rome and worshipped in a temple dedicated to the goddess Dia; but all knowledge of the place stopped there.

From time to time in the following centuries, more fragments of the marble slabs on which the annals were engraved came to light in widely separated places—in the foundations of the sacristy of old St. Peter's; in the catacombs of Sant'Agnese far out in the Via Nomentanai on the Esquiline; under the foundations of a house near the Ghetto; and on the road to Fiumicino five miles outside Porta Portese.

"This last place," wrote Lanciani, "the fifth milestone of the ancient Via Campana, has finally been ascertained to be the true one. The magnificent work of exploration carried on in this spot for two consecutive years by the late Dr. Wilhelm Hanzen under the auspices and with the help of Empress Augusta of Germany brought to light not only the remains of the temple of the goddess Dia, the place of worship of the Arvales, but their banqueting hall . . . and about one thousand lines of the annals."

Not the barbarians but the popes, princes, and architects of the Renaissance and Baroque periods despoiled Rome, Lanciani indicated. "If it were in our power to snatch the secret of the origin and former purpose and use of the marbles, stones, and bricks with which our palaces, our cloisters, and our villas have been built and embellished, or to recall to life the masterpieces of Greek and Roman statuary, hammered or ground into dust or burnt into lime, our knowledge of the city of the Caesars would be almost perfect. The rebuilding of St. Peter's alone caused more destruction and did more injury to ancient classic remains than ten centuries of so-called barbarism.

"Of the huge and almost incredible mass of marbles, of every nature, color, value and description, used in building St. Peter's until the beginning of the present century, not an inch, not an atom, comes from modern quarries; they were all removed from classic buildings, many of which were leveled to the ground for the sake of one or two pieces only."

Between 1540 and 1549, Lanciani said, "the men employed by the contractors of St. Peter's to search for building materials crossed the valley of the Forum from end to end like an appalling meteor, destroying, dismantling, splitting into fragments, burning into lime the temples, the arches, the basilicas most famous in Roman history, in the history of the Old World, together with the inscription which indicated their former use or design, and the statues and bas-reliefs which ornamented them."

In 1540 the podium, steps, and pediment of the temple of Antoninus and Faustina were removed to St. Peter's or otherwise made use of. (In 1602 the temple was given a Baroque facade and converted into the Church of San Lorenzo in Miranda. It remains one of the most conspicuous sights in the Forum Romanum.) Between 1541 and 1545, the marble of the triumphal arch raised to honor Fabius

Maximus, conqueror of Savoy, was hauled away; and the same fate befell the triumphal arch erected to honor Augustus after the battle of Actium, the temple of Romulus, son of Maxentius, and a portion of the Cloaca Maxima. In 1546 the temple of Julius Caesar was leveled to the ground together with the Fasti Consulares and Triumphales engraved on its marble basement; in 1547 the temple of Castor and Pollux was dismantled; in 1549 the temple of Vesta, the temple of Augustus, and the shrine of Vortumnus." And so on.

The men who waged this destruction, Lanciani acknowledged, raised "monuments and edifices which, in beauty and perfection, will bear comparison with the old ones." Still, their cruel treatment of ancient works was inexplicable; they were artists, and an examination of their notebooks and studies leaves no doubt of their immense love and admiration for ancient art. "The most obscure and uninteresting bits and fragments of moldings were taken up by them as subjects of study and investigation," Lanciani wrote. They learned their craft, or improved it, by attending to the genius of the Romans, and then ruthlessly abandoned the old works.

It was quite a game, a gigantic game, played by these masters, and Lanciani shows us some of the intricate moves. The pedestal of the statue of Marcus Aurelius on the Campidoglio was cut by Michelangelo out of one of the columns belonging to the temple of Castor and Pollux. Another fragment of the same columns was transformed by Raphael and Lorenzetto into the statue of Jonah in the Chigi Chapel in the church of Santa Maria del Popolo.

"The coat of arms of Pius IV on the top of the Porta Pia was cut by Michelangelo out of a marble capital of colossal size discovered under the palace of Piero della Valle. The temple of the Sun of the Quirinal furnished the materials for the Cesi chapel in Santa Maria Maggiore, for the fountain in the Piazza del Popolo, for the fountain in the Piazza Giudea, for the pope's palace on the Quirinal, and so forth. The materials for the church of Santa Maria dell'Anima and for some portions of the Villa Medici were quarried from the ruins of the temple of Jupiter Capitolinus; those for the Sistine Chapel in the Vatican from Hadrian's mausoleum (Castel Sant'Angelo, which had been faced with marble and adorned with statues.) The columns of *verde antico* in the Farnese palace and the Villa of Julius III on the Via Flaminia came from Zenobia's bath house at the sulpher springs near Tivoli. The house of Lorenzo Bernini near Sant'Andrea delle Fratte is built with the materials of the baths of Licinius Sura on the Aventine.

"Strange to say, even the work of restoration and preservation of ancient monuments was accompanied with destruction: one monument paid the ransom for another . . . The obelisk raised by Augustus as a sun dial in the Campo Marzio was restored by Innocent XII with the granite of the monumental column of Antoninus Pius discovered in the garden of the 'Casa della Missione.' . . . The Arch of Constantine was restored by Clement XII with the large blocks of marble belonging to the temple of Neptune near the Pantheon. The Pantheon itself, or rather its portico, was restored by Alexander VII with columns from the baths of Severus Alexander and with marbles from a triumphal arch called, in the Middle Ages, the Arch of Piety."

There was no end to the artistic skullduggery, but such questionable practices were hardly new. After Christianity was recognized in the fourth century as the official state religion, the emperors themselves set a bad example by stealing bronze and other valuables from pagan temples and shrines. Constantine carried off works of art from Rome to Byzantium when he transferred the seat of empire to the east; and it was at this time that there began the venal practice of changing heads on bronze and marble statues.

When the first Crusaders sailed past Constaninople, they could hardly credit their senses at the city that rose before them. Constantine had spent sixty thousand pounds of gold on the construction of the walls alone, and imported half a million people to inhabit his new city. The incredulity of the Crusaders is matched by our own, as we read that within a decade of settling the place, the emperor had built a circus, two theatres, eight public and 153 private baths, five granaries, eight aqueducts, four great halls, two pagan temples, fourteen churches, fourteen palaces, and 4,383 houses. Forests of sculpture had sprung up, most of them transplanted from Greece. No part of the empire was safe from the imperial agents.

More than four hundred statues stood in front of the first church of St. Sophia that Constantine built. They included the Pythian Apollo, the Simnthian Apollo, the Samian Hera, the Olympian Zeus, the Pallas of Lindos, the Zeus of Dodona, the four bronze horses of Rome, and Phidias's bronze statue of Athena from the Acropolis in Athens. The porticoes of the forum were cluttered with statues. In the center rose a column that had been transported from Delphi. On the summit of this porphyry column stood a colossal bronze statue of Apollo by Phidias, its original head replaced by a bronze likeness of the emperor. The top of the seats of the Hippodrome was almost solid with statues of Greek gods and heroes, sages and poets.

Rome would survive, but in the matter of statues its glory had been sadly diminished. In the year the Crusaders arrived at Constantinople, 1204, Rome's population had dwindled to that of a backwater. Many stately buildings had collapsed, many churches were roofless and without windows and doors. The future was bleak; in the next century an earthquake would bring down part of the Colosseum's wall. The date is not known for certain but is believed to have been earlier than September 3, 1332, for on that day the Roman nobility staged a rousing bullfight in the arena. Eighteen young patricians were killed and nine others badly mangled.

While the digging in Rome went on and Lanciani's notebooks filled, the archeological bulletins, once few in number and of interest chiefly to scholars, fattened with news and were widely circulated. The whole world was watching and reading as the past—or some small part of it—was brought into the light. Scholars, students, educated layman, and plain curiosity seekers climbed the Palatine to see what was going on.

One of the men who had raised the level of Rome's soil was Gaius Clinius Maecenas, whose surname became a synonym for a wealthy patron of the arts. He was a Roman *eques* of noble Etruscan descent, a close friend and counsellor of Augustus and the benefactor of Virgil and Horace. Virgil, who wrote *The Georgics* at his request, was indebted to him for the recovery of his farm, which the soldiery had taken in the division of lands in 41 BC. To Horace, Maecenas gave a farm in the Sabine country.

Maecenas was famous for the gardens he created on the Esquiline by burying an old cemetery that had become a menace to public health. The cemetery was in two sections, one for citizens who could afford tombs or columbaria for their ashes, the other an area for slaves, beggars, paupers, prisoners, and criminals who had suffered capital punishment. The bodies and great quantities of trash and filth, as well as the carcasses of beasts, were dumped into gaping pestilential holes. Carrion birds and savage dogs prowled the rat-ridden stinking mess under the sightless eyes of rotting corpses left hanging from crosses. After Maecenas suggested to Augustus that the place be destroyed, it disappeared under piles of rock and dirt from eighteen to twenty-five feet high. Orchards and groves of trees were planted; a palace and a belvedere were constructed, and it was said by Suetonius (and denied by Tacitus) that Nero climbed to the tower to watch the city burn.

Other gardens, even lovelier, were laid out, one of them, the Lamiani, across the line of what is today the Via Marulana from the Maecenas property. The Lamiani had yielded numerous works of art, paintings as well as sculptures, including the Esquiline Venus, as early as the sixteenth century.

By Lanciani's time the district had been pretty thoroughly searched, or so it was thought; but Lanciani and every other archeologist who worked in Rome knew how easy it was to overlook something of value that might be lying a few feet below the place where they stood. Lanciani spent a lot of his time on the Esquiline after it was excavated and built over after 1870. The municipal planners would have made it into a most desirable part of the new Rome; but somewhere along the way something went askew, and the large Piazza Vittorio Emanuele developed, under the pressure of mercantile necessity and a pervading neighborhood poverty, into the least attractive open-air space in the city, given over to Rome's biggest and most raucous retail fruit-and-vegetable market and colony of homeless cats.

We were thinking of Lanciani one Saturday evening in November, when we lost our bearings on the Esquiline after a moving visit to the Museo Storico della Lotta di Liberazione di Roma (Museum of the History of the Struggle for the Liberation of Rome in 1943-1944), an apartment house in Via Tasso which the Gestapo had converted into a small prison from which men were taken to be executed at Fort Bravetta or, in the Massacre of March 24, 1944, at the Fosse Ardeatine. The streets were poorly lighted—in the many times we have been in Via Tasso we have never seen anyone, day or night. It is as if the fear the murderous German police created so long ago still envelops the street. A cold wind was blowing, and as we walked away from Via Tasso the houses we passed seemed gloomy and forbidding. We were not alarmed—we knew that if we kept on walking we would set ourselves right, as we eventually did.

But what gave the moment its special relish, apart from the eerie atmosphere of the deserted streets and the conscious indulgence of our fancies, was Lanciani. A brilliant scholar, born January 1, 1847, who seems to have had no gaps in his extraordinary knowledge of history, art, and literature, Lanciani was a restless man who must be up and doing, poking in dirt and debris and smelling the smells of the long-dead on many an occasion when a more cautious and sedentary man would have been at home, certainly on Christmas Eve.

It was the Christmas Eve of 1874 that was in our minds and, quite without knowing it, we were walking to the corner of Via Foscolo and Via Emanuele Filiberto, where Lanciani had found himself that night. In a room of an ancient house far below ground, he and his companions stared at a marble bust of the second-century emperor Commodus under the attributes of Hercules—that is to say, represented with a club on his shoulder and wearing as a helmet the head and skin of the lion Hercules had slain.

On the marble floor were other treasures, abandoned seventeen hundred years before. They are now in the Palazzo dei Conservatori on the Campidoglio, and whenever we go there we pause to salute the memory of Lanciani and to recall the evening we were lost. There are other Esquiline sculptures in the room named for the Lamiani Gardens—an old fisherman, an old woman with a lamb under her arm, a beautiful seated girl, a centaur's head, some statues of females, and the charming Esquiline Venus.

Commodus, the degenerate son of Marcus Aurelius, liked to think of himself as a reincarnation of Hercules. He sometimes appeared in gladiatorial games in the Colosseum. He also liked to wear women's clothes and kiss his male favorites in public. He was thoroughly hated, an obnoxious beast of murderous instincts. When one of his mistresses, Marcia, and other members of his household learned they were on his death list, they conspired to poison him, and he was finished off, strangled by his favorite wrestler, a man named Narcissus.

Lanciani's devotion to the past had a trace of fanaticism. He wrote that when Commendatore G. B. de Rossi, "my master," discovered in the Biblioteca Marciana at Venice the famous codex of Pietro Sabino, "he spent thirty-six hours in devouring, as it were, this volume, with no consideration whatever for food or rest, and did not leave his long-sought-for prey until he actually fainted from exhaustion."

Lanciani was of the same temperament. He worried about problems, and one that gave him no peace for a long tine was the matter of what had been done with the material cut away from the Quirinal Hill by Trajan and his architect, Apollodorus of Damascus, in constructing Trajan's Forum. Lanciani estimated it amounted to twenty-four million cubic feet of dirt and rock, laboriously excavated by swarms of slaves and hauled away in pathetically small ox-drawn carts. This massive piece of old Rome had not been casually dropped anywhere; wherever it was deposited, it had been carried there on purpose.

Trajan's project had been of enormous interest to engineers and archeologists and city planners since the passing of the Dark Ages. Caesar had built his own forum, because the Forum Romanum had become too overcrowded. A ground plan was badly conceived and executed, but there was no other place in the city to conduct judicial, religious, and commercial affairs and to allow people to stroll and chat, argue, gossip, and learn the latest news. To reduce the congestion and the incessant noise, Caesar built another forum; still other fora were built, those of Augustus, Vespasian and Nerva. New temples, porticoes, and basilicas dazzled strangers from all points of the empire.

The new spaces made it easier to move around the center of the city—modern Rome still calls the area of Piazza Venezia its "centro"—but there rose between the fora and Campo Marzio a high barrier, an ugly obstruction, the ridge that connected the Capitoline Hill to the Quirinal and effectively divided the town into two parts, north and south. It could be crossed by following a narrow track, a tiresome climb; or it could be avoided by going westward to the level ground where the spur of the Capitoline hill sloped down to the Tiber.

Trajan removed the barrier, made a passage six hundred feet wide at street level, and then built his forum. The job took fifteen years, and the feat of cutting down the ridge so astonished the grateful people that they paid for a column memorializing Trajan's conquest of the Dacians. The column, made of eighteen drums of elaborately carved marble, is one hundred feet high and is said to represent the height of the ridge.

"I have made investigations all over the Campagna, within a radius of three or four miles from the walls, to discover the place where the twenty-four million cubic feet were carted and dumped, but my efforts have not, as yet, been crowned with success," Lanciani wrote in *Ancient Rome in the Light of Recent Discoveries*. "This fact leads me to suppose that the enormous mass might perhaps have been utilized to fill up some marshy district in the neighborhood of Rome."

His puzzlement ended in May, 1885, when the circular mausoleum of Lucilia Polla and her brother Lucilius Paetus was discovered in Via Salaria, across the street from the Villa Torlonia, formerly the Villa Albani. An inscription sixteen feet long, engraved on marble, states that Marcus Lucilius Paetus, an officer who commanded cavalry and military engineers in the reign of Augustus, had built the tomb for his sister, already deceased, and himself.

It was the largest sepulchral structure uncovered in Lanciani's time, and he compared it in size to the mausoleum of Metella on the Appian

Way. Its basement was 110 feet in diameter, built of travertine and marble; and its top, which had long since disappeared, had borne a cone of earth fifty-two feet high, in imitation of the Mausoleum of Augustus. Trajan had buried it in the second century; it was found in the fourth century by Christians tunneling to make a new catacomb. They had occupied and then abandoned it, and one thousand years later it had been vandalized and much of the interior wantonly destroyed during the fever of ransacking the tombs of the Via Salaria district.

Trajan's reason for his sacrilegious act is unknown. Maybe the decision had been made by Apollodorus, possibly by the contractor. The discovery of the tomb pleased Lanciani, not only because it was a valuable find, but because it ended his conjectures about the soil. He noted that the repeated dumpings had raised the level of the soil about twenty-five feet from Salaria to the Pincian.

My wife and I lived for a few months in the neighborhood and passed the remains of the tomb many times. It looks like nothing but a big deserted hole overgrown with weeds and filled with cats who come to a low wall at the sidewalk to feed on the remnants of the day's *pranzo* left there by people who love cats. The day's dish is usually spaghetti and tomato sauce.

The transformation of the parts of Rome crossed by Via Salaria, Via Nomentana, and Via Pinciana upset Lanciani. "Still," he said, "if anyone has no right to grumble it is the archeologist, because the building of these suburban quarters has placed more knowledge at his disposal than could have been gathered before in the lapse of a century."

He pointed to one instance "famous in the annals of Roman excavations," when, in the years between 1695 and 1741, the vineyard of the Naro family near the Casina of the Villa Borghese was explored and the contents of the graves of twenty-six praetorians and 141 civilians were uncovered. By contrast, in 1887, when the Corso d'Italia was cut through, 855 tombs were discovered in nine months between Porta Pinciana and Porta Salaria, the point in the Corso now designated as Piazza Fiume.

Lanciani's enthusiasm reaches a glowing mark in 1834, when he descends to the tomb of a family of seven Roman patricians murdered at intervals by Messalina, wife of Claudius; Nero; and the praetorian guard. As he stood in the tomb, Lanciani recalled: "I felt more than ever the vast difference between reading Roman history in books and studying it from its monuments, in the presence of its leading actors; and I realized once more what a privilege it is to live in a city where discoveries of such importance occur frequently." The victims of these cruel deaths were the Calpurnii.

The archeological work went on, and Lanciani, who had become the city's official custodian of the treasures, was pressed for room to store them. Many of them, as well as works of art from Villa Ludovisi, were installed in the new Museo Nazionale Romano in the Baths of Diocletian. In 1831, when the foundations of the English church in Via del Babuino were being laid, a collection of bronze imperial busts was found, piled up and concealed in a subterranean passage. A similar discovery was made in the foundations of Madame Ristori's palazzo at the corner of Via Nazionale and Via di Sant'Eufemia.

The two greatest recoveries of Lanciani's years occurred in the spring of 1885: the bronze statue known as the seated Boxer, and another bronze statue of a prince or athlete leaning on a (missing) lance. Both are in the Museo Nazionale.

The circumstances of their discovery began in 1884, when a dramatic society obtained permission to build a national theatre on the western slope of the Quirinal Hill on Via Nazionale near the Colonna Gardens, with the understanding that anything of value found in excavating the site would be the property of the state. Lanciani had received a letter from an old digger friend, Giuseppe Gagliardi, warning him to be on the alert, as he thought some rare bronzes had been buried on the spot. Lanciani knew that Gagliardi was surmising, with no evidence to support his statement; but Lanciani was titillated. Archeology breeds optimism.

In ancient times the Quirinal slope had been occupied by three different edifices: a temple, which the Emperor Aurelian dedicated to the sun in the year 273 after his victories in the East; a shrine dedicated to Semo Saucus, an archaic Sabine god; and a portico built in the reign of Constantine and known in works on the topography of Rome as the Porticus Constantini. What was unknown was that there had been a private house under the towering substructure of the temple. When it was laid bare, the archeologists were surprised; and on examining the ruins, they concluded that, since everything was in disorder, the occupants had fled as if in fear of an impending catastrophe—fire, earthquake, or a sudden subsidence of the foundations. The house had been destroyed.

Toward sunset on Saturday, February 7, 1885, a workman uncovered the forearm of a bronze statue lying on its back at a depth of seventeen feet below the temple's platform level. The contractor for the digging kept the news secret until the following day, and when Lanciani and other officials arrived on the scene the statue had been moved from its place of concealment. Lanciani was annoyed. Archeologists, coming upon something in the ground, move cautiously, taking the most elaborate precautions, measuring the depth of the find, its position, its relation to other points in the field, and so on, knowing that the fullest and most precise knowledge might be of value in solving problems not immediately seen.

The bronze athlete or prince turned out to be a noble figure, seven feet four inches tall and two feet wide at the shoulders. The excitement in Rome—in the world—was great, and a month later it was even greater when the Boxer was found lower down. The second statue had been carefully hidden.

"I have witnessed, in my long career in the active field of archeology, many discoveries," Lanciani wrote. "I have experienced surprise after surprise; I have sometimes and most unexpectedly met with real masterpieces; but I have never felt such an extraordinary impression as the one created by the sight of this magnificent specimen of a semi-barbaric athlete coming slowly out of the ground as if awakening from a long repose after his gallant fights."

A photograph was made of the bronze Boxer before he was lifted out of the pit. As he had been found at a considerable depth below the surface, he appeared to be looking up at the people who gathered to see him. There he sat, as he had sat waiting through centuries of darkness; and as the onlookers stared back at him, their curiosity slowly turned to compassion. He seemed alive. It was the way he cocked his head that touched all hearts, and it was the patient suffering revealed in his battered face, in his big tired shoulders, his tired hands. A century after his emergence from his burial place, the Boxer still stirs the soul—a figure of dignity and humanity.

That same spring the bronze statue Bacchus was taken from the bed of the Tiber—"that mighty reservoir of antiquities which seems to be inexhaustible," in Lanciani's words—by the engineers making the foundations for the middle pier of Ponte Garibaldi, the new bridge that was to cross from Via Arenula to Trastevere, just north of the Isola Tiberina.

Lanciani could not resist telling the public what had been accomplished in the fifteen years since 1870. "If anyone had spoken to us of the probability of an imminent and complete excavation of the Forum, from end to end, we should have denied the possibility of such an enterprise being accomplished by a single generation," he wrote. "But now the golden dream has become a reality. Today, for the first time since the fall of the empire, we are able to walk over the bare pavement of the Sacra Via, from its beginning near the Colosseum to its end near the temple of Jupiter Capitolinus."

He wasn't sure how many works of art had been uncovered in the Forum, the palace of the Caesars, the Baths, or by private individuals who built new houses; but he noted that the city owned about one-third of the land within the walls, and that a lot of wealth had accumulated in the Capital since 1872: 705 amphorae with important inscriptions; 2,360 terra cotta lamps; 1,824 inscriptions carved on marble or stone; 77 columns of rare marble; 313 pieces of columns; 157 marble capitals; 118 bases; 590 works of art in terra cotta; 405 works of art in bronze; 711 gems, intaglios, cameos; 18 marble sarcophagi; 152 bas-reliefs; 192 marble statues in a good state of preservation; 21 marble figures of animals; 266 busts and heads; 54 pictures in polychrome mosaic; 47 objects of gold; 39 of silver; 36,670 gold, silver and bronze coins; and almost incredible amounts of smaller relics in terra cotta, bone, glass, enamel, lead, ivory, iron, copper, and stucco.

And there was—and perhaps still is—more to come. Rome still sat on Hawthorne's cemetery, and no one could guess, not even Lanciani's old digger friend Gagliardi, at the amount of treasure under that precious soil. The Basilica di Porta Maggiore was not unearthed until 1916; in 1950 the lovely sarcophagus of Acilia was dug up on the road to Fiumicino; and in 1958 a Mithraic shrine was found under Santa Prisca on the Aventine.

PART IV

At the Heart of Rome

CHAPTER 23

Bernini's Baldacchino

*I*f it is hard to think of Rome without St. Peter's, it is just as difficult to think of St. Peter's without the Bernini baldacchino.

It looks so right standing there at the crossing of the nave, as if it had sprung naturally out of the earth itself; and few among the millions who have seen it since its rise in the early seventeenth century could guess at the enormous problem it had solved. Urban VIII was the pope who ordered it, and Gianlorenzo Bernini the man who designed and built it.

The builders of the basilica had been concerned, since the laying of the cornerstone, with the construction of the mightiest temple in Christendom. Plans for the interior were anything but clear, and by the time Urban was elected, in 1623, very little decorating had been done, the basilica still appearing to those who came to see it as a barren, cavernous workshop where scores of men painted and hammered, clambered up and down ladders, and chiseled endlessly with dimly ringing blows on distant ledges in the gloom.

Visitors looking up into Michelangelo's modified dome could see in bright colors running around the base of the dome the letters of the traditional words Jesus spoke to Peter about the founding of the church, beginning "Tu es Petrus . . ."; and only when they saw a man up there would they realize its height. The letters they read so easily were, in fact, five feet tall. Day after day pilgrims wandered along the nave and, coming to the crossing and staring upward into the towering emptiness, experienced awe and an emotion akin to terror. The void could not be eliminated. It could be reduced, but whatever was placed there must arrest the eye without destroying the artistic unity.

Urban VIII, Matteo Barberini of Florence, fifty-five when he was elected, was rich, ambitious, intelligent, and in good health. Bernini, thirty years younger, was a recognized sculptor of extraordinary talent when he met the pope. By the time he died, at the age of eighty-two, Bernini's fame had spread throughout Europe. He was one of the greatest geniuses in history—sculptor, painter, and architect-designer of the Colonnades that enclose St. Peter's Square and of the lovely Jesuit Church of Sant'Andrea al Quirinale.

He was the son of Pietro Bernini, a Florentine who had gone to work in Naples and married a pious Neopolitan named Angelica, whose virtues seem to have been transmitted to their son. Gianlorenzo was no skeptic or agnostic like so many of his contemporaries, but an unusually strict Catholic, who attended Mass daily and followed the spiritual exercises of St. Ignatius. He took to stone carving as naturally as other boys played childish games and at the age of thirteen created two marvellous heads, which lay hidden in the basement of the Church of San Giovanni dei Fiorentini in Rome until their discovery in our time.

At the age of sixteen, he sold a carving to Cardinal Scipione Borghese. The Borghese family, untiring competitors in the race of the wealthy noble families for new works of art, became the young Bernini's patrons. He was commissioned at the age of twenty to do the portrait of the Borghese pope, Paul V. His skill as a sculptor steadily improved, and at the age of twenty-five he created his remarkable David, said to be a self-portrait. That work stands today in the Villa Borghese Gallery along with other statues commissioned by the Borghese: Apollo and Daphne, the Rape of Proserpine, and the bust of Scipione Borghese.

No other man, not excepting Michelangelo, left his mark in so many places in Rome. Bernini's works are to be seen everywhere: showy pieces in large public places, others scarcely noticed in obscure churches like Santa Bibiana. His contributions to the glory of Baroque Rome include the Fountain of the Four Rivers, Piazza Navona; the Tritone Fountain in Piazza Barberini; the Fountain of the Bees at the foot of Via Veneto; the chapels in San Pietro in Montorio, Santi Domenico e Sisto, San Crisogono; and the most remarkable of his chapels, the Conaro in Santa Maria della Vittoria, where he portrayed eight male members of the Cornaro family staring at the figure of St. Teresa in Ecstasy. From his workshop—he had so many commissions that he employed other carvers—came the ten madly fluttering angels of Ponte Sant'Angelo, who appear to be caught up in the beginning of a gale that will whirl them away.

The baldacchino was begun in 1626. Three years later Urban appointed Bernini Architect to St. Peter's, to succeed Carlo Maderno. The post gave the young man—he was only thirty-one—full authority over all the work on the basilica. The pope and Bernini had now been in close collaboration for several years. Nothing expresses their relationship better than the pope's words to Bernini: "It is your great good luck, Cavaliere, to see Matteo Barberini pope, but We are even luckier that the Cavaliere Bernini lives at the time of Our Pontificate."

Urban's faith in Bernini was unwavering. A man less steadfast than this stout Barberini might have been appalled when criticism of the baldacchino project became actively hostile. The Romans were an ugly people when angry, and the pope could remember with a shudder the rioting that broke out on the death of Sixtus V, the violence that sent Fontana fleeing to Naples. The baldacchino was no simple piece of ornanental frippery: The fat twisting bronze columns and massive top, though they wore an air of lightness, would rise to a height of ninety-five-and-a-half feet, as high as the facade of the Palazzo Farnese; weigh seven hundred tons; and require a foundation resting on the solid ground far below the pavement.

Bernini's workmen, coming close to Peter's grave, disturbed ancient Christian relics, and when this became known many of the devout and superstitious were outraged. Opposition to the baldacchino quickly developed and spread, helped along by a number of misadventures: The custodian in charge of the high altar died suddenly one morning; his deputy and confidant died the same afternoon; a few days later the custodian's secretary died mysteriously; the secretary's servant was accused of homicide and condemned to be hanged. Urban himself fell sick, but recovered. To cap it all, the workmen, frightened by these happenings, quit. The Roman populace, always ready to be diverted, allowed itself to have a foretaste of hysteria—almost anything could have set off rioting. Bernini remained unperturbed and, ignoring all criticism, persuaded the men to return to their work with promises of extra wages.

The baldacchino was completed and unveiled in June, 1633. Bernini, then thirty-five, for the next forty-seven years would rarely know a moment of idleness. His dedication to his work gave rise to many stories of a romantic nature. In one, he is "*serrato* (locked up) from dawn to the Ave Maria in the rooms of the Vatican," when he is called to meet someone. His response, the story goes, was, "*Lasciatemi stare qui ch'io sono innamorato*" (Let me stay here, I'm in love). He needed time, more time than any man alive, to get on with his multiple tasks.

These tasks included the making of Urban's magnificent tomb. (The pope died in 1644.) At one point in the decorating of St. Peter's, Bernini employed thirty-nine stone carvers to work on medallions close to the ceiling. Before he finally set to work carving the massive statue of St. Longinus on one of the four piers on which the drum of the dome rests, he made innumerable rapid sketches and twenty-two small terra cotta models, as well as one the size of the finished statue.

His vision was limitless. He could foresee problems and solve them when other men floundered. James Less-Milne, in his excellent book on the building of St. Peter's, calls the Scala Regia "a dream staircase," and in describing its astonishing perspective writes, "The aisled and vaulted stairway is one of the world's great architectural triumphs over awkward siting. For although the space provided was not straight, nor wide, nor even of ascent, nor adequately lit, Bernini overcame each obstacle in turn and created by tricks of perspective a long, regular and impressive approach to the papal apartments."

At the request of Urban VIII, he finished the handsome Palazzo Barberini. He designed a new facade for the Palazzo Odescalchi. We see him at sixty-two, working under the fascinated gaze of Pope Alexander VII and Queen Christina of Sweden, chipping away at the marble block out of which will emerge the equestrian statue of Constantine.

The first stone of the Colonnades was laid in 1657. The project actually started two years later and was finished in 1666, when he was sixty-eight. The year before, his inventive powers and energy undiminished by age, he had executed the gilt bronze tribune, the showiest piece of Baroque art, a work which many critics have found to be in questionable taste because of its patent theatricality. But that was Bernini's way: he *was* theatrical, the greatest scene designer of his age.

An English traveler, John Evelyn, described in his diary his visit to the opera when he visited Rome in 1644. Bernini, Evelyn wrote, "painted the scenes, cut the statues, invented the engines, composed the music, wrote the comedy and built the theatre."

Bernini's father, Pietro, created the Barcaccia Fountain, the old broken boat, which is the centerpiece of Piazza di Spagna. Gianlorenzo went him one better in the same piazza, in the north facade of the Collegio di Propaganda. A narrow street, Via di Propaganda, runs along the western side of the building, and the facade on that side is by Bernini's arch-rival, Francesco Borromini. We walked through that little street many times to go to the post office in Piazza San Silvestro, and since the Church of Sant'Andrea delle Fratte lay in our way, we always stopped in: It was cool there, and the cloister was lovely. We thought of the church as Borromini's because of the campanile, but Bernini was even here, in two chaste marble angels intended for Ponte Sant'Angelo. They had been left here when the master's workshop produced those fluttering substitutes.

Bernini married when he was thirty-nine. His wife bore him eleven children. I liked to imagine his young children going to St. Peter's, thinking that it was their own kind "Babbo," so loving and attentive, who built these majestic colonnades—all those white columns, each one sixty feet tall—and who made the horse statue of Constantine and the beautiful lighted staircase up which they were sometimes taken. All this and the shining gold tribune and the altar and the stunning baldacchino!

As the years advanced, Bernini's thoughts reverted to his youth and his beautiful carvings. His splendid achievements at St. Peter's now seemed to bring him less satisfaction than Sant'Andrea al Quirinale, a church he regarded as his architectural masterpiece, which became his retreat. "Often I come here," he told his son Dominico, "to find relief for my spirit. Only here is there consolation and peace."

We thought of him whenever we went to Sant'Andrea—an old man celebrated throughout Europe, a weary old man, whose life was drawing to a close. But it was in St. Peter's that we felt closest to him, when our eyes fell on the baldacchino.

CHAPTER 24

Mass at St. Peter's Church

A
fter breakfast on our first Sunday in Prati, we asked
ourselves whether we should go to Mass at San Giacchino
or Cristo Re. We were still undecided as we walked along
the driveway to the entrance when, on reaching the Lungotevere, I
looked upriver and the matter was instantly resolved.

Crossing Ponte Risorgimento was a bus, and I realized it was Bus
35, the motorized half of ED, our old favorite tram line. This was *Il
Circolare Esterna Sinistra*, and it ran down the Lungotevere with a stop
near Santo Spirito.

"St. Peter's," I said, "will be our parish church."

It could not be, of course—I had made a poor little joke, and we
knew it. St. Peter's was nobody's parish church. The people of the Borgo
who dwelt near it and relaxed, day after day, in the coddling sun on the
inner steps of Bernini's Colonnades, were no closer spiritually to the
basilica than were Catholics from Poland or New Zealand. Nor were the
citizens of Vatican City and the outsiders who worked there entitled to
any special privileges. They had their own parish church, St. Anne's.

St. Peter's was the universal church, built—in the beginning, at any rate—with wealth from the newly-discovered Americas and the money that came so abundantly from the sale of indulgences. How many pilgrims could gape at this marvelous piling-up of massive stones and say to themselves that their contributions—enough to ransom parents from purgatory or guarantee them a place in heaven—had gone into this majestic edifice?

I was aware of what had prompted my parish church quip, but I was also aware that the odd satisfaction I felt was hollow. For several centuries Catholics and people of other faiths, or no faith at all, had journeyed to Rome to see this magnificent Renaissance and Baroque monument to ecclesiastic power and pride, and here we were, a five-minute bus ride away from all this splendor. Yet even as we cherished the notion of intimacy with St. Peter's, we knew it was not and never had been, nor ever would be, the place where one experienced that intimacy felt in the humblest church. Nevertheless, as long as we lived in Lungotevere delle Armee, we went to St. Peter's, except on those Sundays when we drove perhaps to Civitavecchia or Terracina or Bracciano.

Taine, who was unable to resist comparing everything Italian with his native French, had felt keenly the difference between his own familiar Gothic interiors and the extravagances of Rome's churches. Writing about his reactions to Rome, he had called on the cathedrals of Reims, Paris, Chartres, and Strasbourg to affirm the truth. Amid the exuberant decorations of a Roman church, he had thought of the hush and serenity of Strasbourg, the purple dimness of the lofty nave, the silent shadowy figures moving in the choir, the pale light filtering into the apse, and a stranger light—azure, orange, rose—in a single window high above the pavement where an old man knelt. Nothing like this peace was to be found in the ornate churches of the Eternal City.

Taine's criticism may seem harsh to us. "If there is any place on the earth where it is proper to experience compassion, compunction, veneration, the sublime and solemn sentiment of the infinite, of the beyond, it is here," he wrote. "Unfortunately, one feels only sentiments of the opposite character." Roman churches were overly decorated, and the statuary, the frescoes and tombs, were too distracting. Many of the churches, in fact, drew large numbers of visitors because they were museums—Santa Maria in Aracoeli, for example, Santa Maria Maggiore, Santa Maria del Popolo. St. Peter's was the biggest museum of all.

And so, however devout the visitor, and however strong his desire to pray in this place he may have come thousands of miles to see, art put itself between him and God. He might experience spiritual elation when he stood before Michelangelo's Pieta, but the Pieta also appealed to him as a work of art; and the admiration he felt for the excellence of the workmanship—the idea that a man so young, only twenty-six, could create anything so lovely as the Grieving Mother and her dead Son—was overpowering. The emotional pull between esthetic appeal and deep religious feelings of pity and love was inevitable.

There were twenty-nine altars, most of them unnoticed by strangers, to which the piously inclined might retreat. Masses, scores of Masses, were said here, mostly by foreign priests, who were making a record of their own performances. Solitary worshippers attended these Masses, the kind of men and women to be seen at all hours in every Catholic church in the world. Even a big showy ceremony, such as we witnessed on our first Sunday in Prati, yielded little spiritual inspiration; yet it was a most solemn ritual—a canonization of someone, a Belgian or Frenchman, priest or nun, who had died 200 years before.

The basilica was jammed that day, and we learned about the canonization through judicious whispering only after we had wormed our way to a place about one hundred feet or so from the main altar. Small clouds of incense rose and drifted away, as His Holiness repeatedly took from an attendant priest the censer and swung it. The people surrounding the altar on all sides were a faceless mass, except for those close to us; and as we looked toward the distant entrance or gazed at the lofty arches, we thought of the nineteenth-century English cardinal, Nicholas Patrick Wiseman, who like Taine had been put off by Rome's wild taste for embellishments and St. Peter's immense space. The basilica, he thought, was "a grand aggregation of splendid churches, chapels, tombs and works of art," but its very size and the stupendous display of art required a unifying force, and that force, he concluded, was the pope. His presence transformed St. Peter's into "a whole, a single, peerless temple, such as the world never saw before."

This power to turn all the disparate elements of decoration, as well as the emotions of large numbers of strangers, into a satisfying oneness extended beyond the altar. All sorts of people—Europeans, Asiatics, Africans, Americans—came to St. Peter's to see the pope celebrate Mass, and became part of the joyous scenes they themselves created on his entrance. The clamor, the loud and prolonged outbursts of handclapping, the cries of "Bravo!" and "Il Papa! Il Papa!" as he was carried up the middle aisle, were spontaneous.

We watched these unplanned demonstrations of love and respect for the pope and never lost our innocent astonishment at the reaction of men and women whom one would expect to be placid spectators. We saw Spanish nuns weep, American priests climb the bases of the columns and cheer, a German nun giggle hysterically, another nun sigh rapturously when the pope touched the prayerbook she held up for him to bless, and Chinese girls smile. The Japanese led the throng in camera work: Perched on the back of pews, steadied by other Japanese, they fired off shot after shot of flashbulbs. There was no rowdyism, nothing to upset the most devout Catholic. Everybody knew these huge untidy choruses of shouts and cheers were an expression of deeply felt emotions.

We could never get over the way these outpourings of affection began. Here we are on one of those special Sundays, seated not far from the rear and close to the center aisle, with a good view of the congregation. The low insistent muttering rolling through the basilica, the sound of whispering voices, are suddenly stilled, and the air of expectancy intensifies. The lights in the basilica go up, and what sounds like a great sigh rises. The tension breaks, and we can see people turning to watch for the pope's entrance. It comes as if a stage manager had been back there with watch in hand. The great doors open, and in stride eight men in plum-colored trousers and cutaways, bearing on their shoulders the *sedia gestatoria* and His Holiness, whose right hand is already making the sign of the cross.

The first crackle of applause is heard and picked up and runs explosively forward, as the men move briskly. People along the aisle reach upward. Women hold up small children, hoping the pope will touch them. He does touch one now and then, briefly, bringing who knows what delight to the parents, but the plum-colored gentlemen never break step as they proceed to the altar—or, more precisely, to the far side of Bernini's baldacchino. Again I am reminded as my eyes rest not on the altar but on the noble baldacchino, that it was this superb creation that made possible the general physical harmony.

The pope now was out of sight and the noise had subsided to a mild hubbub; in a few more seconds the excitement was over and the basilica silent, as His Holiness and his attendants advanced to the altar. They were so far away that the strain of trying to watch them was too great, and we left off, content to follow the Mass in a manner mostly imaginative. The people around us had settled into an attitude of patient waiting, and the faces I could see when I turned were the faces of men and women quite used to the tedium of a familiar ceremony.

My thoughts, straying from incense and mumbled Latin, moved idly over the mysterious forces that had brought this place into being; the thread of faith, however tenuous, that held everything together, and the strangeness of our being there in that multitude. But, even as my mind rambled in no perceptible order of things, I was aware from time to time of the distant figure raising his arms to heaven or bowing to kiss the richly-patterned linen that covered the sacrificial table, a polished slab of white marble taken from the ruins of the Forum of Nerva.

The peace that lay over the silent throng would be disrupted half an hour or forty minutes hence, as the sixteen plum-colored legs carried their sacred load through a final burst of enthusiasm in the grand exit. For a while I had time to contemplate anew the spectacle and, recalling Cardinal Wiseman, agree on the unifying power of the pope.

For Catholics the pope was the Holy Father, the Vicar of Christ, the successor of St. Peter, who had been crucified on this spot, and whose remains lay in a tomb far below the main altar. For non-Catholics the object of all the cheering was the world's greatest spiritual leader. They need not believe anything he said; but they recognized this power he exercised over millions of others.

www.ingramcontent.com/pod-product-compliance
Lightning Source LLC
Chambersburg PA
CBHW031823170526
45157CB00001B/158